MW00333996

Roots

Global Perspectives on the New Evangelization
Volume 5

Series Introduction

Then he sat down and taught the crowds from the boat. After he had finished speaking, he said to Simon, "Put out into deep water and lower your nets for a catch." Simon said in reply, "Master, we have worked hard all night and have caught nothing, but at your command I will lower the nets." When they had done this, they caught a great number of fish and their nets were tearing.

—Luke 5:3–6

"How beautiful upon the mountains are the feet of the one bringing good news, announcing peace, bearing good news, announcing salvation, saying to Zion, 'Your God is King!'" (Isaiah 52:7). Evangelization is something beautiful. Derived from the Greek word, *euaggelion*, evangelization means to bear a "happy/blessed message." It is safe to say that every human being longs for good news, and the entire drama of salvation history, as revealed especially in Scripture and Tradition, hinges on a claim to the best news there is. In a word, salvation through divine intimacy – Emmanuel, God with us (see Isaiah 7:14; Matthew 1:23). And as for the essence of this salvation? Isaiah's witness makes it clear: a return to goodness, peace, and the lordship of God.

The bridge of meaning between Isaiah's text and the life and teachings of Jesus of Nazareth is unmistakable: "After John had been arrested, Jesus came to Galilee proclaiming the gospel (*euaggelion*) of God: 'This is the time of fulfillment. The kingdom of God is at hand. Repent, and believe in the gospel'" (Mark 1:14–15). Jesus not only proclaims the good news indicated by Isaiah – "Your God is King!" – he manifests and embodies it. Jesus is the good news of God in person: "And the Word became flesh and made his dwelling among us" (John 1:14). In Jesus's humanity united with his divinity, the good news of God becomes sacrament through the perpetual liturgy of incarnation. Yet the totality of God's revelation in Jesus is laced with paradox. He is a servant king. His royal garments are stark nakedness. His crown is woven of thorns. His ministry is unconcerned with the accumulation of material wealth but, to the contrary, is about giving all away. His queen is a vestal virgin, the Church, *in persona Mariae*, and he reigns from a wooden throne of suffering.

In the twenty-first century, the paradoxical message of the Gospel is no less shocking than it was two thousand years ago. If anything, it is even more riveting to scientific sensibilities and to a surging expansion of secularism taking root in virtually every cultural setting of the world. As Pope Paul VI put it in his 1975 apostolic exhortation, *Evangelii nuntiandi*, we have entered definitively "a new period of evangelization (*feliciora evangelizationis tempora*)" (2). In other words, today we find ourselves in a happy and profitable season to evangelize.

This book series, *Global Perspectives on the New Evangelization*, aims to contribute to the mission field of this "New Evangelization." By offering fresh voices from a diversity of perspectives, these books put Catholic theology into dialogue with a host of conversation partners around a variety of themes. Through the principle of inculturation, rooted in that of incarnation, this series seeks to reawaken those facets of truth found in the beautiful complementarity of cultural voices as harmonized in the one, holy, catholic, and apostolic Church.

John C. Cavadini and Donald Wallenfang, *Series editors*

Roots

Catholic Youth Evangelization in a Post-Pandemic World

EDITED BY

John C. Cavadini

AND

Donald Wallenfang

PICKWICK *Publications* · Eugene, Oregon

ROOTS
Catholic Youth Evangelization in a Post-Pandemic World

Global Perspectives on the New Evangelization 5

Copyright © 2022 Wipf and Stock Publishers. All rights reserved. Except for brief quotations in critical publications or reviews, no part of this book may be reproduced in any manner without prior written permission from the publisher. Write: Permissions, Wipf and Stock Publishers, 199 W. 8th Ave., Suite 3, Eugene, OR 97401.

Pickwick Publications
An Imprint of Wipf and Stock Publishers
199 W. 8th Ave., Suite 3
Eugene, OR 97401

www.wipfandstock.com

PAPERBACK ISBN: 978-1-6667-3218-4
HARDCOVER ISBN: 978-1-6667-2557-5
EBOOK ISBN: 978-1-6667-2558-2

Cataloguing-in-Publication data:

Names: Cavadini, John C., editor. | Wallenfang, Donald, editor.

Title: Roots : Catholic youth evangelization in a post-pandemic world / edited by John C. Cavadini and Donald Wallenfang.

Description: Eugene, OR : Pickwick Publications, 2022 | Global Perspectives on the New Evangelization 5 | Includes bibliographical references and index.

Identifiers: ISBN 978-1-6667-3218-4 (paperback) | ISBN 978-1-6667-2557-5 (hardcover) | ISBN 978-1-6667-2558-2 (ebook)

Subjects: LCSH: Catholic youth. | Evangelistic work—Catholic Church.

Classification: BX2347.4 .R66 2022 (paperback) | BX2347.4 .R66 (ebook)

07/12/22

The editors would like to dedicate this volume
to the memory and legacy of
Saint Aloysius Gonzaga and Saint John Bosco,
patron saints of young people.

"I am a piece of twisted iron. I entered the religious life to get twisted straight."

SAINT ALOYSIUS GONZAGA

"Do not put off till tomorrow the good you can do today.

You may not have a tomorrow."

SAINT JOHN BOSCO

Contents

List of Contributors

Joshua Brumfield, IKON Program Director, The Newman *Idea*

Kristen Drahos, Assistant Professor of Theology and Sisters of Saint Francis Chair in Theology, Briar Cliff University

Patrick Gilger, SJ, Assistant Professor of Theology, Loyola University Chicago; Founding Editor-in-Chief, *The Jesuit Post*; Contributing Editor for Culture, *America: The Jesuit Review*

Linda Kawentel, Research Affiliate, Mendoza College of Business and Department of Sociology, University of Notre Dame; Evaluation Scientist, U.S. Department of Veteran Affairs

Clare R. Kilbane, Senior Learning Designer and Director for Research and Development for Digital Education, McGrath Institute for Church Life, University of Notre Dame

Elizabeth Klein, Assistant Professor of Theology, Augustine Institute

Stephen M. Metzger, Scriptor of Latin Manuscripts, Biblioteca Apostolica Vaticana

Timothy Reilly, Assistant Professor of Psychology, Ave Maria University

Bob Rice, Professor of Catechetics, Franciscan University of Steubenville

Sister Damien Marie Savino, FSE, Dean of Science and Sustainability, Aquinas College

Donald Wallenfang, OCDS, Professor of Theology and Philosophy, Sacred Heart Major Seminary

Acknowledgments

It is a necessary duty to recognize those whose support has made this book possible. First, the editors would like to acknowledge the McGrath Institute for Church Life at the University of Notre Dame and, especially, the largesse of Robert and Joan McGrath. Second, we thank the careful and dexterous editorial work of Alexander H. Pierce from the University of Notre Dame. Much gratitude is owed to him for all the editorial fine tuning across the essays of this book. And third, we thank Wipf and Stock Publishers, especially Charlie Collier and Matt Wimer, for continuing to support the *Global Perspectives on the New Evangelization* book series by seeing through this volume to print. May the essays collected herein contribute to making Jesus Christ known and loved all the more in young people's hearts throughout the world today and in the days to come.

Introduction

> Let no one have contempt for your youth, but set an example for those who
> believe, in speech, conduct, love, faith, and purity.
>
> 1 TIMOTHY 4:12

THE THEME OF THIS book drew its inspiration from the 2018 October Synod
on Young People, the Faith and Vocational Discernment, convened by Pope
Francis. This synod of bishops was anticipated by a pre-synodal gathering
of 300 young people from around the world at Rome in March of 2018 in
order for designated bishops to take time to listen to the ideas, feelings and
recommendations of the youth for the upcoming synod. The age group on
which the synod focused its reflections was between 16–29. Following the
synod, Pope Francis published the apostolic exhortation *Christus vivit* on
the Solemnity of the Annunciation of the Lord, March 25, 2019. *Christus
vivit* gives many indications of various cultural malaises affecting young
people today, but also proposes keys to healing, hope and empowerment.

Pope Francis begins the exhortation by proclaiming that "Christ is
alive! He is our hope, and in a wonderful way he brings youth to our world,
and everything he touches becomes young, new, full of life. The very first
words, then, that I would like to say to every young Christian are these:
Christ is alive and he wants you to be alive!"[1] These words are reminiscent
of those of Jesus recorded in the Gospel of Saint John: "I came so that they
might have life and have it more abundantly. I am the good shepherd. A good
shepherd lays down his life for the sheep."[2] This truth cannot be repeated

1. Pope Francis, *Christus vivit*, 1.
2. John 10:10–11.

enough: "Christ is alive and he wants you to be alive!" Fully alive! Who does not want this abundance of life for himself or herself? Pope Francis accentuates the fullness of life offered in Jesus to each person individually in and through the Church communally. He reminds us that young people are a perennial sign of this effervescent life emanating from the Most Holy Trinity even before the creation of the universe. He invites young people to reclaim their inherent dignity as sons and daughters of God the Father.

To everyone in the Church, the pope insists that "each young person's heart should thus be considered 'holy ground', a bearer of seeds of divine life, before which we must 'take off our shoes' in order to draw near and enter more deeply into the Mystery."[3] It is this posture of patient reverence and attentiveness that characterizes the synod as a model for the global Church. The first and most important thing that young people need from their elders is sincere and empathetic listening. Pope Francis never tires of inspiring a Church that listens through the art of accompaniment. Ministry to and with young people never should lack servant leaders whose hearts are attuned to the real feelings and needs of the young. The pope writes later in the exhortation that "young people need to be approached with the grammar of love, not by being preached at," because "the salvation that God offers us is *an invitation to be part of a love story* interwoven with our personal stories." [4] Narrative retrieval is essential for the restoration of the special identity, vocation and mission of every young person today. When the real life-narratives of the youth are comingled with the life-narrative of Jesus Christ, most of all in the unified encounter of eucharistic liturgy, the channel of salvation is dilated to the greatest degree.

Yet in order to arrive at this redemptive liturgical encounter, the suffocating weight of a culture of isolation must be surmounted. The technological revolution in which we live is having drastic consequences on young people around the world. Pope Francis writes that "for many people, immersion in the virtual world has brought about a kind of 'digital migration', involving withdrawal from their families and their cultural and religious values, and entrance into a world of loneliness and of self-invention, with the result that they feel rootless even while remaining physically in one place."[5] The missionary pope goes on to admonish those who may be tempted to inhabit the sidelines of life: "Dear young people, make the most of these years of your youth. Don't observe life from a balcony. Don't confuse happiness with

---

3. Pope Francis, *Christus vivit*, 67.

4. Pope Francis, *Christus vivit*, 211, 252.

5. Pope Francis, *Christus vivit*, 90.

an armchair, or live your life behind a screen."[6] The proliferation of pixels seems to have cast a spell on everyone, especially the young. A solace of screens reinforces social fragmentation and alienation, uprooting in-the-flesh relational connectedness. It is a paradox that we could move so far away from one another without our bodies moving any significant distance in space.

Among all the chapters of *Christus vivit*, chapter 6, "Young People with Roots," looms the largest. Pope Francis clearly wants to encourage young people to recover their roots as a primary means to fashion their unique identities as unrepeatable children of God the Father. A sharp critique is aimed at ideology and cultural colonization. Such powerful currents of thought are resisted inasmuch as young people remain close to the elderly and cultivate a living collective memory by telling stories that take time to tell. Instead of yielding to the illusion of "a culture of the ephemeral" in which "nothing can be definitive," retrieving one's roots vis-à-vis communal elders and the living tradition of the Church recuperates the lassitude of the *anima technica vacua* ("the empty technological soul," Balthasar) by reorienting the soul to the Orient that is the uncreated Light of the world, Jesus Christ.[7]

The present book *Roots: Catholic Youth Evangelization in a Post-Pandemic World* is populated by an eclectic assortment of essays. These essays aim to engage the content of *Christus vivit* intentionally, whether explicitly or implicitly. The range of contributors extends from philosophers and theologians to social scientists to administrators, and even to a scriptor of Latin manuscripts! Each essay offers deeply valuable insights for better understanding Catholic youth evangelization in the twenty-first century. Given the cultural backdrop and recent global viral pandemic, evangelization with young people is no easy task. It requires incredible ingenuity, innovation and intrepid inspiration from God the Holy Spirit. In this volume, the reader will be brought into contact with a wealth of wisdom presented by both scholars and practitioners of Catholic youth ministry. It is our pleasure to introduce the following essays to you with the hope that we continue to turn the corner of a counter-revolution of culture that will result in a renovation of rootedness.

Ex voto suscepto,
John C. Cavadini and Donald Wallenfang

---

6. Pope Francis, *Christus vivit*, 143.

7. See Pope Francis, *Christus vivit*, 264.

Augustine as a Model for Cultural Engagement

Introduction

AUGUSTINE OF HIPPO, WHO lived in the Roman Empire in the fourth and fifth centuries, may seem like an odd choice to be a model for cultural engagement today, especially for engagement with the youth. Augustine, however, is in many ways the perfect figure to whom we should turn in order "to reflect both on the young and for the young,"[1] as Pope Francis challenges us. Augustine faced similar cultural challenges to those of the modern world and he himself struggled with intellectual and moral difficulties in his early life. As a young man, he rejected the faith of his pious (and sometimes overbearing) mother. Generally speaking, as Christianity emerged into the Roman Empire in late antiquity, it was seen as something which was strange, unsophisticated, and anti-cultural. Many traditional Romans felt that Christianity was undermining the greatness of the empire and that Christianity was a religion largely populated by the ignorant. An early Christian opponent named Celsus, for example, sneers at the lack of Christian sophistication, writing that Christianity "is vulgar and . . . only successful among the uneducated because of its vulgarity and utter illiteracy."[2] In the year 410, Rome was sacked by an invading army of Goths. Some Romans felt that Christianity was to blame for the calamity, because the new religion had weakened their society and caused Romans to abandon the worship of their traditional gods. Augustine responded to this challenge with his work entitled *City of God*. Although the sack of Rome was the immediate occasion for the writing of his book, what resulted was a grand

---

1. Pope Francis, *Christus Vivit* #3.
2. As quoted by Origen in *Contra Celsum* 1.27.

theological project which aimed to show what kind of society Christians envisioned, and how that society compared to the one built and revered by the Romans.

As in Augustine's time, Christianity today is sometimes seen as something which is anti-cultural. It is portrayed, at least in popular media, as being primitive, behind the times and soon to become obsolete. This attitude is abundantly clear in the writers of the so-called "New Atheism," who see religion as a hereditary disease which can be cured by clear-thinking, especially the kind brought about by modern science.[3] In short, Celsus' critique sounds as if it could be found on a contemporary twitter feed. Therefore, like Augustine, our biggest challenge in engaging our culture is not simply responding to this or that critique (although Augustine does respond to many particular challenges raised by his opponents), because Christianity as a way of life is rejected out of hand, especially when it is characterized as a superstition. Rather, the ultimate task of any engagement with the hearts and minds of our youth must be to show that Christian community (that is, the Church) is not anti-cultural and outdated, the result of a barbarian human past, but rather, is counter-cultural. We must demonstrate, as the Second Vatican Council proclaims, that "the Church is the real youth of the world,"[4] that it is the source of all true renewal and true life.

That is the task to which Augustine dedicates himself in the *City of God*. This city of God, as Augustine calls it, is a communion which is completely unlike any other human form of communion, because it is based on and founded by God. Augustine famously defines the two cities—that is, the city of God and the city of earth—in the following way: "two loves have made two cities. Love of self, even to the point of contempt for God, made the earthly city; and love of God, even to the point of contempt of self, made the heavenly city."[5] This society that is the Church—which is not based on political allegiances, class, race or accomplishment of any kind, but on the love of God—is sorely needed today, and it is especially needed by our youth who are struggling to belong in an increasingly competitive and globalized society.

Augustine's work *City of God* is divided into two parts. The first part (books one to ten) constitutes a critique of Roman society. Augustine examines the culture around him, and argues that traditional Roman religion offers no benefits either in the earthly life or in the afterlife. Roman society

---

3. See, for example, Dawkins, *The God Delusion*, 25ff.

4. Second Vatican Council, *Message to Young Men and Women* #18. Quoted in *Christus Vivit* #34.

5. Augustine, *City of God* 14.28.

does not promise the fulfillment for which the human heart longs. In the second part (books eleven to twenty-two), Augustine traces the history of the city of God, and presents a vision of a completely different kind of community, which is based on love and worship of God. In this essay, I will accordingly present lessons we can learn about critiquing our culture (taken from the first half of *City of God*) and then some suggestions about how to present the Christian vision of the Church (taken from the second half).

Part 1: Deconstructing the City of Man

How does Augustine approach the monumental task of engaging and critiquing the culture of the Roman empire, which so far as societies go, was one of the most enduring human cultures ever to have existed? And, what lesson can we learn from his method? We may be tempted to say, along with Augustine in the opening lines of *City of God*, "a great work is this and an arduous one; but God is my helper."[6] For the modern reader (or at least for *this* modern reader) sections of the opening part of the *City of God* can be incredibly tedious to read. The reason for this tedium is in no small part due to the fact that Augustine takes his opponents so seriously. Augustine has read Roman history, poetry, philosophy, and rhetoric, and in *City of God* more than in any of his other writings, he wears his learning very heavily. In other words, Augustine does not aim for the lowest common denominator when he engages with his opponents. He refuses to argue against straw men, or to refute only the easiest arguments he can find. He repeatedly asserts that he has looked for the very best and most reliable historian—the Roman author Varro—and that he chooses to quarrel with the philosophers who are in fact the most sophisticated and the closest to Christian truth—the Platonists. He frequently reminds his Roman readers that they themselves revere these authors and consider them authoritative; Augustine calls their attention to the fact that he is not taking an easy way out, and that he understands the narrative about Roman society from the inside. He himself, after all, converted in adulthood.

Few of us are capable of reading and thinking as much as Augustine did, and I am not suggesting that every modern Christian must be incredibly well read to engage with the questions being asked by our youth and by society at large. Nevertheless, we do have to make a concerted effort to understand the narrative that our society tells about itself. I have sometimes seen in my own Catholics friends and students a lack of awareness about what atheists, for example, actually think or how they perceive the world.

6. Augustine, *City of God* 1.1.

Some Catholics seem to assume that no atheist has ever thought about the question of morality or how to live a fulfilling life in a world where there is no God. So what kind of a world do they imagine? What elements of it are persuasive? From what sources are they getting this narrative? We can sometimes be tempted to surround ourselves with those who agree with us, especially in a society becoming ever more polarized, but we really ought to spend some time and energy understanding the narrative of other people, often just by listening to them.

Augustine, however, does not spend all this time and effort understanding the interior logic of his opponents' position simply to concede to them as much ground as possible. He understands their position in order to show how their view of society and the world is, in the end, insufficient. Sometimes when we Catholics engage in dialogue we can give the impression that we are back-pedaling. It can seem as if the Church is playing catch-up with the rest of world when we emphasize only the commonalities that we have with the rest of society and the harmony of the Church's teaching with the insights of modern science or philosophy (for example). We need not be constantly belligerent or argumentative, and we should certainly welcome viewpoints which are complementary to our own, but we, like Augustine, must always keep the larger Christian narrative in mind, the ultimate good or ultimate love, which, as Augustine never tires of repeating, is God himself.

We can find an example of Augustine keeping this grander vision in view in book four of *City of God*. There are long passages in this book where Augustine is deconstructing the Roman pantheon, showing that the Romans have multiplied the gods they worship to such an extent that they have gods in charge of the tiniest tasks. They have one goddess in charge of rural areas, another god in charge of mountain ridges, one in charge of hills and another of valleys. They have a god for germinating seeds, another for sprouting them and another for protecting them;[7] and so on and so on. After Augustine has discussed a number of these lesser gods, he speaks about two Roman goddesses named "Virtue" and "Felicity," felicity being the goddess of happiness. Regarding these goddesses, Augustine writes: "it was not truth but folly that made these goddesses. For these virtues are gifts of the one true God, not goddesses themselves. Still, where there is virtue and felicity, why look for anything else? What *would* satisfy a person for whom virtue and felicity are not enough? Virtue includes everything we should do and felicity everything we should desire."[8]

---

7. Augustine, *City of God*, 4.8.
8. Augustine, *City of God*, 4.21 (emphasis added).

Augustine has already spent most of book four explaining and critiquing very specific aspects of Roman culture and worship, but he never loses sight of the big picture, as we see here. If Roman society does not have as its end, as its highest "gods," human goodness and happiness (i.e. virtue and felicity), what else is worth arguing about? Although polytheism is not so popular in modern America as it was in fifth century Rome, there is an analogy between what Augustine is doing and what we must do. Just like in Augustine's day, we have multiplied (even *ad absurdum*) the factors by which we gauge societal success and by which we measure the health of our country and our world—whether these measures are social, political, environmental or educational. We can become inundated with information and indices for just about anything, and data collection has become its own science. Wrestling with specific data points is, of course, necessary. But if we do not make the final measure of our society that of human goodness and of the happiness found in God, and if we do not have that ultimate end in view, all other arguments will fall short of being persuasive.

Therefore, if we take Augustine as our mentor, we will attempt to critique our culture in a way that is sympathetic and intellectually responsible, while always aiming to keep the most important questions of life in the forefronts of our minds. But coherent and persuasive criticisms of those who have differing viewpoints is only half the battle, in fact, it is even less than half of the battle (indicated by the fact that the second part of *City of God* is significantly longer than the first). Especially in our age of social media and instant reactions, we have an abundance of critique, a glut of clever analysis pieces or witty memes dealing with just about any hot-button issue. So how does one build up a Christian vision of the world rather than simply tearing down a secularist or modernist worldview? To help us, let us turn to the second half of *City of God*.

Part 2: Building the City of God

Augustine spends the majority of the second half of the *City of God* interpreting scripture. He knows that he has taken to task the foundational texts of his opponents, and that he must now show that the Bible tells a different story about the meaning of human existence. Unfortunately, the sections of *City of God* in which Augustine presents the biblical story are often ignored by scholars and casual readers alike. This neglect perhaps reflects a modern tendency to shy away from scripture—it can be difficult to explain, even embarrassing to us at times, and we may not instinctively turn to it when seeking to engage a culture that has rejected it. For Augustine, this tendency is a grievous mistake, one that he himself made in his younger years when he thought that the Bible was poorly written and not as pleasurable to read as Cicero or Virgil.[9] He came to see, however, that reading scripture is an exercise in humility by design, that meditating on God's word is as much about cultivating certain habits and desires in us as it is about communicating certain facts of divine revelation. Pope Francis in *Christus Vivit* likewise reflects this intuition, turning first to the Old Testament and then the New in search of a Christian understanding of the charism of youth, even with the specific view of answering questions raised by non-Christians.[10] If we believe, therefore, that the scriptures not only reveal God to us but also us to ourselves, then the Bible must be the heart of all theology and we need to act in the confidence that the more we read it, study it, and allow it to occupy our hearts, the better we will be prepared to give an account of the faith.

Augustine aims through an exposition of large sections of the Old Testament to tell the story of two cities, of two loves, as Augustine speaks of it. How, then, does Augustine distinguish between these two societies which he claims have existed since the dawn of human history? Through his careful exposition, he determines that these two cities are to be distinguished by their sacrifice. The one city, of earth, sacrifices to itself. The other city, of heaven, sacrifices to God. This enactment of sacrifice is the determining factor and the visible witness to the existence of these two diametrically opposed pulls on the human heart, the attraction or love of these two cities.

One of Augustine's first biblical examples of these two societies at work is the sacrifice of Cain and Abel. In Genesis 4, God accepts Abel's sacrifice but not Cain's. This preferential treatment might seem confusing, since we have just said that Augustine divides the city of God and the earthly city based on whether or not it sacrifices to God, and it seems that both Cain and Abel perform this task. Augustine explains the passage by saying that although Cain "gave something of his own to God, he gave himself to himself."[11] In other words, although Cain sacrificed some material thing to God, he did not sacrifice himself to God. Augustine is not speaking here strictly about spiritualized sacrifice, that is, he is not arguing that Cain's sacrifice was worse simply because his heart was not fully committed. Rather, Augustine interprets his text of Genesis 4, which says that Cain's sacrifice is not "properly divided"[12] to mean that Cain offered something that was not pleasing, or at the wrong time, or kept the best of it for himself. And this

---

9. See Augustine, *Confessions*, 3.5.9.

10. See *Christus Vivit* #4.

11. Augustine, *City of God*, 15.7.

12. Augustine, *City of God*, 15.7.

outwardly deficient sacrifice corresponded to the fact that Cain offered to God in order to get something *for* himself, rather than offering his whole self to God without reservation.

In Augustine's account, then, the *visible* witness to the authenticity of the Church is in her sacrifice. But how can we translate this insight into modern terms? How do we communicate to the world that the Church is based not on any human achievement, but is grounded only on its love for and surrender to God, which is mediated by and displayed in her sacrifice? Unfortunately, this orientation of the love of the Church is all too often obscured by sin, or by the half-hearted and poorly administered sacrifices we make more in the spirit of Cain than of Abel. But, if we backtrack a little way in the *City of God,* we will find Augustine's suggestion.

In book 10, which is roughly in the middle of the whole work, Augustine transitions from criticizing Roman culture to speaking of the Church (it is the book where he is moving from the first part to the second part). It is no coincidence that it is in this book that we find some of Augustine's most beautiful reflections on the Eucharist. For Augustine, the Eucharist is the sacrifice of Christ's body and also the sacrifice of each individual person. He writes: "This is the sacrifice of Christians: *although many, one body in Christ.* And this is the sacrifice which the Church continually celebrates in the sacrament of the altar (which is well known to the faithful), here it is made plain to her that, in the offering she makes, she herself is offered."[13] Unlike Cain's sacrifice, the Eucharist is the proper sacrifice of the whole self. This sacrifice is made possible not by the excellence of the human art of sacrifice (it is not like Roman priestcraft or augury), but by the blood of Christ who is both perfect priest and victim. In uniting our sacrifice to Christ's perfect sacrifice, we can build the city of God.

I do not mean to conclude this essay by gesturing towards the Eucharist as if it symbolically represented the unity of the Church, and so to suggest that we simply must reinforce that central symbol so that people will somehow understand what the Church is by that visible sacrifice. For Augustine, the Eucharist does not simply represent unity or represent the society that is the Church, but the Eucharist *is* the unity of Christians, it *makes* the Church because it is the sacrifice of the Church. In the Eucharist we receive the whole body of Christ, that is, we receive the body, blood, soul, and divinity of Christ, but we also receive Christ's mystical body (what Augustine calls the *totus Christus,* the whole Christ) and so what we receive is one another and what we receive is our own true selves. I do not think that this understanding of the Church is merely an abstraction, and so I

13. Augustine, *City of God,* 10.6

want to briefly share an experience I had as a catechist teaching Augustine's Eucharistic theology.

My experience comes from teaching confirmation class at a large parish in Denver. I was serving as a co-catechist at this parish, and my class was twenty-five girls, all around fourteen years old, and all except one were Latina. Many were there because of cultural pressure, and some (perhaps most) were not from regular mass-going families. We had discussed the meaning of the true presence in the Eucharist, which they seemed to understand quite well. I then read to them the following quotation from Augustine's *Sermon 272*:

> So why in bread? Let's not bring in anything of our own here, but let's listen to the apostle when he says *one bread, one body we being many are. . .* one bread, what is this one bread? The one body which we being many, are. When you were exorcised it's as though you were being ground, when you were baptized it was as though you were mixed into dough. When you received the fire of the Holy Spirit, it's as though you were being baked. Be what you can see, and receive what you are.[14]

After we had discussed which parts of the rite of initiation Augustine was describing in his bread metaphor (baptism, confirmation, Eucharist), I asked them what was being received in the Eucharist according to this sermon. I was quite surprised to hear them get it almost immediately—"I am receiving myself." We had already talked about the renunciations of Satan as being renunciations of finding fulfillment in the promises that the world makes, and we reviewed that: it is renouncing the idea that good grades make me who I am, that having a good boyfriend will make me worthwhile, that getting a good job will make me happy, and so on. I followed that up by saying that instead we receive who we are in the Eucharist, and that we also receive true communion with everyone else, including our relatives who have died and the saints.

By talking to them over the course of the year, I had come to see that these girls were under an incredible amount of pressure to be involved in all kinds of activities, to look good, to have lots of friends and to succeed all the time. Confirmation class could (and probably did) feel like one more extracurricular activity. I hope that emphasizing the Eucharist in our class was a relief for them, and we regularly went to adoration. Adoration might have been the only thirty minutes of their week when they were in complete silence and at rest—not looking at their phone, not listening to music, not talking and not responsible for finishing some task. But I think frequenting

14. Augustine, *Sermon 272*.

adoration (and Mass too, of course) can also help us to put our money where our mouth is, so to speak, because staring at what looks like a piece of bread is basically boring and corresponds to no definition of usefulness or productivity by the world's standard. I hope that by this witness, and by sharing the experience of worship centered on the Eucharist, that we can show forth that the Church really is a completely different kind of society. As Pope Francis recommends then, Augustine brings to his catechumens through his Eucharistic theology, a sense of rootedness[15] (both to their past and to their community) as well as affirmation[16]—the affirmation that their worth derives from their identity as a child of God and is shown forth by Christ's complete sacrifice on the cross.

However, we will also make the same mistake as Cain if the actual material sacrifices that we make fall short of what God demands. Our conformity to Christ's complete offering through the Eucharist entails that our lives, beyond the celebration of the Mass, are sacrificial as well. As with Augustine's interpretation of Cain's sacrifice, we must not see the Eucharist as a spiritualized sacrifice, whose material form is dispensable, and which makes no concrete claims on us and our actions. Augustine's Eucharistic theology implies this dimension of the Eucharist as well—because we are the sacrifice of the altar and yet become ever more committed to that sacrifice, which is why Augustine challenges "be what you can see, and receive what you are."[17] In *City of God* Augustine also parallels liturgical actions with corresponding sacrifices on the part of the worshipper:

> Our heart when it rises to him is his altar; the priest who intercedes for us is his only-begotten; we sacrifice to him bleeding victims when we contend for his truth even unto blood; to him we offer the sweetest incense when we come before him burning with holy and pious love; to him we devote and surrender ourselves and his gifts in us . . . to him we offer on the altar of our heart the sacrifice of humility and praise kindled by the fire of burning love.[18]

In short, Augustine is saying that the sacrifices of the altar are also the sacrifices we perform in our daily lives. However, when Augustine calls our heart the altar, he is not implying that there is no physical altar. When he says the sweetest incense is our love, he is not abolishing liturgical incense. Rather, Augustine is telling us that by participating in the liturgy we prepare

15. E.g. *Christus Vivit* #200.

16. E.g. *Christus Vivit* #216.

17. Augustine, *Sermon* 272.

18. Augustine, *City of God,* 10.3.

ourselves for and commit ourselves to becoming the kind of sacrifice that the Eucharist is. In fact, by mentioning martyrs first on his list (the "bleeding victims"), Augustine reminds us that the most complete conformity to Christ's sacrifice is to sacrifice our entire lives literally, although in practice most of us will not be called to undergo actual martyrdom.

For Augustine, then, we must take the challenges of our modern society seriously and keep our discourse at the highest level that we are able, while always moving our conversations towards the most important questions of human life. But finally, we must win the hearts of young and old alike by showing forth the counter-cultural community that is the Church through our participation in the Eucharist, by our surrender to the merits of Christ and his sacrifice, and by becoming ever more conformed to that sacrifice through the outward works of charity.

The Catholic Institute in the Secular University

Pope Francis' Call for the Mission of the Church in Higher Ed

Joshua Brumfield

THE MAIN THRUST OF Pope Francis' *Christus vivit* might be taken by simply reading the title. Christ is alive! The task of effectively communicating this simple but glorious truth to young people in effective, flexible, and partici-patory modes takes up most of the document. We may paraphrase him to be asking us to consider how to create cultures in which it is easier to be good, easier for young people to encounter the living Lord, to be vibrantly Catholic.

Francis' words in *Christus vivit* reflect the proceedings of the Synod on Young People, the Faith and Vocational Discernment. In the United States there has long been an anecdotal sense that Catholics lag behind our Protes-tant brothers and sisters in effective and formative youth ministry and also a sense that Catholic ministries to the youth and young adult population have grown successful in recent years. However, both people of all faiths continue to disaffiliate with their native faith at a record setting page. More and more people are simply identifying as NONES.

Statistics and surveys can mislead when improperly used, but they can also help us to get a handle on the big picture and to better grasp the ur-gency of this task, especially for college students. They can help us to better understand why our parishes aren't as full as they used to be. In a survey of NONES from 2018, PEW reports that 79% of former Catholics indi-cated they left the Church before age twenty-three.[1] The PRRI's survey of the religiously unaffiliated indicated that about 90% of NONES abandoned their childhood religion before they turned thirty.[2] The vast majority people

1. Vogt, "New Stats on Why Young People Leave the Church."

2. Jones, et al. "Exodus: Why Americans Are Leaving Religion—and Why They're Unlikely to Come Back."

who stop practicing and self-identifying as Catholics do so at a young age. The statistics are depressing. How many thousands of dollars do Catholic parents invest in Catholic elementary and high school education for their children only to see their sons and daughters head off to State U and cease to practice their faith? Why do they end up leaving at all?

One reason may be that we are just not there for them. For example, although over ninety percent of Catholic college students attend non-Catholic colleges, most discussions on Catholic higher education focus on Catholic institutions. We, the Church, are largely neglecting more than nine out every ten Catholic college students simply because they are not attending Catholic schools. What's more, sixty percent of the religiously unaffiliated reported they left their religion because they stopped believing in their religion's teachings. This is a much higher percentage than either those who identify a particular bad experience as their reason for leaving or those who identify the clerical abuse crisis as a primary element in their disaffiliation with their faith.[3] In other words, we are losing a lot of Catholics by then end of their college years for intellectual reasons.

Pope Francis has expressed his concern for young Catholics and his desire for church structures, including education institutions to rethink their work and priorities. For example, in *Amoris laetitia,* Pope Francis spoke of his "dream of a 'missionary option,' that is, a missionary impulse capable of transforming everything, so that the Church's customs . . . and structures can be suitably channeled for the evangelization of today's world rather than for her self-preservation."[4] Can this "missionary option" be applied to Catholic colleges and universities? Francis continues, "The renewal of structures . . . can only be understood . . . as part of an effort to make them more mission-oriented, . . . to elicit a positive response from all those whom Jesus summons to friendship with himself,"[5] to make it easier for students to powerfully encounter the living Lord. Pope Francis' "dream of a 'missionary option'"[6], places responsibility on Catholics in higher education to embrace a paradigm of "missionary creativity" in approaching ways to encounter, form, and inform Catholic college students more effectively. What form might such missionary creativity take? What would it mean to focus our primary concerns, energies, and resources in Catholic higher education to

---

3. Jones, et al. "Exodus: Why Americans Are Leaving Religion—and Why They're Unlikely to Come Back."

4. Pope Francis, *Amoris Laetitia,* #27.

5. *Amoris laetitia,* #27.

6. *Amoris laetitia,* #57.

Catholic college students (wherever they may be enrolled) rather than exclusively on Catholic institutions of higher learning?

Perhaps with one eye on Francis' dream and another on some of these disturbing numbers and trends, the preparatory document for the Synod on Young People, the Faith and Vocational Discernment insisted that "a productive genetic connection exists between evangelization and education, a connection which, in these times, must take into account the gradual maturation of freedom."[7] In light of this connection, Pope Francis observes in paragraph 222 of *Christus vivit* that "Catholic schools remain essential places for the evangelization of the young,"[8] and calls "for the renewal and revival of missionary outreach on the part of schools and universities."[9] In this context he emphasizes that students ought to develop "the ability to integrate the knowledge of head, heart and hands."[10]

How can we better foster profound Catholic living and vocational reflection at non-Catholic colleges? What is necessary for young people to develop a habit of integral knowing? How can we prepare students to be joyful, missionary Catholics in their workplaces and careers after college?

There already exist worthy and creative attempts to minister to Catholic college students. There are excellent Newman centers and Campus ministries on public and secular campuses throughout the country. FOCUS deserves particular mention for its successes but also as an organization embodying Pope Francis' calls for missionary creativity on college campuses. Nevertheless, if FOCUS and other ministries were enough, the data would not be so dire. How can the Church more effectively evangelize and form students on non-Catholic campuses?

The data points to the importance of Catholic intellectual formation for college students. (Let us leave aside for the moment the not insignificant problem of offering Catholic intellectual formation at secular campuses.) Recall that nearly 80% Catholics who disaffiliate do so before the age of twenty-three, and nearly 90% of Catholics who go to college go to non-Catholic institutions. Most of them disaffiliate with the Catholic Church because they no longer agree with some subset of the Church's teachings. In what follows, I assume that the questions which ultimately lead some people to disaffiliate as Catholics, can be convincingly answered by the truth, goodness, and beauty apparent in a robust Catholic community. A

---

7. Synod of Bishops, "Preparatory Document—Young People, the Faith and Vocational Discernment," #4.

8. *Christus vivit*, #222.

9. *Christus vivit*, #222. Cf. *Veritatis gaudium*, #4.

10. *Christus vivit*, #222. Cf. *Veritatis gaudium*, #4.

major movement in the Church's orchestra of answers to Pope Francis' call for missionary creativity must acknowledge this problem.

Truth be told, the problem is not that there is no theology department at Yale or Penn State, much less at less prestigious institutions. Part of the problem is the modern American university itself.

In a sermon preached in the University Church in Dublin, St. John Henry Newman highlighted the purpose of university education—the formation of a devout laity possessing integral knowledge and the philosophical habit of mind.

> I wish the same individuals to be at once oracles of philosophy and shrines of devotion. . .It will not satisfy me, if religion is here, and science there, and young people converse with science all day, and lodge with religion in the evening. . . . I want the same roof to contain both the intellectual and moral discipline. Devotion is not a sort of finish given to the sciences; . . .. I want the intellectual laity to be religious, and the devout ecclesiastic to be intellectual.[11]

Newman's intellectual laity are very hard to find today because a) the modern university doesn't even try to offer the integrated education and formation demanded by both Newman's *Idea* and Pope Francis' call and b) most Catholic college students have no opportunity to receive Catholic intellectual formation.

I encountered a novel approach to these questions before Pope Francis had even posed his challenge. August of 2018 was the first I had heard of Don Briel, one of the founders of Catholic Studies at the University of St. Thomas and until recently Newman Chair of Liberal Arts at the University of Mary. I had the honor of spending time with him on three brief occasions in September and October of the same year. I can't say I got to know Dr. Briel particularly well, and yet, I have been deeply influenced by the weight of his presence and the strength of his humility, by the depth of his faith and the light of his vision. He was diagnosed with Leukemia in January of 2019 and passed from this life about a month later, on Feb. 15. I have spent much of my time since then reading reflections on his life and influence.

I share this because Dr. Don Briel and others have modeled a new paradigm for missionary creativity in higher education. The Catholic Studies programs at the University of St. Thomas and the University of Mary attempt to counter the dis-integration of the disciplines from each other and of information from formation, of knowledge from morality, by developing

---

11. St. John Henry Cardinal Newman, "Intellect, the Instrument of Religious Training," 13.

a "truly Catholic community of conviction."[12] In doing so they seek to help students form what St. John Henry Newman calls a "habit of mind" in a way that organically integrates intellectual and spiritual formation. The University of Mary has begun to transport this successful Catholic program into non-Catholic institutions, partnering with Arizona State University so that ASU students can take Catholic Studies or Theology courses from the University of Mary while in residence at the Tempe campus of ASU. The courses are integrated into ASU's curriculum helping students to more easily coordinate their discipline specific coursework into a Catholic paradigm and in many cases, to earn a double major in Catholic Studies and Engineering, Law, Business, Medicine, etc.

Did you catch that? students at one of the largest public universities in the country can enroll in Catholic courses as part of their curriculum! This is one fruitful direction in which pre missionary creativity must tend. My confidence does not merely lie in my admiration of Don Briel, however. The anthropology and philosophy of education outlined by St. John Henry Cardinal Newman and Pope Emeritus Benedict XVI seem to indicate this approach as well.

In what follows my argument is twofold: 1) the Church—in particular as it exists in academia—has a grave responsibility to offer to Catholic students on non-Catholic campuses what Pope emeritus Benedict XVI has called the "pastoral care of intelligence"; 2) embracing that responsibility by developing Catholic institutes is an essential way to engage in the missionary creativity for which Pope Francis has called. I will first sketch the incongruence of Newman's *Idea* and the modern university, before outlining how a Catholic institute can approximate Newman's idea of integral formation and thereby answer Pope Francis' challenge. Finally, relying on Benedict XVI's notion of Church as creative minority, I will explore the sacramental and missionary value of such institutes and a potential model for this missionary venture.

In 2013 Reinhard Hütter published two articles—in *First Things* and *Nova et Vetera* respectively—in which he turned to John Henry Newman to argue for "putting the universal back in the university."[13] Hütter demonstrates that although the systemic secularity of the modern university and its obsession with the technical and pragmatic might seem to render Newman's *Idea* irrelevant,[14] on the contrary, Hütter insists that Newman's

---

12. Don Briel, as quoted in "Founder: Catholic Studies Programs Help Colleges Fulfill Call to Faithfulness," *Catholic News Agency*, (Bismarck, ND: Sept. 8, 2014).

13. Hütter, "Polytechnic Utiliversity," 47.

14. Hütter "University Education, Unity of Knowledge, and Theology," 1020–1021.

provocative vision demands a hearing. Precisely because Newman calls for the development of a philosophic habit of mind which aspires for integrated knowledge and assumes that "Religious Truth is not only a portion, but a condition of general knowledge,"[15] his remains an important voice today. After admitting that modern universities will nevertheless continue to ignore Newman's proposal (to their detriment), Hütter proceeds to examine the necessary role of natural theology in Newman's vision. Finally, he asks, "what might it mean to take Newman's proposal seriously?"[16]

Now Hütter answers that question by arguing that only theology can save the modern university from its "total functionalization and commodification."[17] Professor Hütter is certainly a more accomplished scholar and a deeper thinker than I. Nevertheless, I here adopt a different approach to taking Newman's proposal seriously.

Instead of making arguments for the necessity and centrality of theology for the university, theologian though I am, my primary focus is not on the university as an institution but on the persons for whom a universal education ought to be offered.

For Newman, undergraduate education is about becoming fully human. Pope Francis agrees. In an address to students he articulated this point at length:

> Today, above all, the right to a good education means protecting wisdom, that is, knowledge that is human and humanizing. All too often we are conditioned by trivial and fleeting models of life that drive us to pursue success at a low price, discrediting sacrifice and inculcating the idea that education is not necessary unless it immediately provides concrete results. No, education makes us raise questions, keeps us from being anaesthetized by banality, and impels us to pursue meaning in life. We need to reclaim our right not to be sidetracked by the many sirens that nowadays distract from this pursuit. Ulysses, in order not to give in to the siren song that bewitched his sailors and made them crash against the rocks, tied himself to the mast of the ship and had his companions plug their ears. Orpheus, on the other

15. St. John Henry Newman, *The Idea of a University*, 62, as quoted in Hütter, "University Education," 1024.

16. Hütter, "University Education," 1025.

17. Hütter, "University Education," 1047: "Newman's vision reminds us all too moderns that theology, and the speculative contemplation to which it gives rise, is about the only thing that can save the university from its total functionalization and commodification. For theology, natural and revealed, constantly reminds all the other disciplines that the greatest freedom comes with the contemplation and communication of the transcendent truth of God."

hand, did something else to counter the siren song: he intoned an even more beautiful melody, which enchanted the sirens. This, then, is your great challenge: to respond to the crippling refrains of cultural consumerism with thoughtful and firm decisions, with research, knowledge and sharing"[18]

Indeed, to be fully human is to become whole, which requires the integration of the intellect and the will, of information and formation, of knowledge and virtue. According to Pope Emeritus Benedict XVI, the modern university disregards "the issues that brought universities into being—the question of the true and the good" and replaces them with "the question of feasibility."[19] Indeed, the modern university, which Reinhard Hütter more accurately labels a "polytechnic utiliversity," practically ignores the formation of the will altogether, and offers to the minds of students disparate facts and skills segregated by discipline. But in truth, as Newman explains, "all branches of knowledge are connected together, because the subject-matter of knowledge is intimately united in itself, as being the acts and the work of the Creator.[20]" Through a true education, "a habit of mind is formed which lasts through life, of which the attributes are, freedom, equitableness, calmness, moderation, and wisdom."[21] For Newman this true education is the development of a philosophical *habit* of mind. Here we are outside of the disconnected model in which a student's business class has no relation to her history class, neither of which have existential significance to her life, except as a means to graduation, which itself is just a means to a job.

No, for Newman true education cannot be reduced to utility because humanity is not made for the technical but for the true, the good, and beautiful. Education is not about learning a skill. It is about learning to think well, in an integrative fashion and concerns the formation of the whole person. A truly intellectual culture "educates the intellect to reason well in all matters, to reach out towards truth, and to grasp it."[22] Our world and our Church sit in desperate need of women and men capable of seeing things in relation, of comparing ideas and evaluating them from multiple perspectives and disciplines. The challenges faced by the church in the modern world call

18. Pope Francis, "Address at the Meeting with Students and Representatives of the Academic World in Piazza San Domenico, Bologna," 1115, as quoted in *Christus vivit*, #223.

19. Pope Benedict XVI, "Faith and Knowledge," as quoted in *A Reason Open to God*, 42.

20. Newman, *The Idea of a University*, 99.

21. Newman, *The Idea of a University*, 101.

22. Newman, *The Idea of a University*, 126.

for Christians who, in the words of Francis, have "the ability to integrate the knowledge of the head, heart, and hands."[23]

In other words, not only does the modern university refuse to address the moral dimension, it also fails in forming the intellect because it recognizes no discipline, science, or perspective, by which the mind can integrate information into true knowledge. Graduates of even the most prestigious institutions, those who become the experts whose alleged wisdom we seek for policy, economic, and medical advice, simply lack the habit of mind necessary for seeing the whole and advising accordingly. Perhaps this has become more obvious and timely in the disagreement of different kinds of experts during the recent pandemic. "Alasdair MacIntyre has pointed out that most of the catastrophic decisions made in the last 20 years are the result of narrowly specialized perspectives of highly educated people misreading the events before them: the economic crisis, the war in Iraq and so on."[24]

How many "expert" decisions have gone awry because the alleged experts never cultivated a philosophic habit of mind? How many of our experts attempt to read and interpret the many aspects of the common good through the narrow lens of their subject area? Just as neither the psychologist nor the optometrist, the oncologist nor the epidemiologist can speak to the good of the whole person, similarly our experts are not trained with the integral habit of mind to advise on the common good.

In this regard Newman can say that "There is a duty we owe to human society as such, to the state to which we belong, to the sphere in which we move, to the individuals towards whom we are variously related, and whom we successively encounter in life."[25] This duty demands we find creative ways to foster a culture of intellectual formation in which students can develop the habit of mind necessary for engaging our current crises with wisdom and subtlety.

Benedict XVI recognized that students have a need for an education which is "Rooted and Built Up in Christ, and Firm in the Faith." But, "where will young people encounter those reference points in a society which is increasingly confused and unstable?"[26] He asks. Benedict directs this question as a challenge to young professors in Madrid, as if to say, "where else will students encounter those reference points if you, young professors, don't make it happen on your campuses?"

23. *Christus vivit*, #222.

24. Lopez, "Coherency in Higher Education & the Integrated Life of Faith."

25. Newman, *The Idea of a University*, 167.

26. Benedict XVI, "The University," as quoted in *A Reason Open to God*, 37.

Similarly, Pope Francis challenges young people, "do not let the world draw you only into things that are wrong and superficial. Learn to swim against the tide, learn how to share Jesus and the faith he has given you,"[27] and adds "Don't let them rob you of hope and joy, or drug you into becoming a slave to their interests. Dare to be more, because who you are is more important than any possession. . . . You can become what God your Creator knows you are, if only you realize that you are called to something greater. Ask the help of the Holy Spirit and confidently aim for the great goal of holiness."[28] Successfully responding to such challenges requires what Pope Francis likes to call "accompaniment," and he recognizes, that "the Church's educational institutions are undoubtedly a communal setting for accompaniment; they can offer guidance to many young people."[29] Benedict XVI and Francis offer us the same challenge. In the spirit of missionary creativity, shouldn't we try to meet these not yet lost sheep of the Church on their own campuses? If so, what does this even mean? How would it be accomplished?

We can start by again turning to St. John Henry Newman who would insist that any environment hoping to foster the development of the whole person must make space for both religious truth and for personal encounter. For Newman religious truth is indeed the condition of general knowledge. As, the pope emeritus reminds us "Blessed John Henry Newman spoke of the 'circle of knowledge' to indicate that an interdependence exists between the different branches of knowledge; but God is he who has a relationship with the totality of the real; consequently, to eliminate God means to break the circle of knowledge."[30] True as these claims may be and despite sound arguments for the necessity of theology, the secular university will not be placing religious truth at the center of its curriculum anytime soon. Nevertheless, the Church must engage in missionary creativity to accompany students at these universities. I will explore this further in what follows, but first let us consider the importance and impact of personal encounter.

We do well to recall that for Newman true education aims to help students develop an integrated life. Benedict echoes this sentiment in *Caritas in veritate* when he reminds us that "Understanding and love are not in separate compartments: love is rich in understanding and understanding is full of love."[31] Commenting on this in an address to young professors, he adds, "If truth and goodness go together, so too do knowledge and love.

27. *Christus vivit*, #220.

28. *Christus vivit*, #107,

29. *Christus vivit*, #247.

30. Benedict XVI, *A Reason Open to God*, 85.

31. Benedict XVI, *Caritas in Veritate*, #30.

This unity leads to consistency in life and thought, that ability to inspire demanded of every good educator."[32] Even highly successful campus ministries who minister wonderfully to the heart, can do little to help students integrate love and knowledge in the course of their studies.

Therefore, we would ideally want college students to be able to adopt an interdisciplinary approach to their education, in order to "overcome the fragmentation of the university" and in order to achieve the philosophic habit of mind. This is important, because, as Benedict XVI puts it, "Faith's recognition of the essential unity of all knowledge provides a bulwark against the alienation and fragmentation which occurs when the use of reason is detached from the pursuit of truth and virtue."[33] Additionally, on the academic level, an interdisciplinary approach cannot be sequestered to classroom learning. After all, we are aiming to pass on an integrated life and Christian culture, not merely interdisciplinary learning. Knowledge and love go together.

Students require the witness of Catholic professors who have integrated not only knowledge and love but also what Newman calls the circle of knowledge. Formation in integral knowledge must differ from an interdisciplinary curriculum where courses from different disciplines are studied side-by-side. No, for true formation and integration to occur, students must encounter professors who have integrated the various disciplines in their faith life and learn from those professors in the context of courses which initiate them into the habit of forming integral knowledge and a communal exercise of faith seeking understanding.

Back in the early 1980s then Cardinal Ratzinger recognized that, "a principal need is for a reconstruction of the existential context of the Catechumenate . . . the common experience of the Spirit that can thus become also a foundation of realistic reflection."[34] The existential context of the Catechumenate was discipleship, a slow introduction into the Christian life. Discipleship at the university means professors should relate to students as something akin to tutors. Because true education is not learned from books but from the personal influence of a mentor who has developed the habit of mind and who exhibits an integrated life. Don Briel explained Newman's position here with typical lucidity: "The university was the work of the lecturer, while the work of the college was conducted by the tutor whose relation to his students was not one of instruction but of education

32. Benedict XVI, *A Reason Open to God*, 39.

33. Benedict XVI, *A Reason Open to God*, 48.

34. Ratzinger, *Principles of Catholic Theology*, 26.

and personal formation."[35] Obviously, the modern university as a "poly-technic utiliversity" makes no space for tutorial practice. We can hardly be optimistic about changing that fact anytime soon. Yet for the good of that ninety percent of Catholic students at non-Catholic universities, we have a missionary responsibility to approximate the impact of the tutorial system on the minds and lives of our students. After all, as Benedict XVI reminds us, "It is certain that only by putting the person at the center and making the most of dialogue and interpersonal relations can the specializing fragmentation of disciplines be overcome and the unitive perspective of knowledge be recovered."[36] If students are to grow in love and knowledge of the Lord, they must be in relation with Christians who bear witness to the integration of liturgical life and the intellectual life. They must be accompanied. Only thus can we hope to help our students strengthen their minds and wills against the confusing plurality of our times.

Yet, all this sounds idealistic. Truly students require an integrated education which makes space for God. Growth in Christian integration has always occurred through discipleship. At the modern university, this fact calls for a tutorial relationship with professors who are further along in their pilgrimage and a communal context within which students can ask their questions, offer their prayers, and pursue the understanding which faith seeks. The Church in academia has a responsibility to develop what Pope Benedict has called "the pastoral care of intelligence."[37] In *Christus vivit* Pope Francis makes a similar call. Nevertheless, the problem of providing such a community seems intractable. How can this be achieved?

Pope Francis

Indeed, the words of Francis, Benedict, and Newman as well as Vatican II's universal call to holiness comport with Leon Bloy's famous statement "the only real sadness, the only real failure, the only great tragedy in life, is not to become a saint." The Church has a responsibility to Catholic college students on non-Catholic campuses to offer them the habit of mind and the liturgical formation necessary for sainthood. Yet one may ask how in the world such a robustly Catholic education can be welcomed at non-Catholic universities, which, as polytechnic utiliversities so often seem diametrically opposed to the vision here described. How can we help Catholics at non-Catholics colleges both experience the Catholic life and develop the habit

35. Briel, "The University and the Church," 27.

36. Benedict XVI, *A Reason Open to God*, 241.

37. Benedict XVI, *A Reason Open to God*, 159.

of mind necessary to answer the questions and misconceptions raised by their atheistic and agnostic peers, since we can't take over the universities themselves?

Several Catholic campuses already boast programs which excellently offer this pastoral care of intelligence, but, if Benedict XVI is right that since the Church shares in the mission of Christ, she "has no option of becoming self-enclosed in her contentment about what she has already achieved,"[38] then Catholic universities cannot be content to offer education and formation to their own fraction of Catholic college students. Although the existence of sound Catholic universities is good and essential, they have a missionary responsibility to find ways to offer integrated knowledge to the Catholic students on secular campuses. Don Briel, Msgr. Shea and others have pioneered a potential solution. Catholic institutes can partner with secular universities to offer classes for students at those universities, a radical and creative missionary venture to infiltrate the secular university, setting up space for the intellectual and moral formation needed by students who wish to glorify God with their lives and to do so by following the examples of Newman and Benedict who shied not away from engaging non-Catholic thinkers in the friendly yet dogged pursuit of truth. Briel summed up his paradigm like this: "It is interdisciplinary, assisting in overcoming the fragmentation of the university for students and faculty; it is a work of the Church and so it assists in overcoming the false separation of the intellectual and spiritual dimensions of education; it provides a foundation for the specialized work of the disciplines (our students double major in another field for example); it offers forums for students and faculty for sustained reflection on the history and relevance of Catholic thought and culture; it cultivates a Catholic imagination; and it stimulates vocational reflection."[39] This could be a bold and creative missionary response to the needs of the ninety percent of Catholic college students at non-Catholic colleges, an attempt to build Catholic cultures of formation in the midst of Babylon. Similarly, there are several "Christian Study Centers" at universities throughout the country. Some of these are more ecumenical in nature and others are more confessional. They all seek through various but similar models to develop a community of Christians seeking to integrate their faith with their learning.

Most recently the Newman Idea, a Catholic educational and religious non-profit of which I am a member, has had its curriculum accredited by a Catholic college and has begun work to partner with various public and

---

38. Ratzinger, *Das neue Volk Gottes*, 110.

39. Don Briel as quoted by Kathryn Jean Lopez, in "Coherency in Higher Education & the Integrated Life of Faith."

private colleges and universities. The global pandemic put many of those conversation on the back burner. Nevertheless, the model has proven successful for students and attractive to some college administrators. First, it involves an integrated curriculum in which interdisciplinary Catholic courses are taught to students at non-Catholic colleges and universities by faculty who have themselves developed that habit of integral knowing. Most interdisciplinary programs aren't actually interdisciplinary, and they certainly aren't integrated. Instead curricula are designed which place students in classes from various disciplines, but since the professors continue to teach from the perspective of their own academic silos they cannot model integral knowing for students seeking to understand how to integrate their faith with their majors and careers.

Second, these professors of integration function less as lecturers and more as mentors or Oxford tutors, in doing so they model for students the activity of bringing various forms of practical, technical, and abstract knowledge together in the unity of the mind. Third, the relationship between tutors and develop into a community which together seeks the understanding which faith demands, driven by the hope which faith provides to act with the love which faith instills. In this way they can function as sacrament of unity in the midst of the secular polytechnic utiliversity. They can call it back to its origins as a true university.

Once last time, we must ask, is this not idealistic? After all, in the "Pragmatic Postscript" to his *Nova et Vetera* article, Professor Hütter concludes by asking "If heeded today, would not Newman's vision fall victim to his own famous verdict of being "unreal," that is, while theoretically compelling, nevertheless being out of touch with the concrete exigencies of real life?—The remedy needed most is often hated most by those who need it most desperately for their cure."[40] It seems to me Hütter hopes for the notional assent which might follow from his arguments to achieve the work of real assent. Even excellent essays by theologians aiming to convince secular academicians that theology is necessary for the university seem unlikely to garner notional assent, much less the real assent that would be necessary to initiate the deep curricular, cultural, and teleological changes which the modern university sorely needs.

But for Newman "The heart is commonly reached, not through reason, but through the imagination, by means of direct impressions, by the testimony of facts and events, by history, by description."[41] Furthermore, as David Delio has argued, "The tangible and social Church as 'idea', not

---

40. Hütter, "University Education," 1053.
41. Delio, *An Aristocracy of Exalted Spirits*, 227.

an interior impression in one's mind or heart, was what Newman exhorted his readers to return to."[42] Insofar as Newman's *Idea* of a university depends upon a certain relation to the Church understood as a tangible and social reality, the way to recall the polytechnic utiliversity closer to that Idea is to offer a concrete albeit germinal image of that reality. Put another way, Catholic institutes can function as ikons, as sacramental communities which witness to the beauty of a university life open to transcendence and to the integration of knowledge.

When Cardinal Ratzinger exhorted the Church to call Europe back to her Christian foundations and heritage, he insisted "the fate of a society always depends on its creative minorities. Christian believers should look upon themselves as just such a creative minority."[43]

Benedict's view of missionary activity exhibits a logic of indirection. While the Church can never eschew her missionary mandate from Christ, she exists to be the community, the body, in which the Father is worshipped in accord with the Logos. What's more, faith is aroused only when God's "closeness is felt." For Benedict, Christian communities have lost their credibility because the lives of Christians are not transparent to God often enough. This transparency and the credibility that comes with it can only come from God: "Only a power and a love that are stronger than our own initiatives can build up a fruitful and reliable community and impart to it the impetus of a fruitful mission."[44] Thus, Eucharist not only makes the church but also sends the church into the world—sends those members on pilgrimage within the modern university as sheep among wolves, to bear witness there.

Of course, a loving openness to the world that is simultaneously an act of nonconformism is necessarily an act of making oneself vulnerable. In that the Eucharist makes the church it also calls upon members of the church to "be what they see," to concretely embody a eucharistic ethos in their lives. These Catholic institutes are called to be His flesh for the life of the modern university—including skeptical colleagues, antagonistic deans, and also students, Catholic and non-Catholic alike. They can bear witness to Newman's Idea and to Christ precisely as communities formed in communion.

Creative minorities,[45] communities in which this communion can be experienced, are existential prerequisites for the church's ability to offer the

42. Delio, *An Aristocracy of Exalted Spirits*, 254.

43. Ratzinger and Pera, *Without Roots*, 80.

44. Ratzinger, *Pilgrim Fellowship of Faith*, 89. Cf. my discussion of this theme in Ratzinger in *The Benedict Proposal*.

45. Pera and Ratzinger, *Without Roots*, 51–81, 107–36.

"pastoral care of intelligence" to Catholics on secular campuses and to bear witness to Newman's Idea in the Babylon of the modern research university. Since being a Christian is not "the result of an ethical choice or a lofty idea, but the encounter with an event, a person, which gives life a new horizon and a decisive direction,"[46] notional arguments are necessary but insufficient. Real assent will be needed. These ikon institutes, as we call them, must become communities where Christianity takes on its nature as encounter, where restless hearts and minds seek to integrate academic knowledge in the Love of He who is Truth, and where they show others the glorious freedom of this search.

46. Benedict XVI, *Deus caritas est*, #1.

Beauty's Surround

The Grammar of Beauty in Daily Catholic Life

KRISTEN DRAHOS

THE WORLD is charged with the grandeur of God.
 It will flame out, like shining from shook foil;
 It gathers to a greatness, like the ooze of oil
Crushed. Why do men then now not reck his rod?
Generations have trod, have trod, have trod;   5
 And all is seared with trade; bleared, smeared with toil;
 And wears man's smudge and shares man's smell: the soil
Is bare now, nor can foot feel, being shod.

And for all this, nature is never spent;
 There lives the dearest freshness deep down things;   10
And though the last lights off the black West went
 Oh, morning, at the brown brink eastward, springs—
Because the Holy Ghost over the bent
 World broods with warm breast and with ah! bright wings.   [1]

GERARD MANLEY HOPKINS

GERARD MANLEY HOPKINS' POEM *God's Grandeur* presents a stark contrast between the shining, radiant glory of divine grandeur and the mundane, tired effects of human existence. His language—"generations have trod. . .all is seared. . .bleared. . .smeared"—puts the "freshness [of] deep down things"

1. *Gerard Manley Hopkins*, ed. Phillips, 128.

and the warmth and light of "bright wings" all the more clearly before our eyes. If we but look, we will find beauty, and beauty will draw us to God. Look up, enjoins Hopkins. Look out and find God's grandeur!

Hopkins admits, though, that this is no easy task. The second stanza of his poem holds aloft the beauty of nature, but the first weighs heavily upon his readers. To find beauty in a world that is "bare now," where the worker has lost sensitivity to "being shod" and the oppression of labor, seems all but impossible. A divide stretches between the objectivity of beauty's presence and the subject's ability to recognize and encounter its power. Although Hopkins gives a word of hope at the end of the poem, where God's Spirit continues to breathe life into the world, his poem presses us to recognize an acute problem. For all that beauty might surround and infuse the world, its potency and durability wanes for the one who encounters and witnesses it.

There are historical reasons for beauty's weakness. Until the twentieth-century, beauty was the ugly duckling of the transcendental tradition, reluctantly borne into the present from the classical religious thought of the middle ages. Fear of aesthetic pleasure distracting from the joy of sanctity brushed beauty into a subdued categorization. It was given greatest sanction when contributed to Christian piety and peace. The concern of too strong an attachment to the external world—present in early Christian ascetics as much as foundational Church bishops like Augustine—exacerbated a fear of external beauty and largely relegated it to an interior, hidden domain.[2] As the scholar Umberto Eco notes, medieval thinkers bore this early conception into their thinking. For them, beauty belonged to a moral category, amplifying the divergence of beauty's interior presence with its exterior façade. Poetry abounded in much of the early writings of central medieval thinkers, such as Peter Damien, Abelard, Bernard of Clairvaux, Thomas Aquinas, and Bonaventure, but ascetic measure left its imprint with fear of what might be "dangerous in the wrong place."[3] Furthermore, beauty received a significant downgrade in status in a post-Enlightenment, and in particular post-Kantian world. Kant's esteem of rational subjectivity made room for beauty's presence, but ultimately prioritized a twofold philosophic alternative as the source of subjectivity's power and freedom.[4] A subsequent

2. Eco, *Art and Beauty in the Middle Ages*, 3–10.

3. Eco, 9. This is not to say beauty did not have a place. On the contrary, Socratic aesthetic contemplation, interior rather than exterior foci, and lamentation of natural transience lead to a view of beauty outlined by its most stable, enduring, and intellectual facets. Beauty projected clarity, proportion, harmony, and light. It showcased the form of created existence that mirrored Greek platonic stability.

4. Kant relies on a category called the sublime in his *Critique of the Power of Judgment* as that which offers human reason unfettered power and scope, even as reason

combination of Kant's preference for the unfettered freedom of the sublime, instead of beauty, and the Romantic affective rejoinder to the Enlightenment degraded beauty's standing even more.[5]

Today, beauty has largely been redefined as taste, or a preferential opinion held by individuals that may or may not cohere with the opinions of others. Beauty is, by and large, a matter of subjective predilection unrelated to either a transcendental norm or form, as well as disconnected from reason's appeals to universality. It is fully and only in the eye of the beholder. Unless beauty trespasses into the realm of ethics, where an aesthetic representation harms an individual or the community in some way—beauty categorized as individual taste cannot be judged. This is not to say that people, and especially young adults, are not deeply influenced by aesthetic decisions made for and by them, from the sleek lines of iphones, contemporary architecture, and web designs to the fashion rebrands that have brought back large eyewear frames, checked flannel, high-waisted jeans, and the chunky heel. Contemporary tastes represent an amalgam of advertisement and individual preference. Beauty's mainstream marginalization is not what startles. What is surprising is that this marginalization extends deeply into contemporary Catholic parish life and stands in stark contrast to the academic revitalization of beauty in twentieth-century theology.

For over seventy years, academics in theology have engaged a steady recovery project in the field of theological aesthetics. In Catholic theology, no one surpasses Hans Urs von Balthasar and his seven-volume theological aesthetics *The Glory of the Lord*. His masterful exploration weaves a dialogue of Old and New Testaments, Catholic and Protestant traditions, ancient and modern philosophy, and a diverse range of literary figures in order to champion the specific issue of beauty as a theological resource. Beauty, be that of the natural world or created art, offers a word of hope and an attractive invitation. Beauty operates as an ontological manifestation of reality that calls for recognition of and response to the splendor that appears in the created world. It showcases the mystery of form associated with the "great radiance from within" that creation itself manifests.[6] In other words, it shows an irreducible connection between *what* is manifest, or the

---

adheres to that which is universal. Beauty stands as that which contrasts with the sublime: "the beautiful in nature concerns the form of the object, which consists in limitation; the sublime, by contrast, is to be found in a formless object insofar as limitlessness is represented in it." Kant, *Critique of the Power of Judgment*, 128.

5. Despite Friedrich Schiller's attempts to revive beauty's uses and navigate between the Scylla and Charybdis of sense and reason as well as form and freedom, beauty's status continued to devalue.

6. Von Balthasar, *The Glory of the Lord, Vol. 1*, 19–20.

form of Being as it appears in existing things, and *how* Being is manifest, namely, through the radiance that accompanies creation. Beauty gives reality its shape, which is anything but "surface deep," as well as its formal brilliance that arrests our attention and attracts us to it. Recognizing the significance and power of this erstwhile transcendental, Balthasar and his successors bring beauty into the height of theology—as part of the nature of God's perfection as divine glory—and into the heart of creaturely existence in a world made for relationship with God.[7] It is "no abstraction," but rather "the living bond between God and the world."[8] For Balthasar and others, the "truth" of the world cannot be thought without beauty as a critical part of what and how created reality appears.

For Balthasar to recognize that this "last word" ought to be "first" was, and still is, a dramatic declaration for what has been forgotten and cast aside.[9] This bounty, however, remains almost entirely unknown and untranslated from its academic revitalization to the majority of Catholic parishes. Catholics thus find themselves at a strange juxtaposition of two practical problems. First, the problem of beauty's historic deterioration to taste has further marooned it as a resource for serious consideration. No one has taught parishioners to understand and mine the richness of what beauty can offer—it largely remains bound to subjectivity's personal preference. Parish programing leaves aesthetic formation out of its biblical, moral, and evangelical efforts. Worse, beauty often devolves into a pawn in liturgical wars between traditional and contemporary parish factions. Either what is old is beautiful and what is new is ugly, or vice versa. Beauty, therefore, deforms in two directions: either its neutrality saps the vitality and fades its presence to the shadow of mere taste, or its weaponization turns beauty into a cudgel. Moreover, Catholic lapses with beauty leave it ripe for further devolution in contemporary society. As Pope Francis notes in his *Cristus Vivit*, today's culture warps beauty through its commodification of youth. Pope Francis warns, "beauty is associated with a youthful appearance, cosmetic treatments that hide the traces of time. Young bodies are constantly advertised as a means of selling products. . . . .Adults want to snatch youth for

---

7. For example, consider works from Hans Küng, John Milbank, Graham Ward, Edith Wyschogrod, and David Bentley Hart. Küng presses us to see classical art as a sign of God; Milbank traces the path of subjective encounter with the infinite depth of objectivity; Ward presses beauty beyond its idolized forms; Wyschogrod navigates the geography of the modern subject's response to beauty's face; Hart turns our steps toward beauty's infinity as a reflection of divine radiance. These are but a few examples of today's fruitful engagement with beauty in theological conversation.

8. Balthasar, *The Glory of the Lord, Vol. 1*, 18.

9. Balthasar, *The Glory of the Lord, Vol. 1*, 18.

themselves."[10] Beauty's idolization turns time into an enemy and promotes a massive robbers' game. All the more is the true depth of beauty is and offers hidden. Catholics of all ages are robbed of the rich heritage and resources of their own tradition.

Beauty, however, need not be sidelined. Furthermore, its reincorporation has profoundly practical benefits. In the remainder of this chapter, I will discuss three notable areas where incorporation of beauty can have a substantial impact: fostering attention in prayer, supporting a habit of everyday wonder, and providing sustenance in times of suffering. In addition to developing beauty's natural contribution, each of these presents something that is under increasing pressure in postmodernity. Today, attention spans continue to reduce with the digitization and atomization of time and history; quantitative fields become dominant expressions of (rather than measurements within) what is valuable; experiences of suffering are increasingly quarantined and marginalized within the fabric of daily life. Beauty has the particular benefit of addressing each of these issues. Its power comes from an encounter with the personal God whose radiance definitively entered and informs the world's innate, analogical goodness. As Catholics, and particularly today, we cannot afford to sideline what beauty offers.

While beauty has the power to matter for all the Church, I will further attune my discussion's scope to the needs of emerging young adults. Young people present a critical audience for beauty's recovery within the Church. On the one hand, they are on the front lines of society's commodification of beauty, not only as consumers of beauty's commercialization, but also as those coded for their own self-exploitation in the project of self-creation and self-consumption of a fetishized aesthetic idol. While digital media is not inherently responsible for beauty's commodification and fetishizing, its emergence and dominance in the presence of young people's daily expressions, social experiences, and cultural creations further its depreciation. On the other, young adults present opportunities to be aesthetic ambassadors. Pope Francis notes that wisdom grows with experience, but he also praises the openness and enthusiasm that press young people to passionately convey important ideas to the Church and world at large. Young adults who are invited to engage the true face of beauty—not its counterfeits—have the energy to bring into their communities the depths of their discoveries and develop the richness that beauty has to offer as part of the Church's ongoing renewal, of itself and of the world it serves.

---

10. *Christus vivit*, #79.

Part I: Beauty and Attention

Beauty's power begins with harnessing attention. This pull differs, however, from the contemporary visual arrest that bombards people with attractive images. With the latter, gazes lock onto screens that flash with advertisements, eyes scan for what appeals through a continuous scroll, and appetites whet with virtual offerings that give glimpses into realities not our own. As Pope Francis points out,

> it is no longer merely a question of 'using' instruments of communication, but of living in a highly digitalized culture that has a profound impact on ideas of time and space, on our self-understanding, our understanding of others and the world, and our ability to communicate, learn, be informed, and enter into relationship with others.[11]

This overstimulation changes the interface between user and medium. Cosmetic appeal operates in a threefold manner: by arresting, detaining, and fragmenting attention. Superficial beauty begins by presenting an imperatival form, where the subject is commanded to "look!" and "remain!" In an increasingly saturated and digitized world, it can seem nearly impossible to escape this imposition. On the one hand, advertisements and images flood the everyday spaces we inhabit. Billboards' presentations invade private spaces through the flashing glare of screen sidebars and the entertainment channels people surf through and click open. On the other, people are encouraged to create and continuously update cosmetic identities online—both professionally and socially. One's virtual presence presents increasing demands to post, upgrade, filter, and curate. Obedience to a culture of cosmetic appearance is both passive (observed) and active (created). In both arenas, people's subjective freedom begins to shift in consequence.

Once the cosmetic command has been obeyed, the subject finds that her gaze is held captive. It is hard, if not impossible, to look away. This kind of appearance maintains the subject's gaze not by an inherent depth, but rather by holding the subject hostage. To be detained by this superficial attraction is not an invitation to remain, but rather a seizure and confinement by what demanded attention. The glamourous appearance promises the subject the enjoyment of what is better with the promise of attractive elevation. In reality, however, the one who looks trades freedom for restraint without even realizing the cost. The subject is placed under increasing pressure to embrace the self-commodification of themselves as image. In the words of philosopher Byung-Chul Han, "one is simultaneously. . .victim

11. *Christus vivit*, #86.

and perpetrator" in the creation and constant curation of one's virtual presence.[12] Moreover, each instance of the superficial competes with the next. Commands to halt and look war upon the subject, whose gaze barely locks onto one image before it is wrenched toward another. It becomes impossible to remain to linger or ponder what is present—cosmetic images are fungible as they quickly replace one another in a seemingly endless litany of selfies, tweets, posts, and updates. Attention becomes the necessary casualty in this assault. The gaze of the consumer is constantly consumed as the subject is stripped of subjective freedom, the capacity for attention so diminished that it is hard to even recognize the process, let alone revolt in response.

While beauty seemingly resembles the cosmetic parade, the two are hardly equivalent. To be pounded by words and drowned by visual caches is both exhausting and destructive. What theologians and philosophers describe as beauty, however, presents a fundamentally different kind of encounter with what attracts and captures human attention. First, beauty begins with an invitation rather than a command. It asks the subject—will you linger? At times, this invitation is subtle, while at others it dramatically halts the subject's gaze. This kind of arrest contrasts with that which detained the subject through cosmetic attraction. In a classical vocabulary, beauty's appearance and invitation appears as fundamentally disinterested. What is beautiful is beautiful because of the depth of what manifests that appears in and through the form that manifestation takes—in short, the *realty* that beauty is communicated through its radiant appearance. Beauty does not need the subjective gaze of the viewer to be itself. Its splendor is all its own and does not feed on gaze of the viewer. As a result, beauty need not force the subject to remain. Its appeal is not predatory, but generous. The beauty of art, nature, or literature give to, rather than take from, those who notice and stay to see what unfurls.

Second, beauty feeds the viewer from the wealth of itself without impoverishing itself in the process. Here too we find a crucial difference from cosmetic glamour, which is limited by being precisely "skin deep." Beauty showcases the bounty of analogical infinity, or a depth that is never depleted in the gift of encounter. No matter how many view beauty or linger in its mystery, beauty never runs dry. Although beauty's depth cannot be measured with the analytic tools of algebra and geometry, it nevertheless demonstrates its presence in human experience. We begin to understand the nature of this depth when we consider why people return to favorite paintings in museums, press repeat to hear the song resound again, or catch their breath at the colors in a sunset they've seen paint the sky before. Beauty

12. Byung-Chul Han, *The Burnout Society*, 19.

unfolds its bounty for the one who would encounter it not by replicating and replacing itself, as cosmetic charms do, but rather by inviting the viewer into a deeper embrace of its own mystery. Its vitality does not grow stale or tired by familiarity. On the contrary, increased time in beauty's presence opens new horizons for the subject to enjoy and explore.

Beauty thus offers a practical redirection for daily life. It begins by developing our capacity for attention. At the outset, working to reclaim, deepen, and develop the power of attention might seem daunting, particularly in a world saturated by cosmetic beauty and its effects. Nevertheless, it is fundamental in order to meet and encounter the God who fits neither into the gross size of complex philosophic systems nor the smallness of character-counted sound bites and flash-point images. As Simone Weil affirms, "the key to a Christian conception of studies is the realization that prayer consists of attention. It is the orientation of all the attention of which the soul is capable toward God."[13] Attention, in other words, is fundamental. Beauty supplies a practical tool that can help recover what has been siphoned and atrophied by its cosmetic doppelganger.

Attention functions like a muscle. "Warmth of heart cannot make up for it [attention]" Weil writes, because to base attention on the pleasurable is to depend upon pleasure's appearance.[14] As a gift that attracts, beauty supports attention's perseverance by reducing the initial burden placed on this faculty. The first part of beauty's nature—invitation—hones attention and invites a subjective encounter with God's presence. Next, beauty supports attention's duration. When we encounter beauty, the effort needed to pay attention reduces. We develop our capacity for attention by a decision to linger and relate to that depth—which is an exercise of intellect and will over some duration of time. The more we encounter beauty, both in the short moments where we recognize it in passing or in the longer experiences of contemplation, the more our capacity to see its presence, acknowledge its distinctiveness, and engage its mysterious depth increases. As in any relationship, the amount and quality of time spent matter.

This is especially true of prayer. The Psalms are perhaps the easiest place to see the interactive mode of content and form as beauty, as well as beauty's effects. For the modern person dealing with the effects of fragmented attention, praying may feel daunting, if not impossible. Beauty, though, comes to aid the one whose mind restlessly shifts yet whose heart yearns for a deeper encounter with God. The Psalmist's words present an initial encounter that invites readers to linger. In Psalm 65, initial words that

13. Weil, *Waiting for God*, 57.
14. Weil, *Waiting for God*, 57.

invoke praise and the might of God transition to creation's powerful beauty. The Psalm's words encourage our minds to weld together the mysterious nature of natural wonders—from the grandness of mountains to the roaring seas, and the wonder of the dawn to the fading mystery of evening's shadows—with the abundance that comes from divine care that blesses and cultivates the earth—drenching its furrows, clothing the hills, and making crops abound and prosper. By praying the Psalms, our minds restless shifting transitions into an intentional journey around what is both recognizable and also wondrously strange. The oracular intention of poetry contours a visual landscape that is familiar, where natural beauty surrounds us, and also foreign, as the world's beauty crescendos to amplify the unassailable and inimitable glory of God. Rather than rush through prayer, the beautiful language of the Psalms forges a path for the experienced as well as the novice. Psalm 48, which begins with contemplation of Mount Zion as "beautiful in its loftiness," concludes with the injunction to "Walk about. . .go around her, count her towers, consider well her ramparts, view her citadels." Invitation grants participation, where there is always more to discover.

The beauty of the Psalms initiates a journey of prayer. Continuing to pray the Psalms invites deepening attention and reflection upon both creation and the God who made it. It is no surprise to see large chunks of monastic life devoted to praying the psalms. Devoting time to this beauty builds a foundation for relationship and attunes our minds to its significance. Beauty is not a distraction from spiritual life, but that which promotes it and attunes modern minds to the richness of its offerings. It both captures our attention and supports our redevelopment of this atrophied, yet fundamental, capacity. The more we learn to see the beauty of prayer and support it in our prayer life—be that when we rise or go to sleep, over meals, and most especially at mass, the more readily and deeply are we able to embrace the mysterious relationship that each of us, as humble created beings, have with the Lord of the Universe.

Part II: Wonder in the Everyday

G.K. Chesterton once wrote, "the world will never starve for want of wonders, but only for want of wonder."[15] Chesterton penned this line at the end of the first chapter of his *Tremendous Trifles* after writing, "Satan was the most celebrated of Alpine guides, when he took Jesus to the top of an exceeding high mountain and showed him all the kingdoms of the earth. The joy of Satan in standing on a peak is not a joy in largeness, but a joy in

---

15. G. K. Chesterton, *Tremendous Trifles* (Cavalier Classics, 2015), 3.

beholding smallness, in the fact that all men look like insects at his feet."[16] With technological advances, it is very easy to feel that we have ourselves climbed to the top of the mountain. Many conflate scientific advancement and truth as though the two were perfectly and exclusively equivalent. In this event, the world is made small before our feet. But to make the world so small is to lose the world as it is, and to lose ourselves as marvelous mysteries made to be in relation to God. The practicality of beauty is the practicality of interruption and arrest that restores the grand dimensions of the world. Beauty halts the gaze and asks a question about the depths of creation and the God who sustains it. It offers an invitation into the vast mystery that this world so desperately needs. One miracle of childhood is to see a world of possibility beyond natural limits. The more we learn to see beauty as adults, the more we are opened to that same infinity of possibility. God's love knows no bounds, and divine infinity outstrips our wildest creativity.

American essayist and poet Annie Dillard challenges her readers to reassume a posture of wonder through everyday experiences. Dillard's first book, *Pilgrim at Tinker Creek*, presents a case for a new way of living in the natural world and of seeing the everyday miracles of one's own backyard. What she discovers is fluid and dynamic, teeming with life and at times brutal in its exchanges. The world bursts with abundance. "This is the extravagant landscape of the world, given, given with pizzazz, given in good measure, pressed down, shaken together, and running over."[17] The more we walk with Dillard, the more our own world opens up to the mysteriousness that this world offers. Her eyes encourage us to look into the intricacies of our own landscape, and especially the intricacies of the natural world we largely ignore. "The texture of the world, its filigree and scrollwork, means that there is the possibility for beauty here, a beauty inexhaustible in its complexity, which opens to my knock, which answers in me a call I do not remember calling, and which trains me to the wild and extravagant nature of the spirit I seek."[18] A walk down a familiar neighborhood street can be as unfamiliar as journey to a new city. In Dillard's case, observations of water beetles, weasels, frogs, and other creatures living around a nearby stream presents opportunities to see the world anew. The smallness of a creek becomes a universe of opportunities. The humbleness of everyday repetition stretches activities into patterns and constellations of activity. "This modified lizard's song welling out of the fireplace has a wild, utterly foreign music; it becomes

---

16. Chesterton, *Tremendous Trifles*, 3.
17. Dillard, *Three by Annie Dillard*, 144.
18. Dillard, *Three by Annie Dillard*, 144.

more and more beautiful as it becomes more and more familiar."[19] Surprise thwarts viewing the world as mechanized order, without reducing the patterns Dillard notices to mere chaos. Although suffering pierces through and marks Dillard's experience of the world, the nibbles, bites, and even chomps that "fray" existence do not destroy the glory she has discovered anew.[20]

The world of Dillard is the world of Chesterton's rediscovered England in his *Orthodoxy*. It is the place that is foreign on account of rediscovery, yet familiar as the place that, really, we have been living all along. Beauty is the hallmark of this world. This rediscovery vested with beauty is the world expanded by eyes attuned to reality's vast depth. To reinvest the world with everyday wonder is not to turn it into a fantasyland, where the goal is to escape reality in search of the extraordinary. On the contrary, training the eyes to see beauty in the everyday presents the opportunity to engage what is really present before us. As with prayer, a habit of attention is required to acquire and sustain this kind of vision. In Dillard's work, the idea of learning to be witness to the world is a lesson learned not once, but rather practiced by the day and even by the hour. Yet it is precisely this kind of attention to the everyday that reveals the sacrality that existence manifests.

For young adults, enthusiasm for life remains high as perspective shifts from imagination's creativity in the meld of fantasy to expanding dreams that make present new horizons of opportunity. Excitement of the young adulthood presents a vision the world filled with openness and fresh prospects. This energy and passion—what Pope Francis describes as the renewal of the "young self"—is a vital aspect of renewal that habits of wonder likewise foster.[21] Here too is beauty eminently practical. Beauty helps to position young adult's creative excitement and passionate energy. It encourages a reprioritization of existence and self within youth's burgeoning domain. To innovate through the lens of beauty and wonder is to be a creator who refuses to eclipse or exploit what is other in one's surrounding. Dialogic creativity engages the other and draws from the depths of what the other offers.

---

19. Dillard, *Three by Annie Dillard*, 106.

20. Dillard does not shy away from creation's horrors. Her prose pushes readers to the brink with suffering. "So much is amiss," she claims" that I must consider the second fork in the road. . .it is only the human feeling that is freakishly amiss. . ..What creator could be so cruel. . .to let them [otters, or creatures] care?" Dillard, *Three by Annie Dillard*, 173. Dillard uses this chapter in *Tinker Creek*, entitled "Fecundity," to interrogate the meaning of the world's abundant suffering and the possibility of a good or loving Creator in charge of it all. All the more does she continue this interrogation throughout her corpus. As she presents an increasingly complex and strained relation to that which she calls God or divinity, she simultaneously refuses to collapse the world's wonder into its darkness.

21. *Christus vivit* #13, 16.

In effect, attention to everyday beauty enacts a fundamental de-centering of the ego. In *Teaching a Stone to Talk*, Dillard embraces the life of the seemingly barren Palo Santo trees. These trees embody the kind of hollowed witness that makes space for the hallowed dimensions of existence. "You empty yourself and wait, listening."[22] If Dillard smothers the world with her own shadow, she distorts the mysterious existence of what surrounds her and misses the engaging the abundance that the world offers. As she writes in *Tinker Creek*, "our life is a faint tracing on the surface of mystery."[23] Dillard challenges her readers to embrace the activity of witness as an inherently de-centering activity with varied images of vacancy, from the trees stark limbs to the cold frosty bareness of polar ice caps. Witnessing becomes a habit of kenotic subjectivity.

The juxtaposition of beauty's fullness and the subjective vacancy required of witness challenges a world where self-creation and self-prioritization dominate social and professional spheres. This lesson, however, is not meant to quash creativity outright. On the contrary, learning to see and respond to the wonders of everyday beauty offers a chance for dialogic, rather than individualistic, inspiration. Beauty harbors wells of unplumbed treasure that challenge, compliment, and refresh the relation we have to our natural environment, our neighbors, and our world at large. Beauty breaks us free from the mundane and small world of ourselves and opens us to the opportunities to be imagine more than our own narrowed perspectives.

Part III: Beauty and Suffering

Beauty's form stretches our imagination in more ways than one. It presses us to engage the meaning of existence's depth and splendor that reveals more about the world than merely our own subjective reflection. It breaks into our world when we look at it and invites us into its mysterious reality and presence. Beauty reveals a form that attracts, an abundance that seems infinite, and a pattern that invites a dialogic relationship. It invests the world with meaning as much as confounds simplified explanations Beauty resists reduction to subjectivity's whim or materiality's externality.

The presence of beauty might seem, at first, to be at once mysterious yet fully recognizable. Not only can we distinguish between beauty and its counterfeits, but we can make judgments about what is not and cannot be considered beautiful. Such judgments are certainly important. They support beauty's restoration as much as weed out what would deplete its power.

22. Dillard, *Teaching a Stone to Talk*, 90.
23. Dillard, *Tinker Creek*, 141.

However, to limit beauty to what we have so far discussed—or what has been inherited and developed out of a classical tradition where light, proportion, clarity, and unity prevailed as classifying features—limits beauty's scope. This is not to say it is not to say such a description is inaccurate. On the contrary, it is significant and vital for Catholic practice. It is, however, incomplete. To *only* think of beauty this way once again shortchanges reality of its presence and power. All of beauty's dimensions necessarily relate to the connection between created existence and the God who creates, preserves, and sustains that existence. The analogous, albeit not synonymous, relationship between divine perfection and the world gives beauty its form, depth, and power. It is precisely because of this relation that beauty has a darkened dimension.

This relationship changes, however, with the impact of the Incarnation on the created world. The Word that becomes flesh leaves an irrevocable mark not only upon history, but also upon the form of existence itself. The Incarnation breaks open the boundaries of glory's relation to beauty and of beauty's potential. Christ becomes the in-forming presence of beauty itself, or what Balthasar describes as the *Urform* of beauty as its ground in origin (divine, transcendent glory) and shape (concrete manifestation in human flesh). Yet for Balthasar, it is crucial to remember that the Incarnation is not a static equation, but rather a dynamic form where the drama of Christ's earthly existence shapes the meaning of the form be creates for the world. In other words, it does not merely matter that Jesus is both divine and human, but that Jesus' whole life imparts meaning upon created reality and the shape of beauty itself. Beauty's form, reformed to and through Christ, directly relates to a living subject. Jesus radiates the beauty of God in himself and through the drama earthly existence. There are no beautiful forms that outstrip his, since he is the exact and fullest expression of divine love and glory outpoured for the world. The radiance, splendor, depth, and mystery of beauty conform to the form of Christ.

Cruciform beauty—or "dark beauty"—explores the meaning and power of the form of God that imprints creation's darkest moments. In Balthasar's words, "the abyss of the unfathomable love has entered the abyss of the meaningless hatred and hidden itself there."[24] Dark beauty signals the reality of the God whose presence empties into the darkness of existence's deformations. Christ's beauty assumes a form that reforms darkness itself. For Balthasar, this is no passing moment in history. Cruciform beauty not only encounters the depths of suffering and creation's deformation, but also

---

24. Von Balthasar, *The Glory of the Lord, Vol. 7*, 210; Casarella, "The Expression and Form of the Word," 128.

penetrates it and carries it into Christ's resurrected body. Balthasar embraces the wounded Lamb from the book of Revelation as the carrier of dramatic, but also the aesthetic expression, of Jesus' death, and resurrection. The glorious body and transfigured wounds of Christ are both meaningful. They are united in the one body of the resurrected Christ, but they are distinct parts of his form, and likewise, they are distinct parts of beauty's expression.

The cross as an active aesthetic form might seem strange to those of us who are used to thinking of the "light beauty" of glory's vitality and light that attend the resurrection. However, the cross also presents particular opportunities for exploring beauty's power in spaces where it seems absent or foresworn. As Balthasar recognizes, there is something fundamentally changed in darkness by the cross' form, which then forever impacts our own experiences of the darkness of life's Good Fridays. The cross and its particular beauty offer a strange kind of attraction that is not simply reducible to the glory of the resurrection. This beauty supplies a moment of encounter not only in abundance, but also in the heart of desolation. Dillard, who so eloquently pulls us into the wonder of nature's abundance, simultaneously finds herself stricken by creation's bleeding wounds and mangled bodies. Dillard's prose increasingly turns to darkened imagery to express an encounter between brokenness and God. In her *Holy the Firm*, Dillard stands transfixed by the horror of a child badly burned in an accident, writing, "Held, held fast by love in the world like the moth in wax, your life a wick, your head on fire with prayer, held utterly, outside and in, you sleep alone. . .you cry God."[25] In Dillard's depiction, the child's pain fuses with the image of a moth burning in a candle, whose flaming body transposes the horror of death to God through an offering of prayer. Dillard does not try to erase the pain of suffering. Rather, she transposes it through the form of one whose body itself is an offering held up and aloft—namely, the body of Christ on the cross. As the radiance of God darkens in death, the fire of divine power ignites and burns bright with another kind of hallowed beauty. Christ on the cross is not simply a standard to look at, but a form to enter into.

It is not that beauty has ceased to be itself, nor ought we celebrate rather than decry and lament the world's violence, pain, and suffering. What dark beauty offers, though, is an expanded domain so that nothing is out of reach, as well as an expanded expression of radiance, so that all can participate no matter how disfigured. In short, there is an invitation for divine relationship even in the deepest darkness. Recognizing and developing an appreciation for this side of beauty further draws us into God's love in the moments that seem to be outside of the good and out of the reach of

25. Dillard, *Holy the Firm*, 76.

consolation, such as the loss of a parent or child, the horrors of a life-altering disease, or the scars created by neglect or abuse. As the Holy Cross motto states, "*Ave Crux, Spes Unica.*" A practical incorporation of such beauty— as a vocabulary for thinking through our own experiences, in the ways we prepare those who minister in times of grief, in the prayers we write for the times of great loss—impacts Catholic engagement and ministry during life's most painful moments. Pope Francis reminds us, "none of this pain goes away; it stays with us. . .the harsh reality can no longer be concealed."[26] Furthermore, it would be a mistake to think that this beauty ought to be sequestered for the more experienced. Young adults are not immune to suffering. On the contrary, the "tragedies of the young" cry out for communal response.[27] As Pope Francis notes, "the worst thing we can do is adopt that worldly spirit whose solution is simply to anaesthetize young people with other messages, with other distractions, with trivial pursuits."[28]

Beauty offers a form for these experiences that neither abandons them to the hopelessness of tragedy, nor simplifies their complexity with superficial gilding. In *Christus Vivit*, Pope Francis urges the Church to remember that "weeping for the young" is a profound, communal act. He disassociates this kind of weeping from tears of self-pity. The weeping he advocates is "an expression of mercy or compassion."[29] These lessons echo ideas in a variety of Catholic spiritual writers, not least of whom is Dorothy Day. In her book *The Reckless Way of Love*, Day reminds her readers that the Latin *compassio* translates "to suffer with." "To love," she declares, "is to suffer."[30] Compassion presses Catholics beyond the territory of sentiment, or the external expressions of consolation, and toward the power of the cross. Compassion as "joined" suffering would be masochistic were not suffering conformed to the cross' meaning.

The cross transects the incommunicable. This kind of beauty is what allows those who suffer, like recently deceased Beth Haile, to reflect: "the Jesus I am coming to know is not so much a healer or a moral teacher or a miracle worker, but a *sufferer*. . . He came to suffer, not to show us a way out of it, but to offer us solidarity. . . I am encountering the Jesus who is still showing us his wounds after the resurrection. And I am encountering Jesus in the countless people who suffer in solidarity with me."[31] Haile—still

26. *Christus vivit* #75.

27. *Christus vivit* #76.

28. *Christus vivit* #75.

29. *Christus vivit* #76.

30. Day, *The Reckless Way of Love*, 86–87.

31. Haile, "Catholic Moral Theology."

young herself in her early thirties—meets the darkened radiance of God in her suffering. She and those who suffered alongside her entered into the mysterious beauty of the cross, where not even Haile's experiences with cancerous tumors would be rendered meaningless. The beauty of the cross made a form for a profound encounter with the mystery of God's own suffering. It provided Haile a way to express that to others, a way for her community to join her, and the assurance that the wounds of this experience would neither be ignored nor rendered insignificant, but rather transfigured and present in the resurrection's glory.

Conclusion

To argue for the practicality of beauty is like shrugging on a dinner jacket tailored for someone with entirely different proportions. While you can get your body in, the sleeves are short, the back stretched taut, and buttoning it in front promises the certainty of failure. The dimensions of modernity's practicality assess by measuring the rapidity of communication, reproducibility by mechanization, and the profitability of a product's commodification. While cosmetic beauty might slide smoothly into these sleeves, real beauty resists at every turn. Yet for all that it cannot fit into modern clothes, beauty is highly practical. It fosters our capacity for deep attention, it expands the domain of our world by the inverted and exploded opportunities of wonder, and it gives us a language for living and compassionately transforming the bleakest moments that shade human life. Beauty's strengths highlight places of poverty that we find in our digitized and commercialized world. It invites us to experience another way of living. It redefines the practical. Beauty does not need our attention, but rather halts our gaze because it has something to offer. Beauty assures us that the world is deeper than the crust we trod. The blear and sear of our toil does not sum up the human experience. Rather, beauty reminds us that the world is a place of abundance, mystery, and surprise.

Beauty teaches us to pay attention to our surroundings so that we expand, rather than shrink, our perspectives. By taking nothing from us and freely giving a world of splendor, it models the love of a God who delights in creation without needing to harvest anything from it. Beauty's invitation to encounter the living God is an invitation into the entire spectrum of divine love—from its splendor, radiance, and glory to the darkness, pain, and abandonment of the cross. This diversity of beauty conforms to Christ. The *Urform* of God's love transfigures all existence, leaving nothing behind. In Christ, the wounds of the world transfigure and are born into the glory of heaven. For God's love knows no bounds, and divine infinity outstrips our wildest creativity. Returning to Hopkins, we indeed look out toward the "bright wings" of the Spirit—be they shining or radiantly dark, beauty indeed surrounds.

The Habits of Belonging

Patrick Gilger, SJ ───────────────────────────────

A FEW YEARS AGO, a friend told me a story. He is also a Jesuit, the president of one our universities, which is relevant only because his story related how he and the university Provost had been invited to dinner by some graduating seniors. The students wanted to say goodbye and toast to their experiences over their four years. Pleased, he and the Provost accepted.

When the evening of the dinner arrived, the two found themselves having a lovely conversation. When the food was finished a last round of wine was poured. It was then that the students summoned the courage to pose some of the questions that had stirred them to make the invitation. "Father, how did you make the decision to become a priest?" asked one. "Provost," another wondered, "how did you know you were ready to marry?"

As all ministers know, it is a joy (and a privilege and a responsibility) to be asked such questions. And my friend, taking it as such, tried to respond both with depth and in a manner that might resonate. "In my prayer at that time," he said, "what I would do is first try to be quiet. Then I would try to pay attention to how my heart felt." As my friend spoke he felt the room grow quiet. But it was not the quiet of attentiveness; it was a disjointed, nervous quiet, as if the unity and joviality felt just a few moments before had been ruptured. Sensing this, he turned to the students and asked them: "Does this make sense? Does it resonate?"

But the quiet held, stretched until the room felt a bit awkward. Piqued, he asked again: "Well, what happens when you pay attention to what's going on in your hearts?" Another pause. Until finally one of the students summoned up the courage to respond. "You know, Father," she said, "most of the time when we pay attention to what's going on in our hearts. . . what we feel is. . . anxious."

A single anecdote does not amount to data. It does not show that such an experience is prevalent among young Americans or young American Catholics (although it is; the data will be provided below). But if, as Simone

Weil has argued, "attention. . . is the same thing as prayer," the challenge anxiety puts to the attention-capacity of young people today ought to be of concern for the Church.[1] In addition to the compassion we rightly feel for those, ourselves included, who know all too well the racing heart, the rapid breathing, the inability to focus that accompany anxiety, other questions emerge when considering the relationship between young people and the Church. To take just one example: how possible is it to develop a relationship with God, much less make a permanent vocational commitment, if anxiety is short-circuiting our capacity for sustained attention?

In this chapter I propose to chart out a social-theoretical and historical framework for how the American Catholic Church ought to understand the increasing-common experience of anxiety among young people today and, then, to offer some ideas for how the Church, as a corporate body, might address it. The first step in fulfilling such a charter will be showing that the above anecdote is not an outlier. After laying out the data, this section will argue that this epidemic of anxiety ought not to be understood—or responded to—as primarily an individual problem but as a shared, a social one.

This turn from the individual to the social will lead us to ask about how we came to inhabit a society in which individual persons are increasingly held responsible for resolving such supra-individual problems. Answering this question will require a turn to history, in this case to an ideal typical reading of how various historical forms of social life have provided common actions and common narratives to those who live and move and have their being within them. What we will see here is that, while the post-everything age in we live has provided us with many freedoms, we have endured losses as well. First among these losses, it will be argued, is our familiarity with common life. We have forgotten—or, better, our society is failing to pass on—the habits of belonging.

Following this historical sketch we will turn our attention to how this framework can aid us in imagining shared, collective responses to the epidemic of anxiety. How, that is, we can unlearn the habit of teaching the faith as a set of ideas to be mastered and begin again to live together as disciples, apprentices of the master teacher whose actions we imitate.

This chapter, then, aims to be nothing more or less than a schematic that incites imagination. It seeks to offer a framework that we in the Church can use to evaluate whether, where, and the extent to which we are succumbing to the all-too-common temptation to offer individuated solutions to shared problems. If successful, it will help us ask whether we are capable

---

1. Weil, *Gravity and Grace*, 117.

of responding to the signs of our times—and begin to sketch the agenda for such a response.

An Age of Anxiety?

But first we must ask whether it is actually the case that we live in an age of anxiety. The data certainly answers in the affirmative. Even a cursory glance at recent statistics about the mental health of young Americans shows that, over the decade from 2005 to 2014, major depressive episodes among adolescents rose 37%. The authors of this study note that this scale of increase translates "into an increase of more than a half million adolescents."[2] Not an insignificant number.

Jean Twenge and her co-authors have recently published a paper in which they followed the same data out a further three years, to 2017. In this paper Twenge and her coauthors noted a continued increase in mental health disorders, which now affect, they note, not just 11.3 but 13.2 percent of young adults. Further, they point out that this trend was limited to young adults (ages 18–25). That is, a corresponding increase has not been found among older age-cohorts. "These trends," Twenge explained, "are weak or non-existent among adults 26 years and over, suggesting a generational shift in mood disorders instead of an overall increase across all ages."[3] This is especially striking given that, as Varun Soni has noted, it is traditionally the oldest generation of Americans who are the loneliest.[4]

Other research has shown that anxiety has become something of a new norm for young Americans. The well-known 2014 study by Penn State's Center for Collegiate Mental Health revealed that more than half of all students visiting campus health clinics that year reported that anxiety was a problem.[5] Similar results have been found in the National Survey on Drug Use and Health. As Twenge notes in her work building off that survey's data, "serious psychological distress, which includes feelings of anxiety and hopelessness, jumped 71 percent among 18- to 25-year-olds from 2008 to 2017."[6] Clearly something is happening here.

It is to be expected that explanations as to the cause of this epidemic of anxiety vary widely. Some argue that increased pressure to succeed is to

2. Mojtabai et al. "National Trends in the Prevalence and Treatment of Depression in Adolescents and Young Adults," 4.

3. Twenge et al., "Age, Period, and Cohort Trends," 185.

4. Soni, "There's a Loneliness Crisis on College Campuses."

5. Locke, "Center for Collegiate Mental Health Annual Report 2014."

6. Twenge, "The Mental Health Crisis among America's Youth Is Real—and Staggering."

blame.[7] Others hold that exposure to violent media has compromised the mental health of the young.[8] Still others insist that exposure to technology, to social media in particular, is a major causal factor.[9] Given the persuasiveness of some of these explanations it strikes me as unlikely that the increase we are seeing is monocausal. Instead, it's likely that each explanation has some validity. In response laudable efforts to support mental health have been constructed: skills to aid students in better coping with pressure have been taught, for example, as have techniques of healthy social media use.

But such strategies, while both laudable and necessary, presume one thing not in evidence: that changes in individual behavior can be made dense enough to counterbalance the weight of anxiety. To be clear: this is not to blame mental health professionals or to say that such work is optional. It is not. On the contrary, the one-on-one work done with young people today by therapists, counselors, and psychologists is both needed and laudable. It is to say that such work is insufficient; necessary but insufficient. Even more, it is insufficient not because our mental health professionals are unskilled or unmotivated, but because the kinds of responses they can offer are, in the main, aimed at one thing: individual capacitation. They are solutions that hinge on personal training.

The mental health professions are not the only one subject to making such a category error. Such a mistake is, in fact, increasingly endemic. This argument can perhaps most clearly be traced in the philosophical analysis being done on the neo-liberal economic form in which we currently live. Philosophers including Philip Mirowski, Eugene McCarraher, and Wendy Brown have traced out the effects of this transition from collective responsibility for the individual to individual responsibility for the (in this case economic) collective.[10] Brown's terms for this inversion is "responsibilization."

In Brown's terminology responsibilization describes the neo-liberal requirement that individuals labor and sacrifice so as to transform themselves into productive members of our economy; workers capable of competing

7. Pew Research Center, "Most U.S. Teens See Anxiety and Depression as a Major Problem Among Their Peers."

8. Madan et al., "The Effects of Media Violence on Anxiety in Late Adolescence." But the causality of the effect has not been established. This experimental study examined the effects of media violence on anxiety, blood pressure, and heart rate in late adolescents. We also examined whether these responses varied by previous exposure to media and real-life violence. College students (N = 209; M age = 18.74; 75 % female; 50 % Caucasian, 34 % African American, 9 % Asian, 3 % Hispanic, and 3 % other racial minorities.

9. Keles et al., "A Systematic Review."

10. Mirowski, *Never Let a Serious Crisis Go to Waste*; McCarraher, *The Enchantments of Mammon*; Brown, *Undoing the Demos*.

within a hyper-capitalistic society. No longer, she points out, is it the case that society is held to be (morally) responsible for helping individuals succeed. Now, instead, it is responsibilized individuals who are expected to sacrifice for the good of the economy, to fend for themselves while so doing and, if unsuccessful in the process, "blamed for [their] failure to thrive."[11]

The analogy to how young people are being equipped to cope with the present epidemic of anxiety is not difficult to make. Just as economically responsibilized individuals are interpolated to undertake "the correct strategies of self-investment and entrepreneurship for thriving and surviving," so the tacit expectation of young people is that they ought to be able to become capable of bearing up under the weight of this epidemic.[12] Too often, and regardless of intention, young Americans are being psychologically responsibilized.[13]

Given this predicament it is particularly notable—laudable, even—that one particular form of psychology seems to have constructed a methodology that, even in such an environment, provides hopeful results. Attending to this small subfield, which has come to be called "positive" psychology—particularly to what it diagnoses as lacking and correspondingly attempts to provide—will deepen our consideration of the category error into which so many of our efforts to care for young people today all-too-readily fall.

Purpose, Personal and Collective

The field of positive psychology consists of the study of the "conditions and processes that contribute to the flourishing" of persons.[14] Under its umbrella is a small subfield that focuses on how the presence or absence of one particular factor, purpose, affects happiness and health.

This psychology of purpose is built off the foundational work of thinkers like Victor Frankl and Aaron Antonovsky.[15] And one of the fruits of the progress in this subfield is that researchers have been able to show that

11. Brown, *Undoing the Demos*, 134.

12. Brown, *Undoing the Demos*, 133.

13. It is important to note that it is not only the young who are being responsibilized in this instance, but mental health professionals as well. This takes place whenever blame is placed on them for the fact that the personalized techniques with which they equip the young fail to produce the hoped-for effect. What we see in such instances is simply a displacement of the blaming process that is set in motion by the category error of attempting to address a supra-individual problem with a necessary but not sufficient individual solution.

14. Gable and Haidt, "What (and Why) Is Positive Psychology," 104.

15. Frankl, *Man's Search for Meaning*; Antonovsky, *Unraveling the Mystery of Health*.

having a strong sense of purpose is relevant for health outcomes across ages. Their research shows that purpose helps to resolve identity crises, is correlated with greater civic engagement, and aids in coping with mental distress.[16] In studies focusing on young adults in particular, it has been shown not only that a lack of purpose is connected to substance abuse and suicidal ideations,[17] but that an increased sense of purpose predicts both "well-being during emerging adulthood" and "developmentally important outcomes such as a positive self-image."[18] Clearly the provision of purpose in life, of an end or a telos, positively impacts mental health in young people. But a question follows close on the heels of this encouraging news: if the provision of purpose, of a telos, makes such a positive difference in the mental health of the young, might it not be precisely because is it this they are missing?

A responsible answer to this question can only be given in the particular.[19] But, taken in the aggregate, the fact that the provision of purpose is making an impact in the lives of young people at this moment in history is striking, albeit not surprising. Not surprising because, as Christian Smith and Melinda Lundquist Denton have shown, many teens inhabit what they have termed a "morally insignificant universe."[20]

Smith and Denton describe such a universe as one in which "moral commitments, decisions, obligations and actions have little if any larger meaning, purpose, significance or consequence; that universe is, in short, a morally empty reality."[21] Their research showed that the moral stage on which young imagined their lives playing out was lacking in meaning. There was no point to the play and because of this their lives exhibited little meaningful drama. But we must take note of the fact that the type of purpose missing from such a moral universe are not the micro-purposes of everyday (surely these young people are familiar with making choices that seek to fulfill their desires), but those purposes located on a macro-level. It is social, or cosmic, purpose that is missing in a morally insignificant universe.

This recognition ought to lead us to take note of two things about such a morally insignificant universe: first, that is punctual—it is focused on the present to the point of severing connections to both the past and the future. And, in part because of this punctuality, such a universe lacks a shared

16. Bronk, et al., "Purpose, Hope, and Life Satisfaction in Three Age Groups."

17. Brassai, Piko, and Steger, "Meaning in Life."

18. Hill, et al., "Purpose in Life in Emerging Adulthood," 237, 243.

19. It *ought* to be given in the particular as well. As the Church teaches, the uniqueness of the person and their circumstance is to be respected.

20. Smith, *Soul Searching*, 156.

21. Smith, *Soul Searching*, 156.

narrative. Second, a morally insignificant world tends to lack commonly shared practices. There is a decreased sense of how to act together toward the same purpose at the same time. These two factors readily weave together to produce a sense of reality in which there is little sense of any lived tradition of excellence, of an embodied knowledge of that to which one ought live up and toward which one can aspire.[22] Instead of such grand visions of the good life, in their analysis of the discourse of many of these young people, Smith and Denton found mainly the self. Instead of a conception of having emerged from a past and being propelled toward a future, such a punctual self attends mainly to the choices it can make and the rewards that can be obtained in the present tense. Little wonder that a positive psychology of purpose might help mitigate some of the more harmful effects of life in such a universe.

But, even in the positive light of such provisions of purpose, the question of the category error remains. We might frame it this way: is it possible for people to provide their own purposes? Can human beings provide themselves with their own teloi?

To some extent the answer is certainly yes. After all, people of all ages establish goals for themselves and set about cultivating the means to accomplish them. But there is a certain type of telos that, regardless of individual capacity, persons cannot establish for themselves: those of collective moral significance. It is not that individual persons are unable to judge for themselves what constitutes, say, a successful life. They are. Even more, after the successive liberations of modernity this capacity to "*sapere aude*" is often experienced as an unshackling, a consoling revelation of a personal identity that takes place through the rejection of false or stultifying standards. We now, and thankfully, live in a world in which women can vote, persons may no longer be property, and a serf owes the fruit of his labor to no Lord. Ours is a world in which we may set our own ends. Yet despite such rightly celebrated freedoms there is one capacity that remains beyond the purview of individual persons: the capacity to construct a morally significant world. Which means, to the extent that it takes the individual as the object of its ministrations, purposive psychology cannot aid young people in providing for themselves what no individual can provide for her or himself: a morally significant world; a cosmos rather than a universe.

The difference, as Seth Benardete has written, between a universe and a cosmos is that the latter is a meaningful whole while the former is an

---

22. Note that it is not presumed here that such a tradition of excellence is Christian in character. As Charles Taylor shows, traditions of excellence vary from Greek honor traditions all the way to the kind of rationalist conceptions of the universe held by Kant (see Taylor, *Sources of the Self*, 16–19).

aggregation: "We see heaven and earth, but we do not see their unity, which we call cosmos. 'Cosmos' puts a label on an insight about the structure of the whole."[23] And the construction of a cosmos is a supra-individual project, one that requires being able to tell not just a personal story about the purpose of my own life, but a collective narrative within which my story finds its place, origin, and vector. A cosmos requires a collective story within which personally stories can be emplotted and so find their moral valence. This is because, as Alasdair MacIntyre has famously argued, identity is narrative.[24] It is because "the story of my life is always embedded in the story of those communities" from which my identity is drawn.[25] We have a limited autonomy with regard to the kind of ends that we can set for ourselves not because we are not yet free enough, but because such a capacity lies perennially beyond our powers.[26] We are, to again use MacIntyre's words, "never more (*and sometimes less*) than co-authors of our own narratives."[27]

It is to be hoped that what this means for the present argument is readily visible. There is indeed an epidemic of anxiety; mental health problems are increasing among the young. And, praiseworthy as they are, current efforts to respond to the crisis by mental health professionals are normally aimed at personal capacitation. And this remains true even for the most effective types of treatment such as purposive psychology. Even more, this insufficiency arises not because the provision of purpose is somehow a mistaken need, but because the kind of purpose needed not individual, regardless of capacity, can provide for her or himself. For a church seeking to hear the cry of the poor, to be something even marginally akin to the field hospital about which Pope Francis has dreamed, this amounts to quite a quandary.

But the construction of adequate responses will be helped little by haste. Instead of rushing ahead, presuming that we understand the problem, we will be aided by an understanding of how we arrived in such a position. It is history that can teach us how to avoid the trap of responsibilization into which many of our best efforts seem to fall. Perhaps it can also teach us something of how we might respond.

23. Benardete, *The Tragedy and Comedy of Life*, 162–63.

24. Argument to this effect have also been made by Ricoeur, *Time and Narrative, Volume 1*; Ammerman, "Religious Identity and Religious Institutions"; and Somers, "The Narrative Constitution of Identity."

25. MacIntyre, *After Virtue*, 205.

26. See MacIntyre, *Dependent Rational Animals*.

27. MacIntyre, *After Virtue*, 199.

The Shape of Traditional Society

Since the birth of the social sciences as disciplines any number of important books have been written with the express aim of grasping the social
transformations that have occurred since the collapse of the medieval synthesis.[28] In the light of such a vast corpus all this section can attempt is a
highly focused synthesis of some of its most essential insights. In particular,
it will focus on the way three ideal-typical social forms—here described as
"traditional," "solid modernity," and "liquid modernity"—have structured
collective action, shared narratives, and social identity. It is to traditional
society that we turn first.

Human culture, in all its different shapes and hues, is at its origin a
hard-won thing, an island of meaning pulled from the chaotic waters of
illness, violence, and scarcity. It is because of this fragility that the aim of
social life in traditional societies is not change but continuity; the collective
preservation of what the passage of time might otherwise obliterate. Within
such social groups, continuity is accomplished in two ways: the provision of
common action and the common narration of a shared story.

By common action what is meant is that members of traditional societies are readily capable of acting together toward the same goal. Many
examples of such could be offered, but an apt one can be borrowed from
Charles Taylor's *A Secular Age*.[29] There he describes a medieval European
ceremony known as perambulation or "beating the bounds." This was a
ceremony in which members of a given community, often following the
Eucharist, processed in a circle around their village. The participants of this
common action performed it in order to create a boundary between the
ordered, safe, internal space of their settlement and the chaotic, dangerous,
exterior space beyond. Notably, the whole community participated in beating the bounds. They all did the same thing, for the same goal, at the same
time, together. Perambulation was a collective good, in other words, one
that could be ensured only by collective participation.[30]

This type of ceremony is marked by actions, postures, gestures, and
words that are carefully ordered and often deployed in repetitive sequences.
It is action marked by what Paul Connerton has called a "potential for

28. A small list of the more significant attempts include Taylor, *A Secular Age*; Anderson, *Imagined Communities*; Elias, *The Civilizing Process*; Durkheim, *The Division of Labor
in Society*; Polanyi, *The Great Transformation*; Weber, *The Protestant Ethic and the Spirit of
Capitalism*; Habermas, *The Structural Transformation of the Public Sphere*; Ong, *Orality
and Literacy*; Connerton, *How Societies Remember*; Bauman, *Liquid Modernity*; Guardini,
The End Of The Modern World; Dupre, *Passage to Modernity*.

29. See Taylor, *A Secular Age*, 43f.

30. See Abrahams, *Everyday Life*, 129–30.

invariance."[31] In fact it is just this invariance, this constraint, that makes this type of acting-together possible.[32] Among the fruits of such invariant action is that they become stable enough to cultivate, preserve, and transmit the common narrative of the community. In fact, in the pre-literary, oral, world of traditional society it was this type of collective ceremony that sustained the group's memory—and did so by embedding this memory not only in participant's minds but in their bodies. Such shared practices are, then, something like embodied, enacted, collective autobiographies that teach "us" who "we" are, how we are to behave toward one another, from whence we come, and for what we ought to hope.

In traditional society such common narration happened not only in action but also in word. This is clearly exemplified in Fr. Walter Ong's *Orality and Literacy*, his classic study of the difference between literate and oral, or traditional, cultures. There Ong offered an answer to a question that had long puzzled scholars of classical texts: why was it that particular words or phrases were repeated so often, and at such seemingly strange intervals? Ong argued that these repetitions sprung from the fact that these texts were initially transmitted not in writing but orally. Which meant that these repetitions were in fact mnemonic devices. They made it possible for the community to remember its essential stories before human beings had learned the preservative technology of writing. It was in this way that narrative repetition, like common action, made possible a cosmos.

Traditional societies are constituted, then, by common action and common narratives. These were the tactics used to preserve a small space of culture, a sacred canopy as Peter Berger called it, that could cover the community from the surrounding chaos.[33] This was what produced the shared life of such societies, the corporate "stock of knowledge" more or less evenly distributed to all members.[34] Yes, the midwife, or the master of the hunt, or the priest had some special knowledge, but generally all the members of traditional societies knew the same things.[35] And it was this shared knowledge

---

31. Connerton, *How Societies Remember*, 57.

32. For more on how constraint empowers forms of action, see Satlow, "Tradition: The Power of Constraint."

33. Berger, *The Sacred Canopy*.

34. See Garfinkel, *Studies in Ethnomethodology*. It is in chapter 3 of this volume that Garfinkel describes "common culture" as "socially sanctioned grounds of inference and action [that] people use in their everyday affairs and which they assume others use in the same way" (76).

35. In Connerton's words, "the presentation of the self in everyday life is unnecessary when. . . the gaps in shared memory are much fewer and slighter." Connerton, *How Societies Remember*, 17.

that provided the members of such societies a corporate sense of purpose, a joint understanding of that in which the good life consisted, a shared appreciation of what actions made sense within this cosmos; of how they could earn glory in the eyes of the community and what would bring them shame.[36] Although I might struggle to live up to such lofty expectations, in such society there could be no conceptual trouble about what would emplot my personal narrative into the narrative of the tribe. Nor was it a difficult task to emplot the tribe's narrative into that of the cosmos. These three stories were, in a sense and to an extent, the same story. And it was that story that was told aloud and enacted in rituals.

The contrast between such societies and our own is self-evident. Our present capacities both for telling a common story and engaging in common action in pursuit of a shared telos is much diminished. The three stories have come apart. Our shared stock of knowledge is much thinner. And this lack of shared understanding prevents us knowing what it means to succeed and from having a lived sense that collective action might be required to secure collective goods. We no longer live in a cosmos. And this is indeed a loss.

But loss ought not allow us to slip into nostalgia. There is a shadow side to traditional society. Their empowerment of collectivity and their emphasis on constraint and repetitive action serve to disempowered personal liberties. The very social actions taken to preserve continuity, that is, came to be felt as intolerably constraining both in regard to the range of actions that could be taken without censorship and the kinds of identities that could be enacted. Traditional societies, that is, empowered collectively purposive lives by restricting and censoring alternate forms of life. It was (and still is) when such censorship grew intolerable that the very members of such societies acted to rupture their constraints and realize new forms of life. Indeed, this rupturing is precisely what Zygmunt Bauman, to whose categories of solid and liquid modernity we now turn, understood modernity itself to be: the ceaseless process of dissolution.

36. In his book *Radical Hope*, Jonathan Lear studies the collapse of the Native American Crow culture during the process of their being forcibly moved onto reservations. This collapse is exemplified in part by the disempowering of irony. And this precisely because irony presumes shared knowledge. This can be seen in the kind of ironic questions that presume a shared understanding of what it means to succeed. For example: "is there a Crow amongst the Crow?" With such arguments Lear lays the ground for the devastating recognition that cultural destruction consists in part in the making-impossible of shared knowledge and shared action. On a reservation, for example, where Crow were banned from taking the kinds of praiseworthy actions that could make one a "real" Crow, the ironic comparison between ideal and average members of society simply ceased to function. See 42–52.

Modernities, Solid and Liquid

In his book *Liquid Modernity* Zygmunt Bauman argues that modernity ought to be understood not as a time period but a process. Modernity simply is, he contends, modernization. This process consists the deconstruction of social forms, the melting down of common practices and narratives that have grown dusty and constraining.[37] One of the consequences of taking such a processual perspective is that "modernity" can be conceptualized as taking place in various ways at various places and in various times. That is, in addition to the forms of life it makes possible, modernity ought to be understood in the light of the social form it is dissolving.[38]

Once modernity is conceived as modernization supportive evidence for this hypothesis arises in surprising places. One such place is Alexis de Tocqueville's masterpiece *The Ancien Régime and the French Revolution*. The question Tocqueville asks therein is a deceptively simple one: what were the conditions that allowed the revolution to occur? Among the strategies he uses to offer an answer is to comb through the now-famous *cahiers de doléances*, the written complaints that members of all three French estates had submitted to Estates-General in 1789.[39] His immersion into how different social classes perceived the problems facing French society before the revolution led Tocqueville to conclude that, although the revolution was experienced as an inexplicable shock—an unforeseen and unforeseeable eruption of modernity amidst medieval France—it should not have been. Instead of being inexplicable he argued that it was, in fact, all but inevitable.[40] This is because the *cahiers* showed him that the traditional society of the *Ancien Régime* was already unstable, already so constraining and dysfunctional that new forms needed to be constructed. The revolution did not knock down a solid structure, but one that was already dissolving. Modernity was happening, that is, before the storming of the Bastille.

As in France after the revolution so in many places, with variations appropriate to changed contexts, did modernization take place. And with

37. Bauman: "Was not modernity a process of 'liquefaction' from the start? Was not 'melting the solids' its major pastime and prime accomplishment all along? In other words, has modernity not been 'fluid' since its inception?" Bauman, *Liquid Modernity*, 2–3.

38. This means that modernity is not, in fact, a monolithic but a plural phenomenon. It will be constructed differently based in part on what is attempting to disassemble. See Eisenstadt, "Multiple Modernities."

39. For more on the relevance of the *cahiers*, and on Tocqueville's research methods in general, see chapter 10 of Swedberg, *Tocqueville's Political Economy*, in particular 247–50.

40. The revolution was "the culmination of a long labor," Tocqueville wrote, the effect of which was to sweep away all feudal institutions and replace them with a "more uniform. . . order based on equality of conditions" (Tocqueville, *Ancien Regime*, 27, 26).

it came a dream, a purpose embedded in this first phase of modernity: the dream of a more just, more equal, more free world. As this dream of liberation swept across the world it produced many things, but there was, perhaps, one key phenomenon: institutional differentiation, the proverbial separation of the spheres of social action.[41] Sociologists have consumed oceans of ink describing the process by which economics and literature, politics and the medical sciences (to pick only a few), emerged from under the thumb of sword and miter. After much struggle the Church came to see in many these liberations the action of the Holy Spirit. This affirmation notwithstanding, for our purposes what must be grasped is how this process of differentiation affected the social capacity to enact common actions and live within common narratives. And what can be seen is that this capacity was, although not destroyed, much truncated. It was not dissolved but constrained.

An example of this shift can be found in Emile Durkheim's *Division of Labor,* a work he wrote in part after seeing so many provincial Frenchmen arrive in the urban center of Paris only to be completely unable to cope with the transition demanded of them.[42] In this work he asks the question of what, if anything, will be capable of binding society together after the division of labor has begun to break down the traditional order. His argument is that a new form of "organic" solidarity can be seen arising. This new solidarity he describes as constituted not by mechanical sameness, not by a universally shared stock of knowledge, for example, but by difference. Organic solidarity is based on the interdependent cooperation of individuals each of whom performs some of the unique and necessary functions that together sustain the whole. The provincial Frenchmen, for example, arriving in the city all of one mind with those from the villages and towns they left, became in Paris workers and citizens, artists and doctors. They differentiated, and in so doing became capable of collaborating to sustain a new, modern, form of society. It was as if Durkheim was saying: Yes, the plot of your life has been ruptured, but it can be sutured back together.

One of the results of this division was the cultivation of new sets of common actions and common narratives. These might no longer be shared among the whole of society, but they still were shared by one's own subgroup: by one's class or trade. There was power in this, as people "disembedded" from the spaces and narratives and practices of traditional society were, albeit often with much struggle and loss, able to find places to "re-embed" themselves.[43] Such places included the factory, where common action

41. See chapter 1 of Casanova, *Public Religions in the Modern World.*
42. Durkheim, *The Division of Labor in Society.*
43. See Bauman, *Liquid Modernity,* 33.

was not only possible but mandated, and the coffee shop, where a certain class of clientele practiced narrating the story of the nascent public sphere.[44] Common action might not take place across the whole society—we may no longer beat the bounds of the village—but we do know how to stand in line, or what it is to vote for the president of the labor union.

Still, there is a difference between these practices (and the narratives to which they give rise) and those of traditional society: the new ones no longer describe or enact a purposefully meaningful world. They are no longer cosmically relevant. Instead, solid modernity begins to confine common narrative and practices to the particular, segmented spheres from which each emerges. As Charles Taylor aptly described it, the cosmic imaginary has been separated from the social imaginary.[45] It's not that values have been eliminated, it's that they have been constricted—they no longer apply to the cosmos but only to this profession, this nation state, this denomination.[46] This delinking of the cosmic narrative from the social narrative means two things: first that in solid modernity it is, for the first time, possible to ask what relevance the segmented spheres of action have for one another. A new form of question arises about what relevance the values of religion, to take one neuralgic example, have for politics or for science.[47] And, second, it means that personal, autobiographical narratives were delinked from a shared cosmic narrative. We human beings could still be embedded in society, but society was no longer embedded in a cosmos.

Further, while for some the zone opened up by the disassembly of old institutional forms gave them the space to become the persons they had felt themselves always called to be, for others this was not the case. For most of the working class, for example, solid modernity amounted to a world of routine and supervision—of time clocks and Ford factories literal and metaphoric. As Bauman says it was a "world of other-directed men and women pursuing fixed-by-others ends in a fixed-by-others fashion."[48] It was because of these constraints, different in particularity but similar in constraining power to those that constituted traditional society, that the dissolving solution of modernization began work anew. Only this time it was the forms of

---

44. These are parts of the story narrated, respectively, in Polanyi, *The Great Transformation*, and Habermas, *The Structural Transformation of the Public Sphere*.

45. See Taylor, *A Secular Age*, 150–52.

46. See Weber, "Science as a Vocation," 147, 155: "The various value spheres of the world stand in irreconcilable conflict with each other. . . .Precisely the ultimate and most sublime values have retreated from public life either into the transcendental realm of mystic life or into the brotherliness of direct and personal human relations."

47. See Weber's "Politics as a Vocation" and "Science as a Vocation."

48. Bauman, *Liquid Modernity*, 63.

solid modernity that were thrown into the smelter. Which means that the same process of differentiation, of separation of spheres and opening up new spaces for new forms of life, was once more repeated.

According to Bauman, however, while the processes of dissolution have continued, two things have changed. First, contemporary society seems to have lost belief in the dreams that originally drove modernity. We have grown cynical, finding it increasingly difficult to believe that the dissolving of corrupt and constraining social forms will pave the way for truly just ones. In his words, we are no longer convinced there is "an attainable telos of historical change."[49] While solid modernity had a purpose (it disembedded French peasants to re-embed them as citizens of the Republic, for example), under the terms of liquid modernity society provides no beds in for re-embedding.[50]

Additionally, and this is the second point, because differentiation continues apace and new, smaller, more personalized, spheres of value are continually being produced, our public institutions have become increasingly fragile.[51] And as they have these carriers of our capacity for common action have become less and less capable of sustaining even the provisional, constricted, sub-cosmic narratives found in solid modernity. Which is why it may strike one as naïve, for example, to rely on a church, or the Girl Scouts, or a union hall to provide the kind of shared narratives in which our lives can be emplotted. Instead, it is up to us, as individuals, to "to find out what she or he is capable of doing, to stretch that capacity to the utmost, and to pick the ends to which that capacity [can] be applied best."[52] In theory, anything is possible, the barriers to virtually any form of social identity have been thoroughly deconstructed. But this permanent freedom, this perpetual state of "unfinishedness, incompleteness and underdetermination. . . is full of risk and anxiety."[53]

Let us dwell on this point for a moment. Liquid modernity is the term Bauman coins to describe a shared state, one in which each of us is individually free to choose any identity for ourselves—as long as we have the personal capacity to carry it off.[54] And we can choose any purpose for

49. Bauman, *Liquid Modernity*, 29.

50. See Bauman, *Liquid Modernity*, 33.

51. See Bellah, et al., *The Good Society*.

52. Bauman, *Liquid Modernity*, 62.

53. Bauman, *Liquid Modernity*, 62. This state is analogous to what Peter Berger termed, in his book of the same name, the "heretical imperative." See Berger, *The Heretical Imperative*.

54. Of course, as Bourdieu has shown, personal capital is conditioned by social, cultural and economic capital. It is the culturally and economically wealthy who, even

our lives—any purpose, that is, that we can provide for ourselves. But no individual, regardless of capacity, can alone construct a collective good. For this a community is required. And it is the common action and common narration necessary for the construction of a cosmos that liquid modernity disempowers; seeks to deny us. Again, while solid modernity succeeded in delinking cosmic and social imaginaries, it is only in liquid modernity that the social imaginary has been severed from the personal.

It is in the light of this historical frame that, I argue, we ought to understand the epidemic of anxiety sweeping our country and the psychological responsibilization of young people today. And it is likewise in this light that the Church ought to construct responses—responses that take seriously two facts: first, that a cosmos cannot be constructed alone; that it must be done collaboratively. And, second, that the goods accomplished in the long work of these modernization processes cannot and must not be vitiated. The ailment diagnosed by the schematic history here traced will not be cured by a nostalgic return to the roles, objects, or social forms of the past.[55]

It is true that the argument given here has traced our declining capacity for common action and common narration. These are real losses. And yet "for freedom Christ set us free" (Gal 5:1). This "us" is not just societies but persons; we ourselves. In none of the responses to which we now turn can we allow ourselves to lose sight of what has been gained.

The Liturgies of Liquid Modernity

Our social imaginary, for better and for worse, has long been disembedded from the cosmic. And now our autobiographical imaginary has become portable, detachable from the social.

Attentive readers can no doubt see already, from the framing of this argument, the kind of responses that will be here proposed: re-creation of common practices that have the capacity to carry a common narrative; attempts at re-suturing the personal, social, and cosmic imaginary; the construction of shared spaces in which young people can find a purpose broader and deeper than they are capable of providing themselves. In other

---

if they too are tilting at windmills, are more likely to be able to produce tenuous and transitory forms of success. See Bourdieu, "The Forms of Capital."

55. This is not least because, as de Certeau has shown, the act of belief is ongoingly produced. It is not the case that social believing, credulity, "remains attached to its object" and that preserving the objects that had in the past contributed to the production of belief (e.g., religious garb, forms of liturgy; social roles) is sufficient to preserve past forms of believing. Rather, belief is ongoingly produced. As de Certeau puts it, it "passes from myth to myth, from ideology to ideology." de Certeau, *The Certeau Reader*, 122.

words, the long corporate process of relearning the habits of belonging. All of this is true. It is what I will argue below. But there is one further consequence of the segmentation of our imaginaries that must be taken into account beforehand, a consequence that alters the character of these anticipated suggestions. It is this: the long process of disembedding has produced not a desert but an ocean of meanings.

Young people today are awash in possible narratives, immersed in available practices. Loosed from their moorings, thousands of disembedded meaning fragments—in the form of advertisements, denominations, brands, self-help practices, workout regimes, Instagram influencers; the list could continue—fill the sea of our liquid modernity. These waters are bursting with stories, each of them a mobile raft of meaning, islands upon which, we are told, we can for a few moments catch our breath. But, as a number of post-liberal thinkers have argued in recent years, these islands do much more that passively float.[56] Siren-like, they call to us to step onto their shores, promising fulfillment in exchange for our participation in the practices of attention control that interweave their narrative and ours: scrolling, shopping, and scrolling again. Never before has the story of our lives been so mobile, so available. Never before has it been so actively courted.

In part we are courted through the offer of a shared narrative and the potential identity to be found therein. The power brands of our liquid age—Amazon, Apple, Nike, Disney—have built economic empires on the narrative identities embedded in slogans like "Think Different," "Just Do It," or "The Happiest Place on Earth." Any of us, for as long as the money lasts at least, can purchase autobiographical embeddedness is these social narratives. It is in this way that the desire to belong drives action—we visit Disneyland because of the story in which we are included. At such times it is the available narrative fragments which shape our practices.

But we are also courted through shared practices. Part of the deep affective power of being a fan of Liverpool Football Club, for example is joining a hundred thousand others in singing "You'll Never Walk Alone."[57] We are linked to the purple and gold, carnival history of Louisiana by standing on a rickety latter on St. Charles street as the Mardi Gras floats roll by. In this way it is by taking part in the practice—in the singing, in the parade—that we emplot ourselves in the story the practice holds.[58] At such times it is the practice that makes available the ephemeral narrative.

56. See Cavanaugh, *Being Consumed*; Milbank, *Theology and Social Theory*; Mahmood, *Politics of Piety*; Bilgrami, "What Is Enchantment?"

57. For more on the power of non-religious corporate practices to replicate "sacred" power see Hervieu-Leger, *Religion as a Chain of Memory*.

58. This is what Hervieu-Leger, drawing on Certeau, meant by saying that "every

Liquid modernity, in other words, has its own cultural liturgies that seek form the desires of those who swim in it.[59] What this means for our consideration of how the Church might respond to these signs of the times is that we must begin to take seriously that our own liturgies, our bundles of practices and narratives, are in competition with other, rivalrous packages.[60] This is all the more true if, as Talal Asad has argued, one of the results of our liquid modernity is the intentional production of "the continual feeling of disruption, of uncertainty" that seeks to disrupt our sense of "fullness."[61] In other words the prize of the competition in which, like it or not, we are always already engaged is not the minds of the young but their anxious hearts.

There is a consequence to the preceding. It is that, in such a set of circumstances, amidst such unchosen constraints, our task is not just to calm personal anxieties. It is to cobble together stable narrative-action packages, to help build local counter-liturgies both persuasive and strong enough to resist the liquid liturgies that treats persons as products, produce constitutive disruption and uncertainty, and profit from that production. It is to take, from the storehouse of our tradition, good things both new and old. It is nothing less than the task of capacitating a living Christianity.

The Church as Holding Environment

There are two temptations to which we may fall prey in such an effort. I name them here because they provide buffers to the proposals that follow.

The first can be seen by noting, with Ann Swidler, that liquid times tend to provoke personal and institutional rigidity. In times such as ours a tradition's plural narratives and practices—bundles that in more stable times were malleable and capacious, in which there was room to maneuver, explore, and imagine—tend to turn rigid and brittle. There is good reason for this. It is because, having forgotten how to act together, we are inclined to relearn this capacity not by heart but by mind. "When people are learning

---

activity secretes the particular form of believing it needs." Hervieu-Leger, *Religion as a Chain of Memory*, 101.

59. Cf. Smith, *Desiring the Kingdom*.

60. It must be noted that it is not only possible but necessary for the Church to collaborate, without anxiety, with a wide variety of other institutions in this process. Many of these institutions arrive at such collaborations equipped with their own packages of narrative-action. And while some of these may well conflict with our own, others will overlap. While differences may remain, there is no question that the narrative-action package of, say, Doctors Without Borders, or the Black Lives Matter movement, hold numerous potential collaborative linkages.

61. Cf. Asad, "Thinking about Religion, Belief, and Politics," 49–51.

new ways of organizing individual action, practicing unfamiliar habits until they become familiar," Swidler maintains, "a highly articulated, self-conscious belief and ritual system" tends to arise.[62] This means that the Church is uniquely vulnerable to taking the capacitation of Christianity to be an intellectual exercise. But this, as Pope Francis has already helped us to see, amounts to Gnosticism.[63] It is ironic that the very necessity of reteaching the practice of faith produces the inclination to "absolutize" theories of the faith capable of "forc[ing] others to submit."[64] This is clearly in contradiction with the type evangelization modeled on the cross.

Instead, then, of turning up the volume on public assertions of the truths of the faith, we ought to consider prioritizing not constraining ideologies but inclusive practices. This means that we ought to teach not primarily through the mind but in the body.[65] Examples of this kind of response can be found anywhere the people of God are coming into contact with the soft flesh of Christ in the persons of the poor, vulnerable, and excluded.[66] We see this, for example, in the regular, undramatic befriending of the elderly performed all over the globe by the community of Sant'Egidio. We see this in the Franciscan Friars of the Renewal and the Catholic Workers of New York City who, every day, again and again, feed themselves with the same food they prepare for the homeless. We see this in the slow, painful, freeing practice of tattoo removal performed by and on former gang members at Homeboy Industries in Los Angeles. And we see this in the unhurried washing of the bodies of the sick and dying by the Sisters of Charity on the streets of Calcutta.

This is not to say that the common practices to which the Church must recommit itself do not include practices of prayer as well—most particularly the mass, of course, but also the liturgy of the hours, common rosaries, and processions. (We do well to remember that Sant'Egidio commits itself to praying together every night in Trastevere, and that the Sisters of Charity each day make space for multiple hours of silent prayer that, they themselves say, sustains their service.) Practices of prayer can also be made common. It is to say that the practices recommended here, in order to resist the segmenting pressures of liquid modernity and the temptation to become brittle ideology, ought to begin with bodily repetitions. It is collective, embodied

---

62. Swidler, "Culture in Action," 278–79.

63. Pope Francis, *Gaudete et Exsultate*.

64. *Gaudete et Exsultate*, #39.

65. Please note the use of the word "primarily" here. The present argument does not amount to a denigration of the Church's long and storied intellectual tradition.

66. See Pope Francis, "5th Convention of the Italian Church."

action that has the capacity to become what Connerton has called habit-memory: "a knowledge and a remembering in the hands [in which it is] our body which 'understands.'"[67]

Another example, which may be surprising for those of us who have grown accustomed to our entertainment being performed for us rather than co-producing it, is song. Here we can note two things: first, that songs provide a powerful example of the kind constraint and repetition that empower a common practice. Songs, as any choir member can attest, constrain not only in their lyrics but also in their tempo, sequence, and volume. And it is strictly this constraint that allows common participation and propels "ritual speech acts in the same direction."[68] But it is repetition that broadens this participation beyond the performers. As anyone who has been caught up in the power of a Gospel song knows, the soloist can lift hearts to the Lord, but it is the repeated refrain that lifts every voice. And second, song provides a powerful example of plurality within restriction. There is a word, in fact, for the type of internal difference produced by vocalists who are singing the same words in the same tempo and at the same volume but in a different note: harmony. It is to these kinds of internally plural, harmonic, embodied practices that, it is here proposed, the Church ought to together turn.[69]

Which brings us to the second temptation. Given the magnitude of the challenges arrayed before us we may, quite rationally, be tempted to withdraw into protective enclaves where the faith can be both practiced and narrated. Because we do indeed need to construct semi-protected spaces where the practices of the faith can be embodied such that they, of their own accord and in plural ways, give rise to narratives new and old. And it is indeed the case that "religious narratives. . . are activated by settings."[70] Indeed, given how much the preceding analysis seems to lend itself to precisely this response we ought not be surprised that such a response has been provided or that it is in some circles quite popular.[71] But the temptation here does not lie in the recognition that is now necessary to reinstitute spaces that can sustain bundles of narrative-action. It lies in thinking that doing so will prove a panacea. It is here, in the attribution to common action and narration of a power it does not possess, that a Pelagian temptation lies.

---

67. Connerton, *How Societies Remember*, 95.

68. Connerton, *How Societies Remember*, 60.

69. On the role of internal plurality in the Christianity, see Brague, *Eccentric Culture*.

70. Ammerman, *Sacred Stories, Spiritual Tribes*, 216.

71. See Dreher, *The Benedict Option*; Chaput, *Strangers in a Strange Land*; Esolen, *Out of the Ashes*.

Again it is Pope Francis who has diagnosed this tendency for us, clarifying that the error of Pelagianism lies in attributing the "same power the Gnostics attributed to the intellect. . . to the human will, to personal effort."[72] While it is certainly true that such a temptation can (and, I can personally attest, does) affect individuals, it can also be present in communities, particularly in the effort to reconstruct in nostalgic miniature a past that never was through the over-exertion of control over persons and the inhibition of their freedom. The "subtle form" of this collective Pelagianism amounts to the attempt to "subject the life of grace to certain human structures."[73]

In contradistinction to such efforts I suggest that the Church's proposed narratives ought to imitate the teachings of its founder, taking on the form of parables or metaphors rather than treatises or monologues. This is because parables do not coerce rational assent but invite the participation of the hearer. They leave space for the action of the free human precisely because of their ambiguity. As C. H. Dodd put it in his famous study, parables leave "the mind in sufficient doubt. . . to tease it into active thought."[74] Further, it is this form and style of common narration that allows personal religious identity to remain on ongoingly accomplished phenomenon[75] rather than to be taken as univocal, unchangeable core.[76] This style of speech, in other words, allow common narratives to be accessed rather than mandated.

But, in our liquid modernity, leaving such access solely to individuals amounts to an abdication of responsibility. It remains true that young people need to be helped in the process of learning how to embed their autobiographical narratives within the social and cosmic narratives of the Church. This learning process is, in part, what new research in Catholic educational theory has begun to uncover and systematize. One example of such is given by Pat Manning in his recent volume *Converting the Imagination*. There he approaches education not as information-provision but as the cultivation of "pedagogical habits."[77] In addition to treating students more like apprentices than empty vaults for the storage of information, this approach to education as habit-capacitation includes the kind of stimulation and expansion of student's imaginations that can pave the way for the embrace of, or embedding

---

72. *Gaudete et Exsultate*, #48.

73. *Gaudete et Exsultate*, #58.

74. Dodd, *Parables of the Kingdom*, 5.

75. Lonergan, *Method in Theology*.

76. Ammerman, "Religious Identity and Religious Institutions."

77. Manning, *Converting the Imagination*, 63.

in, a larger narrative. It helps to facilitate the process of young people, in this case students, emplotting themselves in a wider story.

Still it may seem that one thing may be lacking: a place where these narrative-action bundles, these shared stories and embodied practices, are made available. But this is how Manning understands the classroom, or, on a broader scale, Catholic educational institutions themselves. These micro- or meso-spaces can be understood in this light as "holding environments" in which is possible, with the help of others, for groups of people to make the transition from rootless to rooted. I would, in conclusion, like to propose that we extend this model one step further. It is as a holding environment that, I suggest, the Church ought to understand itself and its role in our liquid modern age.

To understand this suggestion in depth we can turn to the work of psychologist Robert Kegan because it was he who, drawing on the foundational work of D. W. Winnicott, read holding environments as those contexts that capacitated personal human evolution. This took place primarily in his book *The Evolving Self*, where Kegan detailed not only stages through which the self evolves but holding environments as well. Kegan contends that holding environments made personal evolution possible by being, in his words, "cultures of embeddedness. . . psychosocial environments which hold us (with which we are fused) and which let go of us (from which we differentiate)."[78]

This image of the Church in a liquid age as a holding environment that makes the narratives and practices of the tradition beautifully available is one that is both firm enough to serve as solid ground in a sea of narratives and pliable enough to resist the temptations outlined above. This is a Church which understands itself as a culture of embeddedness, an incubator in which young people have space to process the anxious experience of being overwhelmed by the ocean of options in which they swim. It is the framework of a Church that refuses to responsibilize the young by resorting only to individual capacitation but instead teaches them how to act together embodied works of mercy and shared; in story and song.

It is the vision of a Church that does not only talk about such a common mode of life but enacts it, performs it by placing its own body, through bodies of its members, in proximity to the bodies of the poor. It is the vision of a Church which relinks personal, social and cosmic narratives not by force but as Jesus did, by telling stories that make self-appropriation possible. This is the sketch of a Church that does not pretend either that it owns the truth as a rational possession or that it possesses a will capable of

78. Kegan, *The Evolving Self*, 116.

realizing what has been sketched but one that insists on leaving room for its weakness—which is the same thing as leaving room for grace. It is a pilgrim Church that imitates in its own self-understanding the redemptive tactics of the Incarnation by affirming proximity and refusing coercion. It is a Church that is willing to relearn the habits of belong so as to share the joys and hopes, the griefs and anxieties, of the people of the present age.

Thinking Critically about Critical Thinking and its Effect on Young Catholics

CLARE R. KILBANE[1] ─────────────────────────

IN HIS POST-SYNODAL APOSTOLIC Exhortation *Christus Vivit*, Pope Francis, urges young people to recognize the persistent, transformative, and redeeming love of Jesus Christ. He writes, "He is in you, he is with you, and he never abandons you."[2] Yet, to truly accept this good news and fully benefit from it in their lives, young people must develop faith in God. For it is through faith that they will come to know and increasingly practice divine love in an intimate relationship with Jesus Christ and His Church.

Although the development of faith in each young person is vitally important in its own right, it is also critical to the Church because the Mystical Body of Christ is "built up" through every member. Young people make vital and inimitable contributions to the Church as Pope Francis asserts, "the Church needs your momentum, your intuitions, your faith."[3] Adults make important contributions to the Church as well, especially when they assist young people in recognizing and relating to God. In *Christus Vivit*, Pope Francis points to a scriptural example to emphasize the pivotal role adults play in directing the young, he writes, "Samuel was still a young boy, yet the Lord spoke to him. Thanks to the advice of an adult, he opened his heart to hear God's call: 'Speak, Lord, for your servant is listening (1 Sam 3:9–10).'"[4]

This chapter explores a powerful culture of formation, that of formal education, and considers the potential effect of it on the development of faith

---

1. Clare Kilbane is a faculty member, senior learning designer at the McGrath Institute for Church Life at the University of Notre Dame. She also serves as the Director of Research and Development for the Institute's online theological education and produces scholarship on teaching and learning. She is a former Catholic school educator and has worked in teacher education for over 20 years.

2. *Christus Vivit*, #1.

3. *Christus Vivit*, #299.

4. *Christus Vivit*, #8.

and religious belief in young Catholics. Specifically, it explains how critical thinking initiatives, (i.e., intentional, coordinated, and wide-spread programs focused on teaching young people how to think), could influence them—for these initiatives powerfully expose young people to a reduced form of reason and one that makes religious belief seem unreasonable. It suggests how parents, teachers, ministers, and other adults might adapt catechesis so that young people can engage their critical thinking skills in a way that assists them in developing a Catholic worldview, a correct understanding of the relationship between faith and reason, and equips them for a life of faith.

This chapter provides the context required for understanding this problem and presents some suggestions for addressing it. First, it describes the culture of formal education and its significant influence on young people. Then, it defines reason and describes reason's relationship to faith as it is understood by the Catholic Church. It also presents the complementarity of reason and faith which is an essential aspect of the Catholic worldview. Next, the chapter presents contextual information about critical thinking initiatives, including an overview of these initiatives, some history and an example of their impact. Finally, it suggests how adults might adapt catechesis in ways that address the problem.

Young Catholics and the Culture of Formal Education

Although many cultures affect the formation of young Catholics, the culture of formal education is significant for several reasons. The first reason has to do with the time young people spend in school. In developed countries around the world, though the particular schedules and attendance requirements vary, mandated school partition is frequent, regular, and spans an extended period of years. For example, most Catholics growing up in the United States today spend, at minimum, 2,340 days of their lives—generally five days a week, during nine consecutive months, at least 180 days a year, over a period of thirteen years, from 5–18 years of age—in school.

A second reason for formal education's significance as a forming culture has to do with the age(s) of participation in school. It is common knowledge that childhood and adolescence are developmental stages when a person's body, mind, and soul are particularly impressionable. This proverb from the eighteenth century, "as the twig is bent, so grows the tree," captures a truth that has been acknowledge over all human history.

A third reason for the significance of formal education as a culture of formation is its nature or purpose. Because attending school is so deeply ingrained in modern life, it is easy to overlook that its primary goal is to shape young people for a particular end. In schools and school systems knowledge is transmitted, values are inculcated, and a students' anthropology or world-view is developed. Although the efficacy of this transfer varies along with the particular knowledge, values, and anthropologies that are imparted, all schools and school systems share a formative purpose. A school cannot *not* be formative.

Schools also have in common several mechanisms that enable this transfer, including: a) the formal curriculum, (i.e., the intended, planed object or content that is learned), b) the "hidden" or incidental curriculum (i.e., the unintended object or content that is learned), and c) instruction (i.e., the means used to facilitate the curriculum). Other transfer mecha-nisms exist including the attributes of the physical environment (e.g., many rooms that house groups between 15–30 people), rules and procedures that govern activities (e.g., attendance, "indoor behaviors"), and the characteris-tics of their population, (e.g., more numerous children than adults). All of these aspects combine to affect the formation of young people and become more powerful when their influence overlaps. For example, when a par-ticular value (e.g., cooperation) is expressed in curriculum, instruction, the hidden curriculum, and school procedures and unopposed by the members of the school population, the value is more powerfully transmitted.

For these reasons, formal education is an important forming culture. Young Catholics, whether enrolled in public, Catholic, or other types of schools, are profoundly shaped by their experiences in formal education. Anyone in the Church who is concerned with assisting these young people benefits from an awareness of significant educational movements and their impact on a young person's ability to grow in faith and belief.

Reason, Faith, and Their Complementarity

The concept and practice of reason has been central to human existence across history. Universally, regardless of time and culture, the concept refers to a person's mental ability to make sense of, or identify truth in, her experi-ences of reality. The particular boundaries of what constitutes the practice of reason and why one practices it however, have been understood differ-ently during particular eras and within different cultures. For example, one culture might hold that reason describes mental activity that is exclusively intellectual and conscious, logical, and willed. Another could share this no-tion, but hold that it encompasses any mental experience, including those that might not be considered intellectual such as intuition and emotion. These differences reflect the context of the culture conceiving of reason and its particular anthropology or worldview. When using the term reason an operational definition of reason is important.

Etymologically the word "reason" comes to English through French from the Latin word "ratio." As it was understood by the Romans, reason describes the mental processes that allow a person to handle particular objects of thought (or "res") and to do so more precisely[5]. A Roman using reason, for example, could grapple mentally with the particular differences between various philosophical positions or contemplate the attributes of divergent concepts of beauty. It should be noted that this conception of reason reflects the Roman mind, which treated all realities as palpable.[6] In using the term reason, the willed effort to practice intellectual activity is indicated as well as the specific varieties of intellectual activity. A person who reasons is a person who both intentionally engages with an idea and actively applies a particular type of intellectual process (e.g., logic) to do something, like understand possible outcomes or make a judgement.

In the early twenty-first century, the popular concept of reason, is often distinguished as "modern" or "scientific reasoning" because it reflects the modern era and is much influenced by science. This concept is much influenced by the achievements of science, and reflects a worldview that is characterized by materialism and empiricism. Pope Benedict described this saying, "[T]his modern concept of reason is based, to put it briefly, on a synthesis between Platonism (Cartesianism) and empiricism, a synthesis confirmed by the success of technology."[7] One sees this reflected in Webster's dictionary, where reason is defined as, "the power of comprehending, inferring, or thinking especially in orderly rational ways: intelligence."[8] It is this understanding of reason, a one that is purely intellectual, free from emotional bias, and values material and empirical ways of knowing that functions in the educational initiatives addressed in this chapter.

Since the scientific revolution, this understanding of reason has grown in its importance, utility, and practice. The wide-spread and effective use of reason is largely to credit for the sustained development of scientific progress. Observation, or the careful noting of details that accompany natural phenomena (one of the simplest exercises of reason), serves as the foundation of the scientific method and is therefore central to modern science. Reason's impact on scientific progress is also evident in the technologies which result

5. New Advent Catholic Encyclopedia. Accessed June 18, 2020. https://www.new advent.org/cathen/12673b.htm

6. New Advent Catholic Encyclopedia.

7. Benedict XVI, "Faith, Reason and the University—Memories and Reflections," 2004.

8. Webster's Dictionary. Accessed June 18, 2020. https://www.merriam-webster.com /dictionary/reason

from the application of scientific knowledge, including the tools that make scientific study possible, processes for recording and sharing discoveries, and the procedures for refining scientific understanding. In modern science, reason and the things it makes possible, enable the justification or substantiation of beliefs that are held about reality. Scientific reasoning, allows a person to uncover certain, empirical truths about the universe.

The continued development of science and the transformative technologies that come from its application have increased the value of reason and augmented its influence in modern society. Its use to discover knowledge about the material aspects of reality, such as the forces of gravity, characteristics of atoms, and behaviors of organisms, is widely-accepted as both useful and impressive. Given this, it is easy to understand how a culture so influenced by science might come to consider scientific reasoning the "gold standard" or basis for all truth claims. It would even be possible to understand how, over time, this scientific or rational way of knowing could eclipse other non-rational ways of knowing and eventually reduce a person's experience of reality into only that which can be observed, measured, and quantified with material evidence.

Faith

Faith, is a form of belief that is different from scientific belief. Where scientific belief is based on the physical or material aspects of reality and can be known as true through the application of scientific reason, faith is belief based on the knowledge gained through a relationship and known as true through that experience. For Christians, this relationship is with the God who is the creator of all things and who became man in the person of Jesus Christ out of love for all creation. This relationship involves an entrustment or a "handing over of oneself" to God, who in turn reveals himself. Faith opens up recognition of a broader experience of existence than that which is confined within a material, empirical, and rational universe. Faith allows someone to "see more" and therefore expands what reason can know, or the truth reason is capable of recognizing. This concept of reason, one that includes scientific reasoning but is at the same time expands beyond it, is sometimes called "expanded reason." It is at play when faith gives a person deeper insight and clarity into those things she already knows, and helps her to understand God's revelation more deeply.

For the Christian, belief in God expresses a particular kind of truth or certainty—certainty in God's total love for each, individual human person. Further, this love is revealed and manifested through relationship one that culminates in Jesus Christ and His Church. In this way, certainty gained through faith is more like that gained through a loving relationship than that derived from a scientific experiment. Both ways of knowing, faith and science, reveal truth and certainty, but are achieved by different means. Accepting something by faith grants access to a reality that is both more basic and infinitely vaster that any truth that could be reached by scientific reasoning. Reason enables faith, but faith expands reason.

Josef Ratzinger, in *Introduction to Christianity*, considers belief through faith to be a response to God's prior call, the fundamental *decision* at the heart of human existence, a basic mode of being which affirms that reality is not exhausted by what we can materially see, hear, and touch.[9] It is a decision, which he describes as, "as taking up a stand trustfully on the ground of the word of God."[10] Through faith, an understanding of the universe and all of reality is made possible through a gift of divine grace and also an assent or active acceptance of God's revelation. Faith, though distinct from reason, does not exclude the intellect. As the Catechism of the Catholic Church describes, "in faith, the human intellect and will cooperate with divine grace: 'Believing is an act of the intellect assenting to the divine truth by command of the will moved by God through grace' (St. Thomas Aquinas)."[11]

The Catholic Church believes that faith and reason[12] function together to allow a person's relationship with God to begin and grow. Both are necessary for Catholics and complement one another. As Pope John Paul II explains in his encyclical letter *Fides et Ratio*, "faith and reason are like two wings on which the human spirit rises to the contemplation of truth."[13] Reason is a "friend to faith," for faith in God relies on reason rather than its rejection. First, reason enables a person to recognize that God exists.[14] Then, it continues to assist a person as her faith and knowledge of God grows. It becomes a valuable aid when learning about Church doctrine, engaging with scripture, contemplating the mysteries of Christ's life, participating in the life of the Church, and conforming one's life to divine love. Faith without reason would not be possible. Yet a reduced version of reason can exist without faith. If one does not use reason to recognize the limits of reason, or places an over-reliance on reason as the exclusive means of making sense of reality, this makes

9. Ratzinger, *Introduction to Christianity*, 50.

10. Ratzinger, *Introduction to Christianity*, 69.

11. Catholic Church. *Catechism of the Catholic Church*: Vatican City: Libreria Editrice Vaticana. §155

12. In this section, I refer to a more traditional, scholastic understanding of reason than the expanded reason of Pope Benedict XVI.

13. Pope John Paul II, *Fides et Ratio*.

14. See St. Thomas Aquinas, *Proofs for the existence of God*.

faith seem unreasonable. Religious belief cannot stand up to the measure of scientific truth claims. Learning to reason effectively but not rightly creates a threat to the development of faith and religious belief. It is this problem that young Catholics if they do not receive proper guidance as they develop their reasoning ability and critical thinking skills in formal education.

Critical Thinking and Critical Thinking Initiatives

In contemporary formal education settings, the term "critical thinking" is an analog for "scientific" or "modern" reason. Critical thinking it is best defined as, "a disciplined, systematic style of thinking that is intended to be free from bias and other obstacles." Such thinking involves, "the exercise of an integrated combination of distinct cognitive processes, including classical categories such as analysis and synthesis, but also newly recognized categories such as metacognition (i.e., thinking about one's thinking)."[15]

Since the inception of formal education in the United States and other developed countries, efforts to educate young people have emphasized the transmission of knowledge, behaviors, and values—or teaching students "what to think." Increasingly however, this education prioritizes teaching students how to reason, or "how to think." Critical thinking initiatives, which are intentional and coordinated educational programs that attempt to do this, affect all types of schools (e.g., public, private, Catholic) at all levels (i.e., K–12). These initiatives affect educational standards, teaching practices, school culture, and more. The goal of these school reforms is to produce students who are proficient in particular reasoning activities (e.g., generalization, discrimination, analysis, evaluation, etc.) and thus better prepared for twenty-first century living. Students who can engage in critical thinking are, at least in theory, better able to survive and thrive in a pluralistic culture driven by a scientific and technological economy. At a time when so much diversity exists in contemporary culture, support for critical thinking initiatives in schools and school systems is virtually universal. Promoting critical thinking appears to be a common cause that everyone can support.

Efforts to promote students' development of critical thinking skills are apparent in most developed countries. In the United States, one sees them in the K–12 curriculum developed for nationwide implementation called the "Common Core Standards."[16] The creation of the Common Core was sponsored by the National Governor's Association and Council

---

15. Kilbane, *The 4Cs: Critical Thinking*, 12.

16. "Common Core State Standards," *National Governors Association Center for Best Practices & Council of Chief State School Officers.*

of Chief State School Officers with major financial support from the Bill and Melinda Gates Foundation. As of 2020, forty-one states have adopted the Common Core for implementation in their public schools.[17] Many private and Catholic schools also base either some or all of their curriculum on these standards. The Common Core systematically supports students' development of thinking skills across all grade levels and two core subject areas (e.g., Language Arts and Mathematics). It is currently working to produce equivalent standards in Social Studies and the Sciences.

Critical thinking also features prominently in other current curricula authored by professional associations and grade-level advocacy groups. Some examples include, "The C3 Framework for College, Career, and Civic Life" developed National Council for the Social Studies,[18] the "NEXT GEN" science standards,[19] and the Early Childhood Professional Preparation Standards developed by the National Association for the Education of Young Children.[20]

At the higher education level, critical thinking skills are also an important emphasis for learning. The American Association of Colleges and Universities (AAC&U), one of the most influential associations in postsecondary education, has developed a transdisciplinary rubric that, reflects, "the recognition that success in all disciplines requires habits of inquiry and analysis that share common attributes."[21] The AAC&U rubric was developed by teams of faculty experts and refined through deliberation with university instructors. It articulates the fundamental criteria for various learning outcomes related to the application of reason across different learning domains. The rubrics distinguish emerging levels of proficiency with relation to explaining issues, using evidence, acknowledging the influence of context or assumptions, and the like. They are intended for institutional-level use in guiding, evaluating and discussing student learning.[22]

17. National Governors Association Center for Best Practices & Council of Chief State School Officers. http://www.corestandards.org/standards-in-your-state/

18. National Council for the Social Studies. The College, Career, and Civic Life (C3) Framework for Social Studies State Standards: Guidance for Enhancing the Rigor of K-12 Civics, Economics, Geography, and History. Silver Springs, MD: NCSS, 2013).

19. National Governors Association Center for Best Practices & Council of Chief State School Officers. (2010). *Common Core State Standards for Mathematics.* Washington, DC: Authors.

20. National Association for the Education of Young Children (2008). *Overview of the NAEYC Early Childhood Program Standards.* https://www.naeyc.org/files/academy/file/OverviewStandards.pdf

21. American Association for Colleges & Universities, *Value Rubrics.* http://aacu.org/value/rubrics/critical-thinking

22. American Association for Colleges & Universities, 2020.

The impetus for including critical thinking in each of these curricula can be traced to a conceptual model called the "P21 Framework" proposed in 2004 by a group called the "Partnership for 21st Century Learning" (P21).[23] P21, a coalition of business, education, and government leaders, developed and disseminated this model to help schools "position 21st century readiness at the center of US education and to kick-start a national conversation on the importance of 21st century skills for all students."[24] In their framework (see Figure 1–1), P21 proposes the various conditions and competencies believed to prepare students to use and apply the content knowledge they acquire in their education while performing meaningful, practical tasks in life and work. The development of critical thinking skills is part of a complementary skill-set called the "4Cs," that every student requires. The 4Cs are comprised of critical thinking, communication, collaboration, and creativity.

Figure 1–1: *P21 Framework for 21st Century Learning*

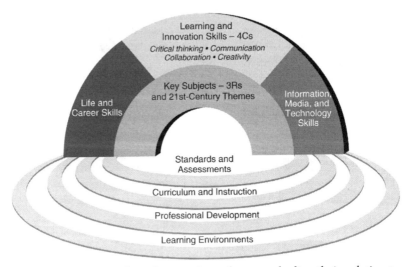

A utilitarian philosophy, one that values people directly in relation to their economic productivity and considers the value of education in relation to this end, is evident in this model. Although there are many espoused reasons for promoting critical thinking skills in schools and school systems, it should be noted that "work-force readiness" is most common among them. It is worth noting that critical thinking skills also contribute to the two other traditional goals of education, namely citizenship and personal

---

23. "Partnership for 21st Century Skills," *Framework for 21st Century Learning*, 2004.
24. "Partnership for 21st Century Skills."

enlightenment, but this is less frequently put forth as a justification for initiatives promoting them.

The History of Critical Thinking Initiatives

The seeds of modern critical thinking initiatives were sown by the scholars, education leaders, politicians, and social activists who were associated with the "Progressive Movement" that influenced American education in the early part of the twentieth century. Progressive reformers aimed to make schools more effective agents of a democratic society. Although the specific views and emphasis among Progressives varied, they agreed that, the education of engaged citizens, "involved two essential elements: 1) Respect for diversity, meaning that each individual should be recognized for his or her own abilities, interests, ideas, needs, and cultural identity, and 2) the development of critical, socially engaged intelligence, which enables individuals to understand and participate effectively in the affairs of their community in a collaborative effort to achieve a common good."[25]

The Progressives aimed to reform the dominant modes of schooling at the time—namely Church schools and public or "Common Schools." They took particular issue with the instructional methods (i.e. didactic approaches) and materials (i.e. the highly moralistic McGuffey Readers) used in these schools—describing the education they delivered as "passive learning, training, and indoctrination."[26]

According to Progressive reformers, education could be improved if its role was limited to two primary goals: 1) provision of the tools needed for democratic participation, and 2) preparation for future occupation. The thrust of educational experiences in Progressive schools then, was to teach students to think independently and solve problems because this was crucial to both of these goals.[27]

Between the 1930s–1970s, the views and values held by leaders of the Progressive Movement gradually moved from the fringe to the mainstream of American education. The ideas of thought-leaders such as John Dewey were widely disseminated, read, and embraced. Dewey's students and followers assumed faculty roles in the colleges and universities where they prepared like-minded teachers and administrators, wrote texts, and shaped education practice.

25. John Dewey Project, *A brief overview of progressive education*.
26. John Dewey Project, *A brief overview of progressive education*.
27. John Dewey Project, *A brief overview of progressive education*.

The success of Progressive schools and school districts became widely known and emulated. But most influential in the "mainstreaming" of progressive ideals was the participation of progressive-minded reformers in the large government-funded educational initiatives which stemmed from programs such as the "War on Poverty." Substantial funding and a national sphere of influence enabled the work of scholars to achieve broad, powerful, and long-standing impact.[28]

Hilda Taba, who had studied with John Dewey, was one of numerous scholars who has been recognized for her pioneering work in supporting the development of students' thinking skills—especially those students growing up in poverty. She expressed views that typify those of Progressives on critical thinking instruction saying:

> One scarcely needs to emphasize the importance of critical thinking as a desirable ingredient in human beings in a democratic society. No matter what views people hold of the chief function of education, they at least agree that people need to learn to think. In a society in which changes come fast, individuals cannot rely on routinized behavior or tradition in making decisions, whether on practical every day or professional matters, moral values, or political issues. There is a natural concern that individuals be capable of intelligent and independent thought.[29]

Taba's recognition of the importance of thinking skills was prescient. Some sixty years later, the speed of life continues to accelerate and the technological and scientific nature of many changes make it virtually impossible to rely on routinized behavior or tradition. It is easy to agree with Taba's prediction that the ability to think will be required by everyone today. But it will be especially so for young Catholics who will need such skills to recognize that scientific reasoning is limited in its ability to explain all of reality and that faith is indeed reasonable. They will need special interventions to sort out the mixed messages they will experience during their long and formative years of formal education.

Illustrating the Effects of Changing Curriculum and Instruction

Although the emphasis critical thinking initiatives place on students' ability to practice scientific reason affects all aspects of formal schooling, the major

---

28. Silver and Silver, *An Educational War on Poverty*
29. Taba, *Curriculum Development*, 49.

impact is made through the mechanisms of curriculum and instruction. Traditional curriculum standards and methods for teaching them are being systematically replaced by new ones. For example, in middle school language arts classrooms, learning how to write a persuasive essay, a practice that was virtually ubiquitous in schools for the last half century, is being replaced with learning to write an argument. At first consideration, it may not seem that these two types of writing assignments are very different. Both involve writing an essay that communicates with others and aims to influence the reader. Each requires careful organization, clear thinking, and thoughtful expression. Each involves the same dispositions for success, including hard work, concentration, and effort. Yet, there are some important differences in these assignments. As demonstrated in Figure 1–2 these assignments prioritize different approaches and reflect different values.

Figure 1–2: Comparison of Persuasion and Argument

Persuasion	Argument
Purpose is to "win over the reader," to appeal to their feelings or wishes in order to make them belief what the author is saying is true.	Purpose is to help reader make an informed (intellectual) decision or consider an idea, even when the author has presented views that are different from those of the reader
Based on passion and emotion	Based on research and logic
Convinces by appealing to the credibility of the author and/or the interest and emotions of the audience	Convinces by substantiating claims with multiple sources of evidence
Considers the perspectives of others, but not always	Involves evaluating the strengths and weaknesses of multiple perspectives
Focuses on the writer's viewpoint.	Addresses counters claims although the piece is clearly written defending one side.

A more careful comparison of assignments surfaces important distinctions. For example, the goal of a persuasive essay is to influence a reader by appealing to his or her wishes and feelings while an argument attempts to inform someone to make an intellectual decision. Further, a persuasive essay is based on passion and emotion while argument is based on research and logic. These are some obvious differences. Yet, much more should be recognized in comparing these two writing assignments. For one, there is an inherent difference in the degree of transparency surrounding the author's motive in these assignments. Both intend to convince the reader and "win them over" to the author's position. However, in a persuasive essay, the author's desire and bias are much more apparent and evident due to its communication of the author's emotion. In an argument, though the author also aims to influence the reader her position (i.e., a way of thinking), she does so in a more objective way, one which might not be apparent to an uncritical reader. An argument has a tendency to obfuscate the author's motive by removing any emotion or apparent bias. Instead, it selectively inserts data that serve the author's goal less detectably.

Although the comparison of these curricular assignments distinguishes some key differences, the change from persuasion to argument should also be considered in how the instructional approaches a teacher might use affect students. Imagine the instructional discourse that would occur in a classroom where a student is being coached to write a persuasive essay. The teacher might encourage a student in selecting the topic for a persuasive essay saying, "What do you care about? What do feel is important enough to you that you would want others to feel the same way? That would be a good topic for a persuasive essay because you'll want to be convincing and the more points you can make to get someone to care, the more powerful the persuasion will be." Now imagine the instructional discourse that might occur in a classroom where a teacher encourages a student as she prepares to write an argument. The teacher might suggest, "In selecting the topic for your argument, be sure to choose one about which there is lots of research and data, one about which you know there are multiple viewpoints but one that is clearly the best. This will make your argument easier to write and ultimately more powerful in convincing your reader."

Although the curriculum in this language arts class involves developing writing proficiency, this example illustrates how the teacher's discourse and instructional approaches impart a "hidden" or indirect lesson to the student as well. It demonstrates how a student can be influenced and formed by both the product chosen as the focus of learning as well as the processes associated with it. A student who spends time writing a persuasive essay and thinking about feelings will be more aware of them and possibly experience them more fully. Further a student whose teacher directs attention and time toward feelings will be more likely to recognize them as valuable and important. Likewise, a student who spends time thinking about issues that can be argued, researched, and associated with lots of data will learn to recognize such issues and wonder why all the things they care about cannot be are argued in this way. A student whose teacher pays attention to argument, data, and research will learn to value data and research. Of course, both of these learning experiences will enable the student to develop her ability to think, organize and express herself in writing. But the experience of the hidden curriculum will affect her development in subtle and more profound ways.

The change in curriculum and instruction evident in this example is similar to other such changes that have happened (and are happening) across grade level and subject area in schools across the country and around the globe. When considered collectively, assignments modified to promote critical thinking skills promise to be effective in teaching both scientific reason and the value or importance of such reason. If left unrecognized, unchecked, and without the intervention of adult guidance, students exposed to critical thinking initiatives, including young Catholics, are likely to identify more with the popular worldview than a Catholic one and accept the popular misconception that faith is unreasonable because its truth claims do not meet the same standard as that of scientific reasoning.

Addressing Faith, Reason and Critical Thinking in Catechesis

Today's young Catholics will need to use their intellect to recognize God's existence. They will also benefit from it as they continually grow in faith. Because of this, the catechesis offered them should incorporate the use of critical thinking skills and be accompanied by opportunities to learn how to these skills properly as Catholics. Such catechesis will reinforce the lessons young people are already learning in their formal education about the value of reason, but it must engage reason so that this capacity can be expanded by faith and practiced rightly. In this way, young people will be challenged to recognize how the Catholic worldview enables them to experience a reality that is not only richer and more beautiful than that realized by scientific reasoning, but also one that is true. Both the curriculum addressed in catechesis and the instructional approaches it utilizes will need to be adapted. In doing so, catechesis will not only teach about the Catholic faith but also equip young people for a life of faith in the twenty-first century.

Identifying Curricular Opportunities for Directly Addressing Challenges to Faith Development

Because Catholics are "in but not of the world," their understanding of certain concepts will always be similar to, but different from those without faith in subtle but crucial ways. They must learn this. It is not enough just to teach young people what to believe, they will also need to understand how it is different, and why it is better. Adults must teach them the faith in ways that meet young people's immediate need (i.e., to develop their reasoning ability) and also prepare them for the future (i.e., the need to use and expand reason across their lifetime) where their worldview will be constantly challenged.

Catechesis that is adapted to address the influence of other educational experiences young people have will be more effective. Because young people are developing critical thinking skills and learning to value scientific reasoning during their formal education, addressing this directly in catechesis is important. Adults should not "side step" this conflict or neglect to recognize the important differences in how the concepts of reason, faith, and belief are understood in different contexts. By confronting these issues "head on," adults will affirm what young people are already learning and stretch them even further. In this way, young people will hone their critical thinking skills at the same time they learn to recognize, appreciate, and develop a Catholic worldview. In this way, catechesis will not only meet an immediate need young people have to learn about the faith, but also prepare them to flourish in a culture where they are different. Whatever curriculum is being used for catechesis should be reviewed to identify; a) existing opportunities where distinctions about the Catholic worldview, especially those related to reason, faith, and belief) can be drawn out and addressed and b) areas where new curriculum (i.e., new standards or objectives) is needed to address contemporary challenges to faith more powerfully. Then catechesis should be adapted accordingly. Some recommendations and examples follow.

Drawing out Distinctions

A review of any existing catechetical curriculum will allow an adult to identify many topics that could be addressed better if they were presented with a recognition of the influence that scientific reasoning and critical thinking initiatives have on young Catholics. For example, when studying a sacred biography such as story of St. Polycarp, Bishop of Smyrna, in the "Golden Legend,"[30] young people would benefit from having it pointed out these accounts of a saint's life and the account of a famous person's life presented in a modern biography are not the same. It would be important to acknowledge that the authors and readers of a modern biography place great importance on veracity, or the extent to which the facts in the biography "stack up" with what really happened according to a modern view of reality (i.e., largely dependent on material and empirical truth). But this is not the case with sacred biographies. In this type of literature, the details included have a meaning that relies on the reader's contextual understanding of the text and a common understanding held by Christians at the time the sacred

30. Jacobus de Voragine. *The Golden Legend*.

biography was written. These biographies placed value on how much the life of the saint reflected the love and example of Jesus Christ who was divine. Understanding a sacred biography today requires that a person develops and shares this context with Christians of another era. Reading a scared biography as though it were a modern one would be rather shocking and unbelievable because our modern sensibilities tell us many of the events that occur within it (e.g., St. Polycarp's body was lit on fire but it did not burn and he had to be killed with a dagger instead) would have to defy what we hold as being possible.

An analysis of the catechetical curriculum would be likely to result in the recognition that there are also many cases of important concepts typically addressed that bear distinguishing as uniquely understood by Catholics and thus different from the popular culture. These include concepts such as family, leisure, time, beauty, truth, virtue, good, and community. In each of these instances, there is considerable overlap between what is understood about a concept in the popular culture and what is understood by those who espouse the Catholic faith—yet the subtle distinctions are of major importance. Taking the time to generalize about the similarities and distinguish the differences will be helpful to young people. Here, curriculum and instruction work together to move young people along the path to faith.

For example, young people would benefit from being actively taught to distinguish the Catholic understanding of the concept of critical thinking from that held by mainstream culture and formal education. Young people would benefit from completing a table, like that included below in Figure 1–3, that reflects the comparison about discussing them or reviewing artifact that demonstrate them (e.g., a curriculum plan, a newspaper article, etc.).

Figure 1–3: *A Comparison of Two Conceptions of Critical Thinking*

	Critical Thinking as Understood by Catholics	Critical Thinking as Understood in Education and Popular Culture
Progenitor- The source of the ability to reason/think critically	Critical thinking is a gift from God. This gift reflects the giver and the intelligibility of all God creates. It is a "good gift" which must be cultivated and developed.	Critical thinking is an innate human capability and people are born with the capacity to perform it.
Purpose- The reason for its existence and use	People require critical thinking to help them grow in their conformation to divine love, develop a relationship with God and participate in God's plan to build his kingdom. They also require it for employment, citizenship and life in the 21st century. Critical thinking helps a person understand how to live their faith in a world that may not share it.	Young people require critical thinking for employment, citizenship, and life in the 21st century. Practicing critical thinking is useful and the more proficiency a person develops, the more success she will experience in life.
Practice- An understanding about its benefits for oneself and others	Critical thinking helps people as they order their thoughts, words, and understanding all of reality. But most importantly it helps them as they grow in faith and come to understand the mysteries of Catholicism. This enables them to live a good life and gain eternal life.	Critical thinking aids people in organizing their thoughts and ideas. People benefit when they learn to do this because it helps them in different aspects of their life including making sense of experiences and solving problems.
Perspective- A recognition of its relationship to reason and also faith	Critical thinking must be considered a capacity that complements and supports the development of faith. Critical thinking is not a direct analog for reason as Catholics experience it. Knowledge gained through the intellect can be expanded by knowledge gained through faith.	Critical thinking allows a person to make sense of the world they can observe around them including material experiences and data. It can be developed and practiced but is not necessarily related to any other capacity that people possess.
Process- The particular way one learns about it and evaluates its effective use	People learn what critical thinking is and how it is useful in life, work, citizenship and also understand how it helps them acknowledge God's existence and live their faith in the world.	People learn what critical thinking is and how it is useful in life, work, and citizenship.

As this example illustrates, the Catholic understanding of critical thinking presents this concept and its capacity in its fullness, richness, and complexity. The Catholic understanding, as theologian Christopher Baglow expresses:

> offers to critical thinking a new, transcendent horizon to explore and within which to situate, to relate and also to distinguish all

other topics which critical thinking engages. This horizon is what God has revealed about His purposes for humanity, and challenges not the methods of other disciplines, nor any of the fruits of critical thinking, but unspoken and unquestioned assumptions that often reduce and fragment one's vision of reality. Within this transcendent horizon, all paths and methods of understanding retain their autonomy, and critical thinking in all disciplines retains its integrity.[31]

By comparison, the other understanding of critical thinking is flat and incomplete. It confines its potential for its use to finite circumstances and diminishes what a person can understand because it does not acknowledge all of existence. Young people will benefit from the training of their thinking an activity like this will involve. This example addresses just one of many concepts that could be profitably explored in an effort to develop thinking skills and also a recognition of the Catholic worldview. Young people will benefit from knowing both that this worldview exists and how it is different.

Additional Curriculum to Incorporate

Although it will be possible to identify existing opportunities in the curriculum where it is possible to draw out and use critical thinking skills to distinguish Catholic understandings of reason, faith, and belief, adults should also incorporate new lessons to support young people if needed. These lessons may work best if they intentionally teach Catholic understandings of these concepts as demonstrated in scripture, literature, art, and theological writings. For example, young people will benefit from exploring logical arguments for the existence of God (e.g., St. Thomas Aquinas' *Proofs for the Existence of God*), consider the relationship of faith and reason (e.g., St. Pope John Paul II's writings on faith and reason), and discussing how faith characterizes religious belief and the notion of expanded reason (Pope Benedict XVI).

If practiced throughout their catechesis, whether this happens in a classroom, parish religion class, or over the dinner table, young Catholics not only stand to increase their thinking skills but also maintain their faith. And when these young Catholics someday encounter individuals who challenge their faith, as so many do in college and in the workplace, they will be prepared.

---

31. Baglow, C. (personal correspondence October, 26, 2016).

Hope in a Time of Despair

On the Origins of the Feast of All Souls and Its Importance for Catholic Culture

STEPHEN M. METZGER

IT MAY SEEM STRANGE, at first glance, to include an essay about death and how society, especially religion, thinks about the dead in a collection of essays responding to a synod concerned with youth and vocation. The literary imagination often associates youth with images of spring, new life, and the hope for, or perhaps even the promise of, a better future. Unsurprisingly then, popular culture in the West since the end of World War II has valorized the young not only as an ideal of beauty and a time of life to be savored at all costs (as well as preserved), but also as the answer to society's many shortcomings. This view can be expressed in one of two ways by older generations, as they approach their dotage and ponder (perhaps for the first time) the future, either with pessimism, e.g., "I hope the younger generation can figure things out," or with optimism, i.e., "after having spent time with young people, I am encouraged and confident in a better tomorrow."[1]

Such romanticization of the younger generation, however, can do a disservice to young people themselves. While it is certainly true that young people many times bring a fresh insight and propose new solutions to old problems and ideas, to look to the young solely as the hope for the future idealizes them to a degree that is hard for them to achieve in reality. It also tends to ignore or at least minimize their hopes, fears, dreams, and anxieties. Many of those fears and anxieties that are associated with school are well known and have been the source of entertainment in print and on film and television. One can think quite readily of the genre of high school oriented movies that flourished in the late 1970s and 1980s in such films as

1. There is, of course, a contrary view that looks at the young as frivolous and ill-educated. This pessimistic outlook will often cause a sigh and a shake of the head as an older person worries about what the future may hold for society.

84

The Breakfast Club and *Fast Times at Ridgemont High*, etc. Indeed, one may be inclined to think that such awkward moments and anxieties concerning social interactions and school work are a normal part of growing up. It becomes a commonplace that such experiences are simply a normal part of being a teenager, especially when adults project their experiences onto those currently attending school.

One aspect that has received not as much attention as it deserves in the popular imagination is the anxiety experienced by young people of potentially imminent death and the process of grief. While it is true that death is a natural component of human existence and while one might expect that this anxiety would diminish as life expectancy has lengthened and medical skill advanced, young people today live under the constant shadow of their potential demise. Indeed, this eventuality is reinforced at school, which may no longer provide a safe haven from the problems of daily life. Young people are routinely conditioned at school to be prepared for a sudden outbreak of cataclysmic violence, a practice which must be unique in human history outside of a time of war.[2] On a quarterly basis, schools practice drills, which are required by law in many states, to prepare for the eventuality of a "live shooter" in their school.[3] These drills include lockouts and lockdowns, but schools also practice at least once a year a "reunification" procedure, in case of the rather frightening scenario that their school has become a crime scene and must be evacuated. In this case, a separate location has been chosen where basic triage and counseling can be provide. This alternative location also provides a safe space for the reunification of the survivors with their families.

Even though laws and governments force such drills and practice onto schools and children out of concern for safety, contemporary society is ill-equipped to mollify the anxiety that they create or to assuage the grief that follows from those outbreaks of violence and the death of classmates and friends. Institutions have protocols for providing counseling services and giving students the space and time that they need in order to rejoin the regular course of their day, studies, and activities. Yet, there is a contradiction in society that makes a return to "normalcy" (whatever that may be

---

2. During the Cold War, school children in the United States were at times drilled in "civil defense procedures" in the case of an attack with nuclear weapons, but unlike the current drills, these were in anticipation of a war with a readily identifiable enemy.

3. The State of Indiana's Department of Education's guidelines for school safety as of 2018 can be found here: https://www.in.gov/dhs/files/2018-Indiana-School-Safety-Recommendations.pdf. This widespread practice began during the 1999–2000 school year in the aftermath of the shooting at Columbine High School in Colorado that took place in the spring of 1998.

perceived to be) particularly challenging. For generations now, death has been either scrubbed from the public consciousness, increasingly relegated to the privacy of the hospital bed, hospice care, or nursing home (the CO-VID-19 pandemic has only intensified this), or it has been lampooned and ridiculed in popular media so that it becomes cartoonish and people are numbed to the savagery of violence. In this sense, even though death is the natural end of life, in real life it can seem more unnatural and shocking.

Added to this consciousness of their own mortality and the struggle to cope and adapt to such realizations, young people enter an increasingly isolating society and lonely world. The advent of the internet has from one perspective made communication easier and shrunk the great physical distance that separates families and coworkers. And yet, in many ways such ease of communication has actually driven people apart, allowing the like-minded to isolate themselves from the broader society, disengaging from reasoned discourse and the practice of polite, social conversation. As a consequence, real human interaction has diminished. The suspension of in-person instruction during the final academic quarter of the 2019–2020 school year has accentuated this. Many students have commented that despite the technological sophistication of platforms like Zoom or Google Meet, they missed the social dimension of school and the basic human interaction of a classroom the most.[4]

This process of separation, isolation, and mental struggle continues into adulthood. Indeed, the modern economy all but demands it. Many young people convinced that their future wealth and happiness can be secured only in an alluring large metropolis find themselves living in cramped apartments away from family and traditional social networks. Starting one's own family no longer ranks highly as a proper part of adulthood, postponed, if not cast aside entirely, to the demands of career aspirations, wealth accumulation, and pleasure. Loneliness abounds.

That young people are entering a fragmented and heartless world should not surprise us. The loneliness and greed associated with success in the modern economy has been commented upon in the literature of the last two centuries. For example, it forms the foundation upon which F. Scott Fitzgerald built *The Great Gatsby*.[5] Fitzgerald's American tragedy reveals the despair, despondency and vacuousness of a life dedicated to wealth and pleasure as pursued in the American capitalist system, as well as

---

4. During the 2019–2020 school year, I taught eleventh-grade English composition. During the online portion of year, the overwhelming answer to my questions about how they were coping with being out of school was that they missed being with their peers and teachers.

5. Fitzgerald, *The Great Gatsby*.

exposes the abrogation of traditional values it causes and the hypocrisy of those who claim to abide by them. That reality still exists, even if it is now varnished with the even brighter polish of digitization, as contrasted to the rather homely advertising and spectacles of the 1920s. This situation paired with a childhood that presents death as both to be feared and cataclysmically inevitable can have a deleterious effect on the psyche of young people. Despite what cheerleaders like Steven Pinker may claim,[6] the world remains a violent place, and young people are perhaps more acutely aware of this than adults. In many ways, they have not been well-prepared to handle these conflicting and harmful mental pressures that exist in the world into which they enter as young adults. Institutions that are especially concerned with the health and well-being of young people have a special duty to correct, or at least minimize, this isolation and anxiety.

It is here that the Catholic Church's long-held theology concerning death, with the Feast of All Souls as one of its highest expressions, can play an important and powerful role. The notion, indeed the reality, that there is a deep spiritual connection between the faithful on earth (long termed the "church militant") with the saints ("church triumphant"), especially in their intercessory role, and the faithful departed yearning for salvation ("church expectant") can provide a powerful antidote to the loneliness and despair that is such an integral part of life in the twenty-first century. It forges a sense of connection and community across time and space, by linking present actions to the experience of the deceased. It can also unite the faithful in a special way to their neighbors and the poor, as prayers for the dead have long been equated with charity for the poor. In this regard a fresh look at the historical emergence of the Feast of All Souls on the calendar of the Roman church is particularly instructive.

The Abbey of Cluny, the Peace of God, and a Special Concern for the Dead

Our story begins in the decades surrounding the year 1000 in the Burgundy region of Central and Eastern France at the great Benedictine monastery of Cluny.[7] Cluny was one of the most powerful monasteries during what has traditionally been termed the "High Middle Ages." It dominated the

6. Pinker, *The Better Angels of Our Nature*.

7. There is an extensive scholarly literature concerning the history and practice of the Abbey of Cluny and its daughterhouses; see, for example, Constable, *The Abbey of Cluny*. It was even remarked upon by Pope Benedict XVI in a General Audience on 11 November 2009; see http://www.vatican.va/content/benedict-xvi/en/audiences/2009/documents/hf_ben-xvi_aud_20091111.html.

religious landscape of Western Europe. Begun as a reform of Benedictine monasticism, practice, and devotion, it quickly developed into what one may quite reasonably claim was the first true religious order in the Latin Church, spawning an immense network of daughter-houses that remained under the authority of the abbot of Cluny. It wielded enormous influence and played a critical role in changing the religious and political sensibilities of an emerging Europe.[8] In many ways, it laid the foundation for the reformation of the church as a whole, in a movement that has come to be known as the Gregorian Reforms (Pope Gregory VII).[9]

Cluny enjoyed a special kind of independence that gave it the space and freedom to have such influence. Duke William the Pious of Aquitaine founded the monastery in 910, endowing it with large estates from which it could be self-sufficient.[10] He then renounced all claim and authority over his foundation, placing the new monastery under the protection and rule of the pope himself. On the one hand, William's decision freed Cluny from the feudal obligations and interference by meddlesome nobles that ensured its future success in reforming and shaping religious life for subsequent generations. On the other hand, by placing his new foundation under the sole protection of the pope when the papacy was just beginning to emerge as a centralized political authority, it left the monastery virtually defenseless at a dangerous time.

As the great medieval historian Jacques Le Goff put it, Europe around the year "1000 was bellicose and violent."[11] The collapse of the last vestiges of the Carolingian empire created a political vacuum and a loss of a strong authority that could command the respect of the aristocracy and their allied troops. With no centralized leadership, the wars of expansion that had created, sustained, and enriched an emerging class of warriors (soon to be known as 'knights') during the Carolingian period were largely over.[12] Without the booty from military campaigns, these warlords turned increasingly to the local population for sustenance and enrichment, plundering and pillaging the countryside, demanding tribute and allegiance. To add to the violence, it was at just this time that the Vikings increased their raids on the continent, taking advantage of the lack of a united front to stop them.[13]

---

8. Le Goff, *The Birth of Europe*, 5.

9. Wollasch, "Monasticism," 163–185; Cowdrey, *The Cluniacs and the Gregorian Reform*.

10. Howe, "The Nobility's Reform of the Medieval Church," 322.

11. Le Goff, *The Birth of Europe*, 42.

12. For one interpretation of these events, see Bartlett, *The Making of Europe*.

13. Le Goff, *The Birth of Europe*, 43.

The poor and religious institutions such as monasteries were a particular target of this increase in localized violence. A place like Cluny was vulnerable precisely because of its independence. It did not have a powerful lord who could come to its aid and protection. Instead, the monks needed to rely on argument, preaching, and persuasion to convince the powerful to renounce a life of violence, especially against fellow Christians. Indeed, the need to impress upon these violent men that their religion demanded that they be peaceful became particularly pressing.[14] For this reason, not only did the monks of Cluny attempt to reform the practice of Benedictine monasticism, but it also became a center for the reformation of society by playing a key role in two movements, the Peace of God and the Truce of God.[15] These two initiatives were aimed at convincing the wealthy and powerful warlords to stop the violence and respect the Christian exhortations to peace and justice.

Reform-minded bishops and other ecclesiastical leaders tried to impress on the warrior class that it was time to end the violence. In a series of councils and meetings, these men attempted to set limits upon whom one could legitimately wage war against (for example, the poor should never be attacked) and on what days it was acceptable to engage in battle (for example, Sundays and feast days should be respected and a truce between warring factions should be observed on those days). This was no easy task to be accomplished by the reformers. Since the time of the civil wars following disputes over territory and power among the heirs of Charlemagne, theologians and lawyers had developed a whole series of arguments justifying warfare, including against fellow Christians.[16] Violence as a means to either political or religious victory had become normalized, and men who had been conditioned to the value of war as both a means to an end and a livelihood would be hard to convince to change their ways.

What could a monastery do to remedy this situation? Certainly it could preach and write against the violence and oppression of the poor. It also participated in councils with other church leaders to denounce unjustified aggression and reform the nobility. But it was in many ways Cluny's monastic practice and liturgical devotion that was most convincing. Cluny became famous for its elaborate rituals in commemoration of the dead. Indeed, as Jacques Le Goff put it in 2005, this development in the understanding about the relationship between the living and the dead was one of the most profound changes for the development of European culture.[17] The monks of

---

14. This point is emphasized by Wollasch in the *New Cambridge Medieval History*.

15. Cowdrey, "The Peace and the Truce of God in the Eleventh Century," 42–67.

16. See the illuminating books by Wynn, *Augustine on War and Military Service*.

17. Le Goff, *The Birth of Europe*, 51; see also Schmid and Wollasch, "Die Gemeinschaft

Cluny became the acknowledged leaders in offering intercessory prayers for the dead. Their liturgies became more and more elaborate, lasting nearly all day.[18] As one observer put it, participating in a liturgical service at Cluny gave one a glimpse of heaven.[19] Their reputation as particularly effective at intercessory prayer for the dead became a source of wealth for the monastery as numerous noble families sought to have their ancestors and relatives remembered in the prayers of the monks. It gave the monks security in both a real and in a monetary sense, and it provided a starting point from which to convince the warriors to change their violent ways. To put it in a rather humorous way, it was as if the monks could say to the nobles, "now that we have your attention, would you mind very much changing your behavior?"

Scholars have dedicated a great deal of attention to the nature of the Cluniac liturgies and their practice.[20] They have also tried at various times to explain why this emphasis on remembrance of the dead was so appealing and transformative. John Howe has argued that the success of monasteries like Cluny was due to a collaboration between the nobility and the monks. Certain nobles, like Duke William the Pious, were interested in reforming religious life and the two groups worked together to reshape religious devotion and by extension alter the cultural landscape of Europe.[21] In a similar vein, Jacques Le Goff has emphasized that the increased emphasis on praying for the dead was a way in which nobles could justify their nobility. It entrenched the notion that their privileged place in society came from their noble lineage as much from their valorous deeds. It thereby reinforced their claims to power and authority.[22] Such assertions became increasingly important as fighting was deemphasized and ideas of nobility were rarified.

Lastly, Barbara Rosenwein provided a psychological explanation for the success of the ritual of Cluny. She drew attention to the martial language associated with the prayers for the dead and how this was interpreted as a way of fighting the devil. The emphasis on combat, found as well in the old expression "church militant," appealed to the monks, a significant portion of which would have been drawn from noble families and passed over for

---

der Lebenden und Verstorbenen in Zeugnissen des Mittelalters," 365–405.

18. Rosenwein, "Feudal War and Monastic Peace," 133–136 for the length of the monastic day and the liturgical activities.

19. Pope Benedict XVI mentioned this in his remarks about Cluny; see n. 7, above.

20. See, for example, Paxton and Cochelin, *The Death Ritual at Cluny in the Central Middle Ages*; there is also the monumental and foundation a study by Sackur, *Die Cluniacenser in ihrer kirchlichen und allgemeingeschichtlichen Wirksamkeit bis zur mitte des elften Jahrhunderts*.

21. Howe, "The Nobility's Reform of the Medieval Church."

22. Le Goff, *The Birth of Europe*, 52.

a military career as a knight. In this way, the signification of "combat" was broadened to include prayer and ritual, thereby appealing to the martial imagination of the noble elite.[23]

There is certainly truth in these interpretations for the success of the commemoration of the dead as it came to be practiced at the Abbey of Cluny. It is interesting that despite all of the attention paid to the liturgy and ritual of this famous Burgundian monastery, little notice has been taken of the significant development at Cluny not only of the commemoration of the dead but also of an annual celebration of such liturgies on November 2, the day after All Saints. As much as the monks' routine of intercessory prayer for the dead played in the reform of noble culture and the diminishment of violence, these ideas were made manifest to the church as a whole in the Feast of All Souls and had a powerful effect on European and Christian culture well into the twentieth century.

The Emergence of the Feast of All Souls

Death plays an important role in Christianity. The sacrifice of Christ on the Cross and his subsequent Resurrection are central to the Christian story and the formation of Christian culture. Early Christians often gathered at the graves of deceased members of the community for prayer and worship during the days of Roman persecution. As Peter Brown has argued, the Christian attitude toward death was transformative, overturning the common view of antiquity that a dead body was a locus of disease and pollution.[24] It was a practice that united social classes, encouraged both by popular devotion and belief as well as the reasoning of sophisticated theologians.

Consequently, veneration and respect for the dead was nothing new by the year 1000. The cult of the saints played a powerful role in the Christian imagination. Once the era of the early martyrs was completed, the Christian community found new saints in the person of those who were deemed especially holy by their exemplary lives, such as St. Martin of Tours. To the intercessory power of the saints was ascribed the conversion of new adherents, the healing of the sick, and the performance of miracles. In this way Christians knew well that the divide between this world and the next was just a thin veil. Indeed, such a distinction between the two, as is common in the Platonic epistemology, was shattered by the Incarnation, which united the things of heaven with the things of earth.

23. Rosenwein, "Feudal War and Monastic Peace," 152–157.
24. Brown, *The Cult of the Saints.*

The monks of Cluny under the direction of their abbot, St. Odilo, instituted a commemoration of the souls of all the faithful departed on the day after All Saints' throughout the Cluniac order sometime around the year 1020 or 1030.[25] The feast would soon be adopted throughout the Latin Church. A medieval account of the origins and rationale for the feast is given in the *Life of St. Odilo*:

> The lord bishop Richard told me of this vision, which I had heard spoken about but without remembering the slightest detail. One day, he told me, a monk from Rouergue (Rodez) was on his way back from Jerusalem. While on the high seas between Sicily and Thessalonika, he encountered a violent wind, which drove his ship onto a rocky islet inhabited by a hermit, a servant of God. When our man saw the seas calm, he chatted about one thing and another with this hermit. The man of God asked him what nationality he was, and he answered that he was Aquitanian. Then the man of God asked if he knew a monastery which bears the name of Cluny, and the abbot of this place Odilo. He answered: 'I knew him, indeed knew him well, but I would like to know why you are asking me this question.' And the other replied: 'I am going to tell you, and I beg you to remember what you are about to hear. Not far from where we are there are places where, by the manifest will of God, a blazing fire spits with the utmost violence. For a fixed length of time the souls of sinners are purged there in various tortures. A host of demons are responsible for renewing these torments constantly: each day they inflict new pain and make the suffering more and more intolerable. I have often heard the lamentations of these men, who complain violently. God's mercy in fact allows these condemned souls to be delivered from their pains by the prayers of monks and by alms given to the poor in holy places. Their complaints are addressed above all to the community of Cluny and its abbot. By God I beg of you, therefore, if you have the good fortune to regain your home and family, to make known of this community what you have heard from my mouth, and to exhort the monks to multiply their prayers, vigils, and alms for the repose of souls enduring punishment, in order that there might be more joy in heaven, and that the devil might be vanquished and thwarted.'
>
> Upon returning to his country, our man faithfully conveyed this message to the holy father abbot and the brothers. When they heard him, the brothers, their hearts running over with joy, gave thanks to God in prayer after prayer, heaping alms upon

25. On St. Odilo, see Hourlier, *Saint Odilon, abbé de Cluny*.

alms, working tirelessly that the dead might rest in peace. The
holy father abbot proposed to all the monasteries that the day
after All Saints' Day, the first day of November, the memory
of all the faithful should be celebrated everywhere in order to
secure the repose of their souls, and that masses, with psalms
and alms, be celebrated in public and private, and that alms be
distributed unstintingly to all the poor. Thus would hard blows
be struck at the diabolical enemy and Christians suffering in
Gehenna would cherish the hope of divine mercy.[26]

This account appears to us as suitably medieval, the stuff of legend. The tale is
told in such a way that it seems familiar as if it was something we might find
in sacred Scripture, epic poetry, or hagiography. Indeed, it has certain reso-
nances with the *Lives of the Desert Fathers*. It relates a medieval conception of
death and the afterlife and marks a waypoint towards what will in succeeding
centuries be a full doctrinal exposition of Purgatory. One might say that the
description in this account is akin to the fuller and more celebrated description of the afterlife that will emerge in the poetry of Dante. It smacks of what
one might call "medieval superstition." It might also bring up allusions to
Martin Luther's polemic against the sale of indulgences, and that old favorite:
"as soon as a coin in the coffer rings/ a soul from purgatory springs."

But let us step back from the legendary origins of the Feast of All
Souls and consider once again the broader historical context. In the power
vacuum created by the demise of the Carolingian Empire, the threat of violence and violent death was real. The situation threatened not just peasants
and serfs but religious institutions, such as Cluny, who were viewed as great
treasure-troves of wealth to be looted and pillaged. If I was keen to use such
terms, one might describe this period as truly the "Dark Ages." As mentioned above, momentum was growing among church leaders and laity to
put an end to the violence and destruction and exhort the strongmen and
warlords, soon to be referred to as knights and nobles, to live according to
the truths of the Christian faith. But how does one do this?

The Feast of All Souls was crucial to this endeavor. It was a way for
church leaders and the faithful to reinforce not only the Christian teaching
concerning death but also equality. Death is after all the great leveler. The
monks of Cluny could say to the strongmen and the warlords, "You might
be powerful now, but there will come a day when you will be absolutely reli-
ant on the mercy of God and the supplications of your brothers and sisters.
Your rank and your possessions will no longer matter." To put it another

---

26. Text as appears in Le Goff, *The Birth of Purgatory*, 125–126.

way, the monks could say to the powerful, "there will come a day when you may need the help of someone who does not even know your name."

This was an ingenious way for medieval Christians to reinforce the teaching of St. Paul, "There is neither Jew nor Greek, there is neither slave nor free person, there is not male and female; for you are all one in Christ Jesus" (Gal 3:28). In a world, much like our own, marked by oppression and inequality, the Church found a way to make manifest and relevant an ancient truth of the faith. For example, in the days of Early Christianity, when processions would go out from the cities to worship at the shrines of the holy martyrs, no protocol would be followed: aristocrat and peasant, rich and poor would walk side by side.[27] Such a conception had a powerful effect on the Catholic imagination. For example, it persisted into the twentieth century at imperial funeral masses. When the procession for the funeral of the Austrian Empress Zita reached the doors of the church, the retinue found the doors locked. Upon knocking, a church official asked who it was. The members of the retinue replied giving the Empress' full titles and honors. The church official replied that he did not know this person. Once again they knocked, upon being queried gave the same or similar answer, and once again were denied entry. Finally a third time, the members of the procession knocked on the doors. This time in answer to the question they responded "We come with the sinful mortal, our sister Zita." At that reply, the doors opened.[28] It is in death that we most forcefully realize not only our mortality but our frailty, our equality and dependence on our brothers and sisters, and how much in need we are of the mercy of Christ. In this way, the Feast of All Souls is as much about the living, if not more so, than it is about the faithful departed.

This facet becomes particularly clear in the link between prayers for the dead and alms for the poor. In the passage describing the origins of the feast quoted above, great emphasis is laid on the need for alms as much as for prayers. Rosenwein emphasized only the martial language in this passage to make the point about the appeal of the Cluniac life for young nobles. There can be little doubt that such language was convincing, but the far greater emphasis in the passage is on the care for the poor. Such charitable work is mentioned three times, including their rather striking phrase that the alms should be given "unstintingly."

The poor and the faithful departed occupy the same mental space then in the Christian worldview. They are in a sense powerless and must rely on

---

27. Brown, *Cult of the Saints*, 42–43.

28. Schmemann, "Hapsburg Grandeur is Dusted Off for Burial of "Our Sister the Empress Zita," 3.

the actions of the powerful to help them, one with shelter, clothes, food, and drink, the other with prayers for their salvation and their eternal rest. One is a spiritual work of mercy and the other is a corporal work of mercy, but both are to the credit of the believer who performs these tasks. As the example from Cluny makes clear, it is of crucial importance that one cannot truly pray and care for the dead without also praying and caring for the poor. In this way, the radical call of the Gospel to pull us out of ourselves and see in all, both living and dead, our brothers and sisters is put into action.

Conclusion

This is a time in a time of great economic inequality with a looming financial and ecological crisis brought on by our desire for comfort and financial gain as remarkably detailed in the Pope Francis' encyclical, *Laudato si'*. Young people feel the pressures of this reality intimately. They are also regularly presented with a world that fears the outbreak of sudden and cataclysmic violence. The challenge of our time is how can we enflame the hearts and imaginations of young people to follow Christ and commit themselves to his service and the service of all of humanity. How can we give them hope?

I do not claim that a re-emphasis of the Feast of All Souls is the only answer. But I think it is incumbent upon religious institutions and the Church herself to create or emphasize structures, devotions, and practices that will support young people and the entire faithful in the practice of their faith, and thereby create a lasting Catholic worldview that will guide and sustain them. Young people are yearning for substantive ideas, but also for something that makes sense and is opposed to the dominant economic and cultural model that chews up its adherents and spits them out. In this sense, the full and beautiful traditions of the Catholic faith are countercultural.

Moral arguments should be made for peace, for the care and protection of the poor and marginalized, and for the stewardship of our common home, but the eschatological teachings of the Church provide powerful tools upon which to found and support these arguments. This can be done not in the terms of fire and brimstone like the sermon by Jonathan Edwards, "Sinners in the Hand of an Angry God." Similarly, there is no need to fear that such practices and devotions will be ridiculed as superstition and unappealing to the rational, scientific mind.

There is no need to fear death. It is after all the common destiny of all mortal life, and Christ promises eternal life to those who are close to him. *Pie Jesu Domine, dona nobis requiem.*

Forming Young Catholics in Faith and for Vocational Discernment

Considering the Implications of Social Science for Pastoral Practice

Timothy Reilly and Linda Kawentel ——————————————

Renewed interest in the religious and spiritual development of youth is clear, not just within the Catholic Church (e.g., Francis, 2019), but within the culture and social science scholarship more generally (e.g., Hardy & King, 2019; Smith, Ritz, & Rotolo, 2020; Bengston, Putney, & Harris, 2017). Despite this, too rarely within the Catholic Church has this led to productive collaborations between social scientists and formators. This is especially worrying amidst the ongoing decline in religious participation and affiliation. We seek to address these challenges, bringing social science research and theory into dialog with pastoral documents of the Church.

We approach this as a conversation between pastoral theology and social science, seeking to acknowledge the contributions each can make to the challenges of formation in the contemporary world. We begin with an overview of current pastoral documents of the Catholic Church on young adults. We then turn to recent sociological research on Catholic young adults, which both raises concerns about current trends and offers insight into the social processes at play in the spiritual and vocational formation of Catholic young adults. Expanding upon this research, we present developmental science research and theory as it applies to faith and vocational formation. Next, we use this as the basis for a constructive model of faith and vocational formation and consider this model in light of *Christus Vivit*, addressing the particularities of Catholic faith and vocational formation. Finally, we elaborate upon the pastoral suggestions of *Christus Vivit* in light of social science and consider next steps for continuing the conversation between social science and pastoral theology.

The Synod Preparatory Document and other pastoral documents.

In October 2016, Pope Francis made his announcement that a Synod of Bishops would take place on "Young People, the Faith and Vocational Discernment." Preparation for the Synod, which would be held in 2018, involved the drafting of the Preparatory Document, which described the purpose of the Synod as an opportunity for the Church "to examine herself on how she can lead young people to recognize and accept the call to the fullness of life and love, and to ask young people to help her in identifying the most effective way to announce the Good News today" (Synod of Bishops, 2017). The Synod Preparatory Document emphasized a focus on discernment and vocational formation, both of which are appropriate tasks for young people. However, many young people are insufficiently prepared for these tasks, lacking the knowledge and experience of prayer to be able to perceive and relate to God in the way such discernment demands. These young people are especially in need of a more basic spiritual formation, which would plant the seeds for vocational formation. As such, pastoral consideration of their particular needs is especially urgent.

Christus Vivit, Pope Francis' apostolic exhortation encapsulating the work of the 2018 Synod, responds to this issue well, at once exhorting faithfulness and vocational formation and considering the role of faith communities in fostering it. It especially emphasizes the need to encourage young people to engage actively and autonomously in their communities, spiritual and secular, at once being formed and becoming who they are called to be. It also emphasizes the role of faithful Catholics in accompanying young people, not as children who are to passively receive the faith, but as friends with whom to build up the Church. Further, it defines this friendship and notes that growth in faith is dependent on such friendship, friendship with Christ and committed friendship with other Christians. These then are the foundations of basic spiritual formation, laying the groundwork for vocational discernment.

Given this, a focus on the relational formation of young people is essential, preparing them and modelling for them friendship, amongst Church communities and with Christ. Yet, this relational formation, encompassing both human and spiritual formation, depends, if it is to be mature, on the other pillars of formation: intellectual and practical[1]. Understanding this formation fully is likely to benefit from engagement with social science, the subject we turn to next.

---

1. These pillars emerge from concepts of priestly formation in Pope John Paul II *Pastores Dabo Vobis* and lay formation in Pope Paul VI, *Apostolicam Actuositatem.*

Social Science and Faith Formation

Sociology and the Catholic Young Adults: From Investigating Attitudes and Behaviors to Faith Formation

Sociology is concerned with understanding how society shapes people's lives and experiences and with how people's actions maintain and transform those social structures. Some recent sociological inquiry into Catholicism centers on understanding the religious beliefs and practices of Catholic young adults (Wittberg, 2016; Pew; 2015; Smith et al., 2014; D'Antonio, Dillon, & Gautier, 2013).[2] Researchers have found notable differences between young adult Catholics and older Catholics, particularly on issues concerning marriage, family, and sexuality. For example, young adult Catholics tend to be less traditional than older Catholics same-sex marriage and pre-marital cohabitation than older Catholics (Pew, 2015). Young adult Catholics are also less consistent in their participation and less attached to the institutional Church within the United States. As illustrated in Table 1, young adult Catholics attend Mass at lower rates than older Catholics. While only 30% of Catholics ages 18–29 reported attending Mass at least weekly, 37% of Catholics ages 30–49 and 50–64 and 49% of those over 65 said they attended weekly.

Table 1.

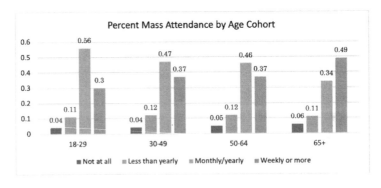

Source: Pew Research Center Survey of U.S. Catholics and Family Life, May 5–June 7, 2015. See Pew (2015).

2. Importantly, researchers have used both different terms and different cutoff ages to describe Catholic young adults. Some studies refer to this population by their generational cohort, i.e., millennial Catholics (born 1982–2004) (Gray & Hagan, "Catholicism"), whereas others use 'emerging adult,' a term that refers to one's stage in the lifecycle. See Smith et al., *Young Catholic America*.

A 2015 study by the Pew Research Center found that 56% of Catholics ages 18–29 said they could never leave Catholicism, in contrast to 70% for those 30–49 and 50–64 and 80% for those over 65 (Pew, 2015).[3]

While research on the beliefs and practices of young adult Catholics has been a topic of interest within sociological circles for some time (Drake, 2004; Hoge et al., 2001; Fee et al., 1981; Greeley, 1980), current research has focused on understanding why some young adults continue to affiliate with and practice Catholicism, as well as why many young adults raised in the Catholic Church no longer attend Mass or have left Catholicism altogether. Largely conducted by sociologist Christian Smith and colleagues, existing scholarship on the formation of young people reveals some important factors at play in whether a teenager raised in the Catholic faith continues be religiously active in the Church come young adulthood. Among these are having relationships as teens with adults who have a strong faith life, internalizing Catholic beliefs as teens, and regularly practicing one's faith as a teen (Smith et al., 2014). In particular, parents have been shown to play a critical role in both the faith formation and later religious practice of Catholic-raised young adults (Smith, Ritz, & Rotolo, 2019; Bartkus & Smith, 2017; Manglos-Weber & Smith, 2015; Smith et al., 2014). Parental religiosity is associated with teenagers' later religious affiliation as young adults:

> [T]he religious commitments and habits of parents matter tremendously. Using our survey data, we can anticipate quite accurately whether a given teenager will continue to identify as Catholic into emerging adulthood based primarily on what we know about the religious home environment in which they were raised. Whether an emerging adult continues to identify as Catholic has much to do with whether his or her parents valued and modeled a rich, multifaceted, and consistent religious faith.[4]

Indeed, parents are so influential to the formation of young people that "parents represent not simply an influence of the development of children's religious worldviews, but the *arch*-influence over it."[5]

---

3. It can be difficult to untangle whether the differences between young adult Catholics and Catholics of other age-groups are due to membership of an age cohort ('generation effect') or simply to their phase of life ('age effect') There is some evidence that today's young adult Catholics are different from those of previous generations. While in the 1970s more than one-third of 18–25-year-olds attended Mass at last weekly, by the 1990s and 2000s only one-fifth of those in this age group attended weekly or more often. Smith et al., *Young Catholic America*.

4. Manglos-Weber & Smith, *Understanding former young Catholics*, 18.

5. Bartkus & Smith, *A Report on American Catholic Religious Parenting*, 8

This is not to say that schools, youth ministry, and CCD programs do not matter in the faith development of Catholic young people. Rather, parents should be understood as the primary formators of their children. They do this by acting as the point of access between the Church and their children, by acting as "gatekeepers" of the Catholic faith (i.e., controlling the religious content their children encounter), and by interpreting the Catholic faith to their children. In other words, parents play a definitive mentorship role. To quote Bartkus and Smith, "If children do not "see" Catholicism in the "face" of their parents, they will likely never gain sufficient familiarity with it to commit to practicing the faith in the long run."[6] These researchers argue that parenting should be seen as the building of a culture, a project in which children are initiated (or not) into certain core values, practices, and modes of experience regarding religion. An important implication of Smith's work is that not only must the Church invest in the faith formation of young people, but also in the formation of parents and those who will become parents.

While this research sheds light on how parents, in collaboration with their local parishes, can help retain Catholic youth, it also highlights the striking lack of faith formation among today's young adults. Among young adults in the U.S., there are now nearly as many who have left the Church as there are who identify with Catholicism (Bartkus & Smith, 2017). Many young adults have not had religiously involved parents. Of those who left the Catholic faith, 30 percent have had parents who attended Mass weekly or more. In comparison, among young adults who remain Catholic, 52% had parents who attended Mass weekly or more.[7] In her edited volume *Young American Catholics*, sociologist Maureen Day (2018) notes that the lack of religiosity among today's young adult Catholics is not just something that just happened naturally, and that parents should not take all the blame. Rather, Day sees the decline as a result of many years of inadequate faith formation. Day writes:

> The number of cracks that can occur in this broad offering of faith formation are many. Focusing just on the Smith team's data, first, one's parents might not have had the time, awareness, or personal convictions to have been strong first teachers in the faith, which resulted in Catholic beliefs and practices worn lightly rather than a more intense socialization. Second, one's parish might not have networked these youth with other adults who could have served as mentors in their parents' stead. Third,

6. Bartkus and Smith, *A Report on American Catholic Religious Parenting*, 15
7. Manglos-Weber & Smith, *Understanding former young Catholics*.

this faith formation might not have presented material in a way so that it was truly internalized and incorporated into one's belief system . . . Finally, religious practices that were relevant to youth were either not regularly available or were not preserved in a way that made the religious meaning apparent (e.g., service as a good deed rather than as an act of compassionate and just charity).[8]

Day suggests that the Church not only put resources into youth faith formation, but also think creatively about how to reach young adults who have left the Church or who are thinking about leaving.

Sociological studies on Catholic faith transmission are useful in pointing to the actors and institutions most important in socializing young adults into the faith. At the same time, the field is limited in what it can say beyond the social processes present in faith formation and faith transmission. Next, we turn to the social science field of developmental psychology to explore psychological processes at play in the faith and vocational formation of young adults.

Developmental Science, Faith Formation, and Vocational Discernment

Questions of human becoming are challenging and have undergone considerable empirical and theoretical scrutiny by social scientists. As such, developmental science provides an invaluable resource for understanding how one is to become who God calls them to be. Further, developmental scholars have taken a growing interest in the religious and spiritual development and formation of young people (see especially Hardy & King, 2019).

We present a selective and integrative account of how developmental science can inform the Church's efforts to accompany young people and support them in their vocations. Two areas of theory and research are especially applicable to these efforts: identity (e.g., Schwartz, Cote, & Arnett, 2005) and moral and spiritual development (e.g., King & Defoy, 2020; Frimer & Walker, 2009).

The classic approach to identity in developmental science emerges from the writings of Erik Erikson (1968) and a concurrent model (Marcia, 1966). This approach suggests that a healthy identity emerges from self-understanding and consideration of one's commitments. Such self-understanding requires thinking about one's values and goals, exploring them, and, with time, committing to these values and goals. Through successful resolution of this identity decision-point (crisis), the young person can

8. Day, "Going, going, and some are gone," 292–93.

make healthy commitments to identity in a number of domains: intellectual, political, spiritual, religious, vocational, and relational. However, such resolution isn't to be taken for granted, many young people form unhealthy identities, in one or more domains, and the development of an integrated and agentic purpose, directing one's identity toward a good beyond oneself is especially rare (Damon, 2008).

Recent scholarship has shed new light on this theory, elaborating on the original dimensions of exploration and commitment with the addition of reconsideration, acknowledging that young people, even after making identity commitments remain open to new values and commitments (Meeus, Van de Schoot, Keijsers , & Branje, 2010). Such reconsideration allows for ongoing development, as young people experience new situations and learn new things, allowing them to change their commitments in light of these experiences. What does this research tell us? Exploration, reconsideration and commitment are all healthy, to a point. Further, they are ideally engaged in progressively, with exploration amidst tentative commitment and reconsideration leading to the best emotional outcomes for young adolescents and a movement toward firm commitment amidst ongoing reconsideration, with diminished exploration, leading to the best emotional outcomes for young adults.

Parallel research, adopting the individualization theory of identity formation, considers two primary pathways to identity development, a default pathway and a developmental pathway (Schwartz, et al., 2005). Default individualization occurs when a young person passively and uncritically goes along with social norms and expectations. Developmental individualization, in contrast, entails an active, personal, and critical consideration of who one desires to become. Here again, the active and critical approach is associated with better outcomes, consistent with all developmental approaches to identity formation.

However, these theories provide little insight into the ideal identities for individuals to develop, emphasizing process over outcome. Such consideration is largely reserved to scholarship on spiritual and moral development, areas in which normative claims about what is good are unavoidable. Studies of exemplary individuals (e.g., Colby & Damon, 1992) ground this work, and have recently received renewed attention (Bronk, King, & Matsuba, 2013; Frimer, Walker, Lee, Riches, & Dunlop, 2012; Damon & Colby, 2016). Exemplars have served to ground inquiry into moral and spiritual identity, which are often intertwined (Colby & Damon, 1992; King, Clardy, & Sanchez Ramos, 2014).

King and Defoy (2020) propose a model of spiritual development in which human potential is reached as a result of the developmental integration of the (1) relational self, (2) authentic self, and (3) ethical self, through engagement in a transcendent narrative identity. Transcendent narrative identities are those identities that faith traditions of all kinds are intended to support, in which individuals come to be a part of a story and community larger than themselves. As such, this story orients the relational self, how one thinks of others and their proper relationship to them. Similarly, this story generally demands that one be oneself, knowing oneself and participating *as* oneself utilizing one's gifts and talents and recognizing one's flaws and weaknesses, rather than participating in a generic and impersonal way. Finally, this narrative requires that one seek moral and spiritual excellence, cultivating an ethical self.

This model bears striking similarity to research on moral exemplars and highly generative adults. In all of these cases the kinds of stories that individuals tell about their lives are associated with the objective goodness of their lives. There is also a self-transcendent end, divine and/or prosocial, in each case. Yet, though it seems to some paradoxical, the integration of the self with something larger than oneself seems to orient individuals' agency and personal capacities. This is to say that spiritually and morally well-formed individuals' selves are always selves-for-others. Walker and colleagues (2012) address this most directly, noting that for moral exemplars, their goals and efforts are subordinated to a desire for the good of particular others and consideration of the greater good of all.

However, it is worth noting that none of these studies consider explicitly Catholic exemplars, indeed, in one of the few studies revealing the religious traditions of the exemplars, all of the exemplars were Protestant or Jewish (Colby & Damon, 2016). Thus, while a general understanding of likely optimal processes, exploration, reconsideration, and commitment, and outcomes, a transcendent narrative directing one's agency and integrating the self toward participation in one's community and contribution to the transcendent narrative.

Constructive Model—Integration of Developmental Science Perspectives

Drawing from this account of moral, spiritual, and identity development, a constructive model of faith and vocational development begins to emerge. This model emphasizes the need for self-understanding, exploration of options, and growing commitment to one's faith and spiritual identity suggested by identity development research. Further, young people are understood to be relational beings naturally oriented toward particular moral and spiritual ends, though not always aware of these ends. In addition, experiences throughout life shape young people's developing faith and capacities for vocational discernment.

King and Defoy's (2020) model of spiritual development provides the most comprehensive articulation of the ends of this development. In this model, individuals come to flourish as a result of prudently seeking God's glory and seeking to enjoy the divine. This entails coming to see oneself as part of a transcendent spiritual narrative, as a participant in the ongoing gospel, rather than seeing the gospel as merely a historical or personally irrelevant account. Through this, young people can come to participate in the life of God virtuously and to better understand their purpose and vocation, as they participate in God's life *as themselves*.

The greatest challenge in applying this model in a Catholic context is its non-denominational Christian nature, emphasizing only baptism and otherwise sacramentally sparse. This requires an understanding of the emphases and uniqueness of Catholic teaching and pastoral contexts. It is to these topics that we turn next.

Pastoral Insights: *Christus Vivit* and Social Science in Dialog

Christus Vivit (Francis, 2019, see especially Ch. 7) provides some guidance for thinking through the particularities of faith development and vocational formation in the Catholic tradition. It recognizes the agentic and relational nature of young people, expressed through their participation in religious and spiritual practices. It also emphasizes their capacity for leadership and need for friendship and mentoring. *Christus Vivit* (Francis, 2019) also examines formation in doctrine and morality, centered in the *kerygma*, the central narrative of the Catholic faith, a narrative of which all Catholics are a part. The *kerygma* then, is the transcendent spiritual narrative (see King & Defoy, 2020) that a well-developed Catholic young person will come to call their own.

Agency

This encourages a focus on practices already common for maintaining the involvement of young people in Catholic practice: mission trips, involvement in ministry, retreats, and encouragement of youth initiatives to address local spiritual or material needs. However, access to these practices is uneven, and support for exploration and youth commitment, rather than simple participation is valuable. Further, these opportunities are often collective, rather than personalized. For instance, everyone on a mission trip often shares the same schedule and participates in similar activities throughout the day. Some variation or agency in selecting one's manner of being involved, social science suggests, could enhance the value of these programs for identity and faith formation. This implies that parental and pastoral support for these involvements, fostering agency and autonomy (see Mabbe, Soenens, Vansteenkiste, van der Kaap-Deeder, & Mouratidis, 2018), rather than resistance to youth agency and creativity is important.

Relationality

How are parents and pastoral staff to support the faith formation of young people? Certainly by teaching, but also, and perhaps more centrally by listening, in alignment with the listening central to the preparation of *Christus Vivit* itself (see also Dollahite & Marks, 2019). Thus, mentoring should be a response to and support for youth as they are formed, rather than strictly directive. Such relationships support agency and faith formation through providing youth a space to discuss and make sense of their active involvement in the Catholic faith. Further, youth thrive in formation not just on the basis of relationships with adults, but also through relationships with peers. In our own research, a common refrain among young people is a lack of spaces and contexts in which young people have rich and supportive conversations about spiritual matters with other young people. This is especially important during the transition from living with parents common among young people today. Finally, young people can provide life and vibrancy to the Church through their involvement in the leadership of the Church, relating to the Church as a whole as participants and agents, rather than simply as consumers of Church ministries.

Narrative

Relationships and agency are part of helping youth to participate in the ongoing work of the Catholic Church, and so of participating in the *kerygmatic* narrative. This narrative, centered on the Gospel narrative of the life, death, and resurrection of Christ recognizes the Church as continuing the work of Christ in the world. Mentors can play a central role in helping youth to see the ways that their involvement is valuable in this work, and can help young persons to understand the personal ways that they are called to participate in the life of the Church. Further, through relationships, young people can come to understand the ways that the sacramental life of the Church, young persons desires, concerns, and contributions, and the missional life of the Church are interwoven. This can foster an awareness of the ongoing nature of the *kerygmatic* narrative and the living faith of the Church as sources of life and inspiration for ongoing formation and vocational discernment. It can also help young people to more fully appreciate the variety and necessity of others calls and contributions to the Church.

Pastoral Implications of Social Science Research

Given this, we strongly recommend *Christus Vivit* to pastors and ministers as a guide for ministry to young people. Drawing on social science, we also wish to suggest some elaborations on this account, which we believe stay true to the spirit of the document. Specifically, further emphasizing the personal nature of relationality and agency. These include ministerial considerations of the kinds of formation that particular young people may be best prepared for (e.g., different attitudes toward the *kerygma*), adaptable and agentic approaches to formation, and increased involvement of youth as ministers themselves, for youth and adults.

Given the personal nature of faith formation and vocational discernment, accompaniment during this process is valuable. Assessment of faith formation processes and progress can facilitate this. Such assessment would include spiritual (relating to God, especially through prayer), human (relating to others, individually and in community), practical (acting with and for God), and intellectual (understanding, God, the world, and oneself) pillars (John Paul II, 1992; Paul VI, 1965) and relational, agentic, and narrative components. For instance, it would emphasize the ways that the young person relates to other Catholics and non-Catholics, lives out their Catholic faith, through involvement in the sacraments and ministries, and describes their life and calling in light of the *kerygmatic* narrative. Central to this is a focus on personal growth and formation rather than impersonal standards. This approach allows mentors and others involved in formation to provide appropriate forms of support and response to sustain and continue growth, advancing formation. It also requires ongoing relationships with mentors, who through these relationships come to know young people well enough to provide valuable support in formation and discernment.

Further, social science suggests that default universal patterns of formation may be counterproductive. As such, processes of formation, in adolescence and young adulthood, should allow for personalization. This might mean a shift toward young people as instigators of sacramental participation in Confirmation, varied 'tracks' of expected ministerial involvement for confirmed young people, or other forms of at once flexible and engaged involvement in the life of the Church. Young people are less likely to identify with the Catholic faith and to become well-formed and discerning if they are mere consumers of Church ministries or the sacraments.

What kinds of ministerial involvement are most appropriate for young people then? This knowledge would ideally emerge from accompaniment and assessment of formation. Some young people may be prepared to lead ministries within the Church, others may be better served to work alongside more fully formed Catholics, learning from them. Here it is important to remember that, institutionally, vocational discernment is not strictly a matter of individual choice, but rather of selection, on the part of both the individual and others in the faith community. Mutual discernment may mean that young people are sometimes restricted from involvements that they would pursue. However, it also requires an openness on the part of those in authority, allowing young people to prudently explore their gifts and so to cultivate experiences which will foster discernment and active commitment to the faith. One example of this is to consider peer mentoring, a valuable process, especially for young people, who often identify more strongly with those of a similar age. Recent confirmandi might be especially valuable mentors for young persons seeking the sacrament, able to share their own experiences and struggles, while inspiring those to be confirmed in a way that others cannot.

Proposals for Future Development and Integration of Social Science and Pastoral Practice

While we have proposed a number of ideas above, much work remains to be done. Generally this work falls into three domains: (1) additional research and intervention development in developmental science as it relates to faith and vocational formation, (2) sociological research on the role of institutions in faith and vocational formation and cultural effects of demographic change, and (3) pastoral collaborations between ministers, theologians, and social scientists, supporting the ongoing development and evaluation of ministries for young people. Ideally, each domain would remain in conversation with the others, fostering integration and collaboration between researchers, ministers, and the faithful.

Developmental scientists could contribute to richer faith formation and vocational discernment through developing assessments, understanding of general patterns and trends, and elucidating the processes that foster and undermine faith formation and vocational discernment These assessments could include rubrics for interpreting what young people share during mentoring sessions, along the lines of Weddell's (2012) 'threshold conversation' approach. These assessments could be aligned with research to understand patterns and trends, within and across facets of formation, for instance, understanding ways in which moral formation might help to motivate greater integration of intellectual formation with spiritual formation. Finally, developmental scientists can assist in understanding how assessments and patterns and trends within individuals relate to appropriate supports and practices in faith formation and vocational discernment. This could lend itself to models of formational progressions, similar to learning progressions popular in science education (e.g., Wilson, 2009). These progressions help to understand typical trajectories of development within a domain, and can guide mentors and ministers in supporting young people and meeting them where they are, whether they are advanced or in need of more basic formation.

Sociologists also have the potential to further contribute to faith formation and vocational discernment in their work. This contribution could be furthered by the inclusion of additional measures of spirituality and religiosity, vocation and purpose, and decision-making strategies on large-scale surveys. While measures of religious attendance, religious identification, and frequency of prayer are common in large-scale surveys such as the General Social Survey, they fall short in providing sociologists the necessary data to answer important questions around formation and discernment. Additionally, sociologists could further contribute knowledge of religious formation and vocation by further focusing on how different racial and ethnic communities support the faith and vocational formation of young people. Sociologists have already taken up this charge in looking at religious trends among black, Latinx, and Asian Catholics (e.g., Pratt, 2018; Ospino, 2018; Cherry & Bruce, 2018), though more research is needed to understand the practices at play in these communities that may be important to fostering faith development.

All of this work would benefit from collaborations between Church leaders and ministers and developmental scientists and sociologists. These collaborations could help to attune social scientists to the needs and concerns of the Church, and provide Church leaders and ministers with robust data and information to help them improve programs and allocate resources. This could mean involving social scientists more actively in university programs to form ministers as consultants or instructors, sponsoring more social science research into faith formation and vocational development, and working with social scientists to evaluate existing and new programs and ministries. Indeed, the Center for Applied Research in the Apostolate (CARA) provides one model for this work, conducting some research on faith formation and vocational development and evaluating programs and ministries throughout the United States. However, much more work remains to be done, and CARA generally emphasizes a sociological perspective over a developmental one.

Conclusion

Social trends make this an important time for the Church to be more attentive to the faith formation and vocational discernment of young people. The work of the Church in this area would be well served to draw on research in sociology and developmental science. This would assist the Church in better assessing and addressing declining participation and broader concerns about faith formation. Sociology and developmental science suggest some avenues to support this work of the Church, including through parenting and the development of spiritual identities and faith narratives. These avenues align well with the suggestions of *Christus Vivit* and help to understand how robust faith formation and vocational discernment might be best supported. We close with suggestions for future work in this area, emphasizing a need for increased collaboration between developmental scientists, sociologists, and church leaders and ministers.

The History (and Future) of Catholic Youth Ministry in the U.S.

Bob Rice

Introduction

St. John Paul II wrote that the Church has always had, "an intense love for young people,"[1] and the Catholic Church in the United States has, in many ways, reflected that love in her history. Unfortunately, her passion for youth has not often translated into a successful pedagogy for passing on the faith, as young Catholics in the beginning of the twenty-first century reflect the lowest levels of religious involvement ever recorded in our country.

It can be argued that the issues with youth are merely symptomatic of larger issues within Catholic families, the culture, and the Church as a whole. While acknowledging this to be true, the recognition that there are many things outside of our control when it comes to ministry with youth should not lead us to abdicate our responsibility to act on the things that are, for history has shown that when the Church courageously and creatively invests her "time, talent, and treasure" in an outreach to young people, great results can occur.

What Christopher Dawson wrote regarding the history of the Catholic Church can be applied to her history with youth ministry in the U.S.: "the successive ages of the Church are successive campaigns in this unending war, and as soon as one enemy has been conquered a new one appears to take its place."[2] Those who do ministry with youth face new "enemies" than those of fifty years ago. However, as will be shown, though the outward appearance of youth culture is a constantly shifting landscape of fashion trends, musical genres, and technology, its core characteristics have remained unchanged

---

1. John Paul II, *Iuvenum Patris*, #1.
2. Dawson, *The Historic Reality of Christian Culture*, 48.

since its inception. When the Church has taken a missionary approach to accompany young people in the light of that culture, lives are changed and disciples are formed.

This article seeks to briefly examine the history of ministry to youth in the United States and apply the lessons learned to propose what needs to occur for more effective youth ministry in the future. In the context of this article, "youth" refers to those in junior high (or middle school) and high school, as young as eleven or twelve and as old as seventeen or eighteen. Furthermore, the word "youth" will be used synonymously with "young people," "teenagers," and "adolescents."[3]

The "Pre-History" of the Adolescent

It is generally agreed that our contemporary understanding of a "teenager" or "adolescent" reflects a social construct that occurred in the wake of the Second World War.[4] But it was not created *ex nihilo*. At the time of the Revolutionary War, the country was young, both in terms of its government and the average age of its citizens. Half of the population of the United States was under sixteen by 1776 and teenagers played a significant part in the American Revolution.[5] This may account for Joseph Kett's suggestion that the modern idea of the teenager is consistent with the creation of America itself. He began his "prehistory of youth culture" at 1790, saying it was the beginning of, "uprooting young people from agriculture, their migration to cities, a dramatic rise in the degree of occupational and intellectual choice available to youth, and the increasing disorderliness and violence that marked their educational and social institutions."[6]

Thomas Hine compared the teenagers at the start of American history with the teens of the later twentieth century:

> Throughout history, most young Americans have not lived sheltered lives of study and preparation (high school). They have

3. Those words (with the exception of the word "teenager") are how the United States Conference of Catholic Bishops' document *Renewing the Vision* described youth in the document. Of those terms, "adolescent" was the most used.

4. This perspective is characterized as the "inventionist" view and is the predominant conclusion of the authors quoted in this research. Cf. Santrock, *Adolescence*, 4.

5. "It's still worth bearing in mind the youthfulness of the country at the time of the revolution and the many roles young people played in it. We can argue about whether the revolution could of happened in a country with an older population. We cannot, however, escape the truth that the revolution happened when we had, by percentage, more young people than any time in our history." Hine, *Rise and Fall*, 89–90.

6. Kett, *Rites of Passage*, 5.

supported their families as they struggle to survive. They've been pioneers and entrepreneurs. They have been poor or displaced, left to scramble on their own as bootblacks or newsboys, or as pickpockets and prostitutes. They've been soldiers and sailors and cowboys and miners and schoolteachers and physicians. At most times, only a few have been students, living at home, devoting their second decade to preparing for the future.[7]

In 1789, John Carroll was named the first bishop of Baltimore, the first diocese of the United States. His inaugural pastoral letter, released in 1792, began by emphasizing the importance of Christian education. He wrote, "I have considered the vitreous (*sic*) and Christian instruction of youth as a principal object of pastoral solitude."[8] His concern for educating the young was like, "a kind of melody that courses like a theme song in and out of his writings, correspondence, and sermons."[9] Subsequently, the importance of Catholic education became a constant theme in numerous pastoral letters.

Another prominent figure in early Catholic American history was Cardinal James Gibbons of Baltimore. In a Pastoral Letter from 1884, the Third Plenary Council of Baltimore (which he chaired) declared that Catholic schools should be multiplied until:

> Every Catholic child in the land shall have within his reach the means of education. . . There are still thousands of Catholic children in the United States deprived of the benefit of a Catholic school. Pastors and parents should not rest until this defect be remedied. No parish is complete till it has schools adequate to the needs of its children, and the pastor and people of such a parish should feel that they have not accomplished their entire duty until the want is supplied.[10]

The industrialization and urbanization of the late nineteenth century moved American society away from a family-centric agricultural lifestyle and began to physically separate young people from their families and other caring adults.[11] At the same time, there also began a new psychological un-

---

7. Hine, *Rise and Fall*, 300.

8. Carroll, "Pastoral Letter." in Nolan, ed., *Pastoral Letters of the United States Catholic Bishops*, vol. 1, 17.

9. Bryce, *Pride of Place*, 12.

10. Third Plenary Council of Baltimore, "Pastoral Letter" in Nolan, *Pastoral Letters*, vol. 1, 225.

11. "Whereas in the decades of agrarianism and apprenticeships, young and old worked side by side in skills were passed on through working together. In the high school young people spend most meaningful hours with their peers, away from the work of parents and other adults." Root, *Revisiting Relational Youth Ministry*, 32.

derstanding of the difference between adults and teenagers, spearheaded by the work of G. Stanley Hall.

Born in Massachusetts in 1840, Hall was awarded the first doctorate for psychology in the United States.[12] After a time studying in Germany, he returned to the US and began to examine the psychological characteristics of adolescence. In 1904, he published a two-volume work titled, *Adolescence: Its Psychology and Its Relations to Physiology, Anthropology, Sociology, Sex, Crime, and Religion*. He wrote:

> Adolescence is a new birth, for the higher and more completely human traits are now born. The qualities of body and soul that now emerge are far newer. The child comes from and harks back to a remoter past; the adolescent is neo-atavistic, and in him the later acquisitions of the race slowly become prepotent. Development is less gradual and more saltatory, suggestive of some ancient period of storm and stress when old moorings were broken and a higher level attained.[13]

His phrase, "storm and stress" became a popular description for the period of adolescence. By suggesting that an adolescent was ontologically distinct from an adult, Hall's theories would be later used as a reason to withhold adult privileges and responsibilities from teenagers. It has been argued that this notion has impeded healthy relationships between adults and youth:

> The traditional "storm and stress" model of adolescence accurately depicts only a minority of teens. . . and, in our view, is a counterproductive lens through which adults view youth. That lens unnecessarily and unhelpfully creates distances when what is greatly needed is connection. Adults need alternative mental and discursive models that emphasize grown-ups' similarities to, ties to, and common futures with youth.[14]

From 1905 onwards the "Problem of Youth" became a staple item in newspapers and mass-market magazines. One solution was an increase in the number of high schools[15] which offered not only further education, but also

12. "A Brief Biological Sketch of G. Stanley Hall." Hall founded the American Psychological Association, launched the first American journal for psychology, and personally instructed the majority of the first generation of American psychologists.

13. Hall, *Adolescence*.

14. Smith with Denton, *Soul Searching*.

15. "School was seen as virtually the only safe place for the menacing young. Only a few years after Hall's book appeared, a prominent Missouri educator called for all young people to be 'sentenced' to high school, both to give them essential training and protect the public. He argued further that universal schooling would provide an opportunity

many of the types of social institutions that could be found on college and university campuses.

Cardinal Gibbon's dream of having every Catholic child in a Catholic school became unrealistic in light of the immense poverty the country faced, especially in urban areas, due to the Great Depression.[16] In 1933, the US Bishop's Welfare Committee released a statement on, "Family, Youth, and Business" expressing their concern for the large number of divorces and the indecent media that threatened youth.

> The divorce courts have crowded calendars, and some communities have resorted to the degrading device of adding to their revenues by turning their halls of justice into divorce mills. Theaters and amusement places have been converted into centers for the exhibition of lewd and indecent performances, and for the presentation of plays and moving pictures that are constant stimulants to prodigality and vice. The printing presses have poured forth a never-ending stream of obscene books and pictures that are a menace to the morals and characters of the youth of the land.[17]

There were two major movements that sought to reach those "endangered young" who could not attend a Catholic school. One came from the farms, the other from the city. They were the Confraternity of Christian Doctrine (CCD) and the Catholic Youth Organization (CYO).

The Confraternity of Christian Doctrine, originally created by Pope Pius V after the Council of Trent, found its way onto American shores in 1902 in a New York City parish.[18] As it was in Catholic schools, the emphasis was on *instruction,* believing that regular study of the Catechism (and observance of what they studied) would bring about salvation.[19] Though mostly focused on younger children, the CCD also sought to educate people in their early teens. While the program grew over the next thirty years in cities such as New York City and Pittsburgh, its real growth was in the farmlands that dominated America at that time.

---

for weeding out the feebleminded, who can be sent to institutions that would ensure they would not have children of their own." Hine, *Rise and Fall,* 162.

16. The economic crisis of the time was not exclusive to the United States. In 1932, Pope Pius XI compared it to the Flood. See Pius XI, *Caritate Christi Compulsi,* #2.

17. National Catholic Welfare Conference, "Statement on Family, Youth, and Business" in Nolan, *Pastoral Letters, vol. 1,* 405.

18. Cf. Bryce, *Pride of Place,* 101.

19. Cf. Pius X, *Acerbo Nimis,* #19.

Bishop Bernard J. Sheil, an auxiliary in Chicago, sought to bring young people into the Church through another way: sports. He established the Catholic Youth Organization in 1930, "to promote among Catholic youth recreational, educational, and religious program that will adequately meet their physical, mental, and spiritual needs in their after school hours."[20] Though it became most well-known over the next few decades as organizing the nation's largest basketball league that involved teenagers of every race, creed, and color, the CYO also provided a wide range of community centers and social services.[21]

Through those three organizations—Catholic Schools, CCD, and CYO—Catholic ministry to youth was at a high point in its history. Catholic schools provided not just faith formation but education needed by a growing immigrant population.[22] CCD provided the instruction about the faith for those who had no Catholic school available. Both of these were focused on education as the primary means of Catholic youth formation. CYO was the most innovative of the three. It reached teens through what they were attracted to (sports) but also provided opportunities to help young people grow in their faith.

It is important to mention, successful as those movements were, the family was the primary place a young person learned about what it meant to be Catholic:

> Most Catholic youth grew up in practicing Catholic families where the Catholic faith was lived at home. Youth had more contact with extended family. They attended Mass on Sunday and participated in a wide array of festivals and social gatherings. . . the programs of CYO and CCD complemented and extended what was already happening at home and in the parish. They were not replacements.[23]

---

20. Francis G. Weldgen, "A Brief Look at the Growth of Catholic Youth Work" in Murphy et al., eds., *Hope for the Decade*, 2.

21. See John Roberto, "History of Catholic Youth Ministry" in Thomas East, ed., *Leadership for Catholic Youth Ministry: Second Edition* (New London, CT: Twenty-Third Publications, 2013), 25–43: 28.

22. "By the mid-1900s, the American Catholic parochial school system had developed into an impressive and unique institution— there was nothing like it in scale and character in the rest of the world, even the Catholic world." Christian Smith, et al., *Young Catholic America*, 17.

23. Roberto, "The History of Catholic Youth Ministry," 30.

The Creation of the "Teenager"

As part of the government's response to the Great Depression, Franklin D. Roosevelt established the National Youth Administration in 1935 with a mission to get more teenagers off the streets and into high schools. His strategy worked. In the beginning of the 1930s, only twenty percent of teenagers attended secondary school. By 1940 that number had grown to ninety percent.[24] Only twenty-five percent of sixteen to twenty-year-olds participated in the military during World War II, the lowest teenage participation in a major war up to that point.[25]

In the United States, the high school became (and still is) the *de facto* place for youngsters to spend their adolescent years. High schools became the crucible that shaped youth culture and, in time, defined it. Though the high school was created, in part, to standardize the experiences of teenagers in the US, separating them from society and putting them together in the same age group allowed young people to create their own standards, quite different from what society may have intended:

> The universalization of the high school did not bring uniformity as had hoped; rather it brought the pluralizing forces of modernization into the world of the adolescent. . . The hoped for monolithic high school experience fragmented into a diversified youth culture in the 1940s and beyond.[26]

The isolation that was the catalyst for a new "youth culture" also contributed to a prolonged immaturity of young people. If there are no, or few, family members or caring adults to mentor a young person into responsible adulthood, he or she is less likely to reach that destination. Being a "teenager" in the immediate post-war years was, for those so labelled, a very transitory period. The teenagers of that era seemed eager to grow up by settling into careers and raising families. The next generation was different. Twice as many children were born from 1946 to 1956 than in the previous decade (forty million births vs. twenty-six million births). It was this "Baby Boom" generation that shifted toward a greater prolongation of the youth experience, especially as more young people opted to go to college.

From the mid-1940s and beyond, "teenagers" became identified (by themselves and others) by what they purchased, wore, watched, or listened to. This emphasis on consumerism was fueled by numerous forms of media,

24. David F. White, "The Social Construction of Adolescence" in Mahan et al., *Awakening Youth Discipleship*, 12.

25. See Hine, *Rise and Fall*, 228.

26. Root, *Revisiting Relational Youth Ministry*, 34–5.

such as movies, radio, television, and music, which is itself a product and a promotion for other products. Jon Savage suggested that from the beginning, the concept of "teenager" was driven by business:

> During 1944, the words "teenage" and "teenager" become the accepted way to describe this new definition of youth as a discrete, mass market. Teenagers were neither adolescents nor juvenile delinquents. Consumerism offered the perfect counterbalance to riot and rebellion: it was the American way of harmlessly diverting youth's disruptive energies.[27]

In the 1950s, products created for and about teenagers became more popular. The creation and marketing of movies, music, and clothing was a significant trend of youth culture in the fifties. By the end of that decade, teenagers spent fifty million dollars a year on records alone. Ten years later, teens were spending over one-hundred million dollars on music and teenage girls spent three-and-a-half billion just on clothing.[28]

By the 1960s, the Baby Boomers became teenagers, and it was the first time in US history since the American Revolution that teens were the most populous age group. This time, the revolution was social. Youth culture went mainstream and has never relinquished its grip. Some go so far as to propose that a separate adolescent culture no longer exists, not because it has vanished but because it devoured everything around it: "Today, *all* popular culture is youth culture, and vice versa, and *all* age groups participate in it."[29]

Three foundational characteristics emerge from this historical overview of the creation of the "teenager" as well as "youth culture." First, it occurred out of *isolation*. In the beginning of the twentieth century, teenagers in the US became isolated from their family and society due to a number of factors, such as the Industrial Revolution, the Great Depression, two World Wars, and the establishment of high schools. Second, this culture became defined by *consumerism*: their music, their fashion, their media. One author defined youth culture as, "in essence, a series of decisions about personal appearance and entertainment."[30] Created out of isolation and fueled by consumerism, this led to a *prolonged immaturity*. High school expanded the youth experience; college prolonged it even further.

Though youth culture constantly changes its outward appearance, its fundamental characteristics remains the same. Whether the music of the moment is rock, rap, or K-pop, whether the hemlines rise or fall, whether

27. Savage, *Teenage*, page unknown.

28. See Palladino, *Teenagers*, 155.

29. Root and Dean, *The Theological Turn in Youth Ministry*, 32.

30. Hine, *Rise and Fall*, 226.

the cause is just or frivolous, or whether teens gather in a dance hall, a mall, or on Facebook, these three elements of isolation, consumerism, and immaturity are a lens through which one can understand youth culture in order to more effectively evangelize teenagers.

The Birth of Catholic Youth Ministry

Protestants, particularly Evangelicals, were to be more in touch with the cultural changes occurring among teenagers and quicker to adapt effective strategies and movements to minister to them than the Catholic Church in the 1940–60s. Two Protestant organizations stand out during this period: Young Life and Youth for Christ.

Though both started in the early 1940s, Youth for Christ—which emphasized large gatherings of youth—was initially more popular but faded by the end of the 1950s. "While the youth rallies could provide cool events in a popular nationalistic flavor, they could not provide the one thing adolescents desired most: intimacy through self-chosen relationships."[31] Young Life, on the other hand, emphasized strategic relationships and one-on-one contact. They did not fill stadiums in cities but instead preached the Gospel in the living rooms of suburban homes. Their "church" was the high school. By the 1960s, Young Life became the largest youth ministry organization in America and a model that other churches and para-church organizations sought to replicate.[32]

No such innovations occurred, at least on a large scale, within the Catholic Church. Changes in family life and youth culture seemed not to be programmatically recognized by the Church over these decades, at least on a national level. Judging by the literature produced by the bishops over that time, the needs of Catholic youth received almost no attention.[33] Gone was the "melody" of the importance of Catholic education that flowed through the writings of Carroll and Gibbons; absent was the concern of delinquent and uninformed youth in the time of the Great Depression.

31. Root, *Revisiting Relational Youth Ministry*, 51.

32. Root, *Revisiting Relational Youth Ministry*, 51–54.

33. In over 50 pastoral letters written between 1934 and 1970, young people were only addressed twice. There was a brief mention of young people in context of the family in the 1949 pastoral letter, "The Christian Family." Cf. "The Christian Family" in Nolan, ed., *Pastoral Letters of the United States Catholic Bishops, vol. 2*, 90–96. The second was in, "The Child: Citizen of Two Worlds" released November 17th, 1950. "The Child" was a letter addressing the importance of Catholic education and how children should be raised as good citizens both of the country they are in and the Kingdom of God. See "The Child: Citizen of Two Worlds," 97–105.

During these decades, the three organizations of Catholic Schools, the CCD, and the CYO remained the main mechanisms through which Catholic teenagers learned about their faith. These became less effective as the faith lives of Catholic families in the US began to diminish. The causes for this are many and beyond the scope of this article to examine. Christian Smith proposed a major reason was due to the upward mobility and greater social acceptance of Catholicism in the US:

> Everything that sociologists of religion know about how socio-economic status and cultural differences shape religiosity...predicts that this upward mobility and social and mainstream cultural integration would have had the consequence of weakening American Catholic's religious identity and commitment. By most accounts, this is precisely what has happened... In the second half of the twentieth century, U.S. Catholicism saw a significant decline in regular church attendance, in the strength of religious orders, in the number of new priestly vocations, and in ordinary American Catholics' readiness to learn, embrace, and live out Church doctrines and teachings.[34]

Thanks in part to an emphasis on evangelization and ecumenism from the Second Vatican Council, the 1970s saw a shift in the way the Catholic Church in the US approached teenagers. Early attempts to apply some of the methods used by Protestants to evangelize Catholic youth showed great promise. The first official Catholic use of the phrase "youth ministry" is found in the 1972 Bishop's document, *To Teach as Jesus Did*, where it suggests youth ministry could, "compliment the formal religious education carried on in Catholic schools and out-of-school programs."[35]

At the Synod of 1974 (from which the encyclical *Evangelii Nuntiandi* was inspired), Cardinal Krol (president of the US bishops' conference) titled one of his interventions as "Reaching Youth and Inactive Catholics"—the two groups he felt had the most special concern. Another member of the delegation, Archbishop John Quinn of Oklahoma City, gave a written and a spoken intervention specifically addressing youth ministry. His spoken one was titled, "Youth Ministry: Do Joyless Heralds Dull the Good News?" where he put the blame for the lack of youth participation upon the Church itself.[36]

---

34. Smith, *Soul Searching*, page # unknown.

35. National Conference of Catholic Bishops, *To Teach as Jesus Did*, 133.

36. "The chief problem for many young people is not the gospel or Christ. It is the church... The problem for youth of the dichotomy between the Gospel and the church does not lie principally in structures or in approaches or methodologies. It is chiefly

It was his written intervention that would have the most significant impact on youth ministry in the United States. Simply titled, "Youth Ministry," he defined it as, "the church's mission of reaching into the daily lives of modern young people and showing them the presence of God."[37] He also specifically mentioned the success of Young Life and wrote, "Anyone seriously considering opening a campus ministry may want to take their leadership course."[38]

However, the most significant "wake-up call" came through a study commissioned by the US bishops in the early 1970s that investigated how many children and teenagers were not receiving faith formation of any kind. Its conclusions were published a few months after the 1974 Synod. The study was titled, *Where are the 6.6 Million?* Between 1965 and 1974 the number of declining youth involvement had grown more than 100 percent, from 3.1 million to 6.6 million—and 3.2 million of them were teenagers.[39]

In light of this, there emerged an awareness that a new approach to ministering to Catholic teens was necessary. In 1976, the Bishops' Department of Education published a document titled, *A Vision of Youth Ministry.* The document described youth ministry as "the response of the Christian community to the needs of young people, and the sharing of the unique gifts of youth with the larger community."[40]

It is hard to overstate the significance of this document. The introduction of *Renewing the Vision* called it, "the catalyst for a dramatic increase in new and innovative pastoral practice with adolescents."[41] Over the next five to seven years, many offices of youth ministry were established in numerous dioceses. Michael Warren reflected on how quickly the document impacted the Church:

> Thus a unified theology tends naturally to a unified pastoral action. . . within a recent three year period almost a third of all Catholic dioceses combined their efforts to minister to youth into either a single office or a single person charged with directing this ministry. In many dioceses there had been three

the problem of the minister of the church who, rightly or wrongly, frequently does not reveal to them that Christ whom they find in the gospel." John R. Quinn, "Do Joyless Heralds Dull the Good News?" in United States Catholic Conference, *Synod of Bishops* (1974), 58–59.

37. Quinn, "Youth Ministry," in United States Catholic Conference, *Synod of Bishops* (1974), 60.

38. Quinn, "Youth Ministry," 66.

39. See Paradis and Thompson, *Where Are the 6.6 Million?*, 1–2.

40. *A Vision of Youth Ministry*, 6.

41. *Renewing the Vision*, 3.

separate agencies serving youth: the youth division of the religious education/catechetical office; the Catholic Youth Organization, which carried on non-school-based (but often highly educational) programs; and the Catholic high schools' organization. Often though, these agencies, working separately, ended up competing with each other in the struggle for adequate funding and even in the matter of programming. What seems to have allowed them to unify under a common effort is the concept of youth ministry.[42]

Because of *A Vision of Youth Ministry*, being a "youth minister" started to become part of the Catholic vocabulary in the US. The key word is *started*— Catholic youth ministry would not be more fully embraced by the Church until the 1990s.

A High Point for Catholic Youth Ministry

As young people are usually quicker to adapt to new technologies than those who are older, the technological innovations of the seventies to nineties widened the gap of isolation between teens and adults and offered a new means of consumerism. The Sony Walkman provided a young person an opportunity to listen to his or her music in any location. The VHS gave the freedom to watch movies or television shows on their own schedule (and offered exposure to new media they did not have access to before). Video games provided a new form of entertainment. In 1991, the Internet was open to commercial uses. The World Wide Web was launched and would take only a few years before it went mainstream.

According the Child and Youth Well Being Index (CWI), teenage risk behaviors in the late 1970s (which included violent crimes, drug use, and teen pregnancy) were at an all-time high. Though at-risk teen behavior seemed to improve in the 1980s, it was short lived. The CWI reported that by the early 1990s children and youth were at their highest (worst) levels since the mid 1970s. The study also showed concern over a teenagers' health, social relationships, and emotional/spiritual well-being.[43]

Catholic schools hit their peak in the early sixties when they had 5.2 million students in almost thirteen thousand schools. After three decades of decline, by 1990 there were less than nine thousand schools with 2.5 million students.[44] CCD and parish faith formation programs saw similar losses.

---

42. Warren, "Youth Ministry—An Overview" in Warren, ed., *Youth Ministry*, 4.

43. Land, "Child and Youth Well-Being Index."

44. "Data and Information," *National Catholic Educational Association*.

When it came to the traditional means of Catholic education, the disturbing statistics given from *Where are the 6.6 million?* had only gotten worse. What had worked in the 1930s was no longer effective in the late twentieth century. Christian Smith wrote:

> . . .the organizational means that the Catholic Church historically employed to more or less successfully accomplish its work with youth, Catholic school and CCD, have in recent decades had the world around them change and have themselves changed in ways that, for whatever good they do accomplish for Catholic and other youth, render them inadequate to serve as the primary vehicles for contemporary youth socialization, education, formation, and ministry. The old wineskins skins cannot hold the new wine, and so it is often spilled and lost.[45]

While school and parish formation programs declined, youth ministry grew in popularity, especially with the arrival of John Paul II in Denver for the 1993 World Youth Day. Previously, World Youth Days were targeted at eighteen to thirty-year-olds. In the US, they lowered the age to high school. This decision, based on a concern they wouldn't get enough numbers,[46] had a tremendous impact on high school youth ministry in the US. Much of the success of the event was because of the work of the National Federation of Catholic Youth Ministry, an organization made up of diocesan youth directors that was formed in 1982.[47] Coordinators of youth ministry brought numerous busses of teenagers to Denver. They also organized three-day catechetical sessions, which was a first for World Youth Day and became a staple afterward. The original estimation by the bishops' conference was sixty thousand participants. Instead, half-a-million young people attended, many of them teenagers.

Almost every bishop in America was present as hundreds of thousands of young people chanted, "JPII, we love you!." George Weigel commented the event gave many in the episcopate new hope in reaching the young:

> Many of them thought "youth ministry" was virtually impossible. The culture, the music, the lifestyle of the teenagers of the 1990s struck them as alien; so did young people's struggles with drugs and sex. . .Those who had thought the Pope's moral challenge could not be heard in the American cultural context had

45. Smith, *Soul Searching,* page # unknown.
46. Weigel, *Witness to Hope,* 679.
47. Pascione, "25th Anniversary Review, 1992–1997," *NFCYM.*

to think again, as did those who felt that youth ministry was impossible.[48]

After World Youth Day, almost every diocese in the United States had an office dedicated to youth and/or young adult ministry. At the next national bishops' gathering, they called for new documents to be written, which were published in 1997: *Renewing the Vision* for youth ministry and *Sons and Daughters of the Light* for young adult ministry.

Renewing the Vision had an even greater impact than its predecessor, *A Vision of Youth Ministry*.[49] It was a more substantial document, both in authority (coming directly from the USCCB as opposed to a department within it) and in length (twice as long). Its three goals, seven themes, and eight components created the framework for "comprehensive youth ministry" and became the normative outline for books, resources, and training programs. *Renewing the Vision* also had a significant international influence.[50] Arthur David Canales praised the document for setting a "gold-standard"[51] and leaving "an indelible mark upon Catholic youth ministry."[52]

Attendance at Catholic youth events skyrocketed after World Youth Day. The National Catholic Youth Conference, sponsored by the NFCYM, went from six thousand attendees to twenty thousand in that decade. The Franciscan University of Steubenville Summer Conferences went from three thousand participants to thirty-five thousand. Ministries providing resources to youth ministers, such as Life Teen, also grew exponentially.

As the century came to a close, another significant event drew the country's attention to youth. On April 20, 1999, teenagers Eric Harris and Dylan Klebold marched into their own school, Columbine High School in Littleton, Colorado, armed with a variety of weapons. They killed twelve students and one teacher, injured twenty others, then killed themselves. As the story was reported, one of the gunmen asked one of the students, Cassie Bernall, "Do you believe in God?" She replied, "Yes." He asked, "Why?" and then shot and killed her. The story of Rachael Scott was similar, but her response was more defiant: "You know that I do." She was also shot and killed.

---

48. Weigel, *Witness to Hope*, 679, 685.

49. "The document has sold over 126,000 copies in print form in addition to hundreds of thousands of downloads... *Renewing the Vision* continues to be a driving force in leadership training, resource development, and parish renewal of ministry." East, *Leadership for Catholic Youth Ministry*, vii.

50. Numerous bishops' conferences around the world have used *Renewing the Vision* as the template for their own statements on youth ministry, such as New Zealand, Australia, and Ireland, all of which used the same goals, themes, and components structure.

51. Canales, "The Ten-Year Anniversary of *Renewing the Vision*," 58.

52. Canales, "The Ten-Year Anniversary of *Renewing the Vision*," 67.

Another teen, Valerie Schnurr, was shot and exclaimed, "Oh my God!" One of the gunmen (there is uncertainty as to which one) asked her, "Do you believe in God?" She answered, "Yes." He asked, "Why?" She responded, "Because I believe and my parents brought me up that way." The gunman walked away, and Schnurr survived.[53]

According to Pew Research, the Columbine shooting was the biggest news story "by far" in 1999.[54] It raised a greater societal concern for teens. Bernall was active in her Protestant youth group; both Scott and Schnurr were active in a Catholic one. The horrors of Columbine and the stories of martyrdom that came from it gave Christian youth ministry a high profile in 1999.

The next year, John Paul II celebrated World Youth Day in Rome for the year 2000. It was the second largest WYD event up to that point and attracted an estimated one-and-a-half million pilgrims, well above original estimates.

Catholic youth ministry in America hit a high point (perhaps its highest) in the years 2000/01. The language of *Renewing the Vision* had become normative, there was strong diocesan support, the country had been inspired by the sacrificial faith of teenagers (some of whom were Catholic) at Columbine, the world breathed a collective sigh of relief at the uneventful entry into the new millennium, and the Holy Father celebrated the jubilee with over a million young people in Rome and millions more through mass media.

There are a few important caveats for this "high point." First, it is in reference to the dominant Catholic experience in the US at the time, which was primarily white, suburban, and with some affluence (the "upward mobility" referenced earlier by Smith). Successful youth ministry programs were usually done at larger parishes that could afford a full-time lay person to oversee the ministry on the high school and/or junior high level, and it could be argued that *Renewing the Vision* was written with this audience in mind (this article will examine a critique from the Hispanic community in the next section). But even those programs could only be found in about one fifth of the parishes in the US.[55] Furthermore, proposing that youth ministry hit a "high point" is not to imply that it had been given enough time to flourish and impact the Church on a national level, but only that it had the potential to do so until the events of September 2001 and January of 2002.

---

53. See Watson, *The Martyrs of Columbine*, 96.

54. See "Columbine Shooting Biggest News Draw of 1999," *Pew Research Center*.

55. There is not data from the 1990s that examined how many full-time youth workers were in Catholic parishes, but the National Study of Youth and Religion in 2004 said that 21% of Catholic parishes had a full-time position, compared to 37–44% of Protestant churches. Cf. Smith, *Soul Searching*, 211.

Decades of Scandal and Decline

Author Leon J. Podles in his book, *Scandal: Sexual Abuse in the Catholic Church* made a connection between the terrorist attacks of 2001 and the sexual scandal that rocked the Church in 2002:

> Something happened to heighten the anxiety of the American public: September 11, 2001. Parents realized that American society was vulnerable to massive attack, and that our government had spent trillions of dollars in defense but could not protect us from nineteen unarmed men. Then came the revelations about the bizarre sexual hungers of John Geoghan and Paul Shanley in Boston, and the public was shocked at what certain priests had done to children and, perhaps even more, what bishops had allowed priests to do.[56]

The epicenter of the sexual scandal was in Boston but it soon was felt throughout the entire country.[57] Publicity over the scandals caused many to come forward and admit they were abused.[58] One author commented that, "Without a doubt, this was the worst scandal to ever face the Church in America."[59] Reading about what had happened and what had been allowed to happen is both saddening and sickening. The largest numbers of victims were boys "at or a few years after the age of puberty."[60]

The US Bishops responded by creating the "Charter for the Protection of Children and Young People" in July of 2002. It instituted a zero-tolerance policy, promised complete transparency for any accusation toward deacons or priests (but did not mention bishops, something that would become a serious issue later), and established offices in every diocese for Child and Youth Protection to make sure children and young people had a "safe environment."[61] Though the details and training required for safe environment policies varied from diocese to diocese, they all included training on how to recognize signs of abuse, how to recognize potential abusers, and

---

56. Podles, *Sacrilege*, 2.

57. The *John Jay Report*, commissioned by the US Bishops, said the average amount of clergy sexual offenders ranged from three to six percent. Cf. John Jay College of Criminal Justice, "The Nature and Scope of Sexual Abuse of Minors by Catholic Priests and Deacons 1950–2002," United States Conference of Catholic Bishops

58. See The *John Jay Report*, which stated that one third of sexual abuse allegations between 1950 and 2003 happened between 2002–3.

59. Plante and McChesney, *Sexual Abuse in the Catholic Church*, 10.

60. Podles, *Sacrilege*, 241.

61. See "Charter for the Protection of Children and Young People," United States Conference of Catholic Bishops

mandated background checks for anyone working with children or teenag-ers.[62] Most dioceses, if not all, created safe environment policies that forbid volunteers to be alone with young people or meet young people outside specifically planned parish activities. Required forms for parental consent became necessary for almost all activities sponsored by the parish. It was a necessary and important step to rebuild trust and create safer environments for young people. Mandating background checks and requiring more ad-vanced training for volunteers has made parishes and schools a safer place for children and teenagers.

I would like to highlight three specific ways the sexual scandal nega-tively impacted Catholic youth ministry in the United States (other than the obvious: the abuse of the very young people the Church was called to min-ister to). The first was a lack of trust. The story of sexual scandal first broke in the *Boston Globe* in January 2002, but stories of Catholic sexual abuse remained in the media for many years (even decades) after. This particularly impacted many forms of Catholic youth ministry that regularly took teens away for weekend retreats, camping trips, etc., all of which became more "suspect" in light of the stories of abuse. For many Catholics, the cover-up by the bishops was as scandalous as the sexual crimes. Many families left the Church and took their children with them.

Second, the incredible number of lawsuits over the crisis caused at least thirteen dioceses to go bankrupt and virtually all were forced to cut staffing.[63] Youth ministry offices on the diocesan level lost staff or were shut down.[64] This led to less advocacy on a diocesan level, and often less activity, for youth ministry. For those diocesan positions that remained, job responsibilities sometimes shifted from supporting youth ministers in their diocese to focusing on safe environment policies.

A final effect was that some safe environment policies had a negative effect on adult/teen relationships within Catholic youth ministry. Frank Mercadante, in his book, *Engaging the Soul of a New Generation*, wrote:

> In an effort to protect young people, the responses we have formed through legal policies and guidelines may be ham-pering, limiting, challenging (and perhaps even driving to

---

62. See Kettlekamp, "Ten Points to Create Safe Environment for Children," United States Conference of Catholic Bishops. Kettlekamp was the executive director for the Secretariat of Child and Youth Protection for the USCCB.

63. See Gibson, "Duluth Catholic diocese latest to file for bankruptcy over sex abuse payouts," *Religion News Service.*

64. This article does not propose that youth ministry fared worse than other de-partments in a diocese, but all diocesan ministry suffered in order to pay back debts incurred from legal costs.

extinction) significant relational ministry. These policies often wind up protecting teens from much more than predators. In the end, we protect them from any meaningful contact with adults. The result is that Millennials highly value relationships and are quite comfortable with adults, yet adult church leaders are afraid to get too close to teens. . . Overly stringent policies lead to a Church that is more concerned about financial and legal protection than on the active, personal, pastoral care of young people. This results in the loss of the Church's credibility and the far greater loss of our teens.[65]

Mercadante made it clear he was not encouraging readers to ignore the policies, but instead suggested people in youth ministry need to advocate for a change so that "'protection and prevention' can meet 'practical and pastoral.'"[66]

While the Church was struggling with sex scandals, a new form of communication emerged among youth in 2005: social media. "What the drive-in was to teens in the 1950s and the mall in the 1980s, Facebook, texting, Twitter, instant messaging, and other social media are to teens now."[67] Many dioceses forbid any type of social media communication with teenagers because it did not know how it might fit within safe environment policies which were still being developed. Young people began speaking a new language but the Church was not able to translate.

As the Church moved into the third millennium, more disparaging news. The National Study of Youth and Religion found that Catholic teenagers reflected the lowest levels of religiosity than any other Christian group in the US.

There are, of course, U.S. Catholic teenagers who are very religiously engaged, but they are not typical. In our study, Catholic teenagers, who represent nearly one-quarter of all U.S. teens, stand out among the U.S. Christian teenagers are consistently scoring lower on most measures of religiosity. . . Perhaps more important for Catholics, our findings regarding Catholic teenagers show many of them to be living far outside of official Church norms defining true Catholic faithfulness.[68]

65. Mercadante, *Engaging a New Generation*, 52–53.
66. Mercadante, *Engaging a New Generation*, 53.
67. Boyd, *It's Complicated*, page number unknown.
68. Smith, *Soul Searching*, 194.

Other surveys found a significant increase in young people who would not identify with any religious affiliation, making the "nones" the largest "religious" group in America.[69]

The cultural demographics of the Church have changed significantly since the end of the twentieth century. In 1990, there were an estimated 22.6 million Latinos in the United States. By 2010 that number almost doubled.[70] Those numbers have only continued to grow. Today, the largest population of Catholic teenagers are Latino.[71] This growth is an incredible blessing for the Catholic Church in the US and the main reason that Catholicism in America is growing instead of shrinking.[72] The influence of a profoundly Catholic Latino culture is a welcome change from a modern European culture which is trending toward atheism.

Unfortunately, the number of Latinos who identify as Catholic is diminishing (dropping from 70% in 2000 to 52% in 2016[73]) and Latino youth are at the forefront of that trend. It is felt by many in the Latino community that documents such as *Renewing the Vision* do not speak to their needs:

> Both documents (*Renewing* and *Sons and Daughters of the Light*) recognize the presence of different cultures in the Catholic Church in this country and were translated into Spanish as *Revovemos la Vision* and *Hijos e Hijas de la Luz*, respectively. However, their focus continued to be on the middle class of the dominant culture, ignoring the tradition and the work of Pastoral Juvenil Hispana, despite the efforts of the Hispanic leaders who were consulted.[74]

The end of the second decade produced two initiatives that have had a positive impact for youth ministry in the United States. The first was the V Encuentro, an initiative launched by the US Bishops with the theme, "Missionary Disciples: Witnesses of God's Love." The Encuentro process included ministry leaders from across the nation to discuss a range of important

69. Lipka, "Millennials Increasingly are Driving the Growth of 'Nones,'" *Pew Research Center*.

70. See Krogstad and Lopez, "Hispanic population reaches 55 million, but growth has cooled," *Pew Research Center*.

71. See Johnson-Mondragón, "Hispanic Youth and Young Adult Ministry," *Instituto Fe y Vida*

72. "Catholics are not losing their share of the U.S. Population for one reason only: The Roman Catholic Church is becoming more Hispanic." Lugo, "Becoming Latino: the Transformation of U.S. Catholicism," *Fordham Center on Religion and Culture*.

73. "Fact Sheet: Hispanic Catholics in the US," *CARA*.

74. National Catholic Network de Pastoral Juvenil Hispana, *Conclusions*, 22.

topics, one of the foremost being how the Church might more effectively minister to Hispanic youth.

The second was a synod called by Pope Francis for, "Youth, the Faith, and Vocational Discernment" (also known as the "XV Synod"). It was a multi-year process that sought to listen to youth from around the world, both from diocesan input and directly through social media. Pope Francis had a "pre-synod" with three-hundred young adults, and feedback from young adults permeated the XV Synod proceedings that occurred in October of 2018. The following April, Francis published *Christus Vivit*, an exhortation that not only highlighted what he felt important from that process, but also encouraged the Church to look at other documents that came from the synod, such as its Final Document. The United States was the first country to hold a conference that examined *Christus Vivit* and the implications of the XV Synod on youth and young adult ministry in the United States.[75] Organizations such as the National Dialogue sought to bring ministry leaders together to implement the findings of both the synod and the V Encuentro.

Sadly, much of the "good news" of the XV Synod and the V Encuentro was overshadowed as numerous states (such as Pennsylvania) subpoenaed dioceses for more detail in previous abuse cases, and the discovery in 2018 that Theodore Cardinal McCarrick of the Archdiocese of Washington had abused seminarians and used his position to cover it up. Such stories further eroded the trust many US Catholics had toward the Church, fewer were willing to give financial support, and more cut-backs ensued. To add to this "perfect storm," parishes were shut down for months in 2020 due to the COVID outbreak, and in-person ministries came to a halt. National programs for youth ministry had to cut staff and many parishes, unable to support full-time lay ecclesial ministers during a time of inactivity, reduced or eliminated staff positions in youth ministry.

Faith for the Future

Writing this article in 2020, it is hard not to feel that almost everything is at its nadir. History tells us there are reasons to believe things can get better. These "successive campaigns in this unending war" are not all failure and retreat. In fact, when things seem at their worst is often when God intervenes most powerfully.[76] The Gospel has overcome more dire circumstances than these.

---

75. The "Voice + Vision" Conference, held July 31st–Aug 2nd at Franciscan University of Steubenville.

76. See the Bible.

However, things won't improve on their own. As a faith community, we can't keep looking around the Church hoping someone else will do something about this escalading exodus of Catholic young people. All of us—bishops, priests, religious, parents, school teachers, members of the laity—must ask ourselves how we can be a part of positive change. Our study of history gives insight on what we need to do to succeed in the future.

From Absence to Awareness

The history of the past century shows that adults in the US have had a sort of "super-hero" relationship with teens: they show up when there is trouble, but fly away when the situation seems better. This often means youth don't get attention unless something is seriously wrong: the Great Depression, *Where are the 6.6 Million?*, severe levels of high-risk behavior, or Columbine. The good news is that when the Church, on both the national and local level, becomes aware of the needs of young people and is willing to act, great things have happened. Though teens may live down the street or even in the same house, they exist in a very different cultural milieu than adults, and successful ministry to youth requires loving adults who are willing to invest time and energy in better understanding their needs and culture. Young people need to see Christ in their midst, not Christ somewhere else. As a Church, we need those willing to have a greater awareness of youth culture to create "cultural parables" so the young can have the Good News explained to them in a way that will resonate with their daily lives. Ministry to youth must become more missionary in its nature.

From Isolation to Accompaniment

The US Bishops 1976 document *A Vision of Youth Ministry* and the XV Synod had the same foundational Scripture in common: the Road to Emmaus. Jesus walked with his disciples, even though they did not recognize him, even though they were heading in the wrong direction. It was only by accompanying them that they were eventually able to recognize who he was. Youth culture started because teenagers became isolated from adults. Too often, adults' attitude toward youth are "out of sight, out of mind" or, even worse, some are hostile to the younger generation. For many young people, it feels like the world rolls out the red carpet but the Church gives them a cold shoulder. Over twenty years ago, *Renewing the Vision* conveyed surprise at a survey that found, "Many adults no longer consider it their responsibility to play a role in the lives of youth outside their family."[77] Sadly, many today might be surprised it has been any other way. Faith communities need to take responsibility for the faith lives of their young and the Church will need to create more opportunities for adults to interact with youth and accompany them on their journey, helping them navigate safe environment policies (some of which may need to be revisited) as they do so.

From Consumerism to Kerygma

Consumerism is the religion, not only of youth culture, but of society in America. Older generations remember getting a driver's license as a "rite of passage" for their teenage experience; today's teens are more excited about getting their first iPhone.[78] Such devices become the lens through which they view the world and primary means by which they interact with others. Many base their identity on the amount of likes and followers they have. It is a false Gospel. The Church must be bold in preaching the *real* "Good News": "Jesus Christ loves you, he gave his life to save you, and now he is living by your side, every day, to enlighten, strengthen, and free you."[79] This must be done in a way that speaks the language of their culture and is the context of loving accompaniment. As we walk with young people, we must also break open the Scriptures and break the bread, as Jesus did on the road to Emmaus. The faith must be proclaimed as more than just something complimentary to what they are already doing. It should bring about conversion, a change of heart. Because the growth of the Church in the US has historically resulted from immigration rather than evangelization, such dramatic proclamations feel foreign to many "cradle Catholics" and aren't always primary in many programs for youth. The kerygma must be proclaimed with boldness, and proclaimed often, in all forms of youth ministry.

From Immaturity to Discipleship

Renewing the Vision stated that the first goal of youth ministry was to "empower young people to live as disciples of Jesus Christ in our world today."[80] When the two on the road to Emmaus recognized Jesus in the breaking of the bread, "they set out at once and returned to Jerusalem"[81] where they

77. United States Conference of Catholic Bishops, *Renewing the Vision*, 54.

78. See Twinge, *iGen*, 26.

79. Francis, *Evangelii Gaudium*, #164.

80. United States Conference of Catholic Bishops, *Renewing the Vision*, 9.

81. Luke 24:33.

joined the Apostles. They found purpose. This is the path of discipleship. We must share with young people, through word and witness, a different way of living that can only happen through the power of the Holy Spirit: an identity based on who we are instead of what we do, and a purpose not driven by love of self but love of others. The culture they live in seeks to prolong immaturity and responsibility. The Lord told the prophet Jeremiah, "Do not say, 'I am too young.'"[82] History has shown that teenagers are capable of changing the world, and none more so than the teenage girl who said "yes" to Gabriel's invitation. Pope Francis wrote that, "young people themselves are agents of youth ministry... they need to be helped and guided, but at the same time left free to develop new approaches, with creativity and a certain audacity."[83] We must empower young people to live the Good News and share it with others, in both word and deed. This can only happen as they grow in intimacy with Jesus Christ.

Conclusion: From Fear to Faith

For ministry to youth to be successful, those within the Church need more "courage and creativity."[84] It is not about creating more programs but re-thinking our entire approach. "The young make us see the need for new styles and strategies,"[85] wrote Pope Francis. "At the same time, we should take into greater consideration those practices that have shown their value."[86] We should re-consider the effectiveness of parish-based youth ministry, which is subject to pastor changes and financial challenges, and be more open to (and supportive of) ministry done by apostolates specifically focused on youth. We should not only examine what is successful in Catholic youth ministry but also Protestant youth ministry. Perhaps Archbishop Quinn's suggestion that we can learn from Young Life (currently the largest youth ministry in the world) is as apt today as it was in 1974? Since documents on youth ministry (*A Vision of Youth Ministry, Renewing the Vision*) have created successful moments of youth ministry in the past and could well be a key to its future, it is reasonable to hope for a new document from the US bishops that synthesizes the best of *Renewing*, the XV Synod, the V Encuentro, and other insights from the past two decades. However, the real

82. Jeremiah 1:7.

83. Francis, *Christus vivit*, #203.

84. Pontifical Council for the Promotion of the New Evangelization, *Directory for Catechesis*, #244.

85. Francis, *Christus vivit*, #204.

86. Francis, *Christus vivit*, #205.

work needs to happen not from the pulpit but the pews, a grass-roots movement that doesn't narrowly view youth ministry as an opportunity to send teens away to another program but is rather an invitation and participation in the community of faith. It can be argued that the Church, in light of the many sexual scandals, has in a way become afraid of youth. We must move from fear to faith, willing to step out of the boat and into the storm because Jesus invites us to. We have waited too long for better weather. The time for boldness and creativity is now.

Evangelizing through Land-Based Experiences and Dialogue with Science

Sɪsᴛᴇʀ Dᴀᴍɪᴇɴ Mᴀʀɪᴇ Sᴀᴠɪɴᴏ, FSE _____

> "Dear young people, please, do not be bystanders in life. Get in-
> volved! Jesus was not a bystander. He got involved. Don't stand
> aloof, but immerse yourselves in the reality of life, as Jesus did."[1]

Introduction

Iᴛ ɪs ᴀ sᴜᴍᴘᴛᴜᴏᴜs spring morning, cool and crisp, the pleasant odor of
petrichor emanating from the grass as the sun brightens the sky after several
days of rain. Passing by the chicken coop and barnyard, I make my way
to the *Laudato Si'* Sanctuary, a restored prairie on our 230 acre farm and
environmental center in Michigan. As a Franciscan Sister of the Eucharist
with a background in environmental science and theology, I take particular
delight in this place. For several years, we have been working bit by bit to
restore what was an abandoned pasture into a native prairie. Before the restoration, the old pasture was overrun by invasive species like garlic mustard,
autumn olive, and thistle. These aggressive, introduced species have very
few or no predators, so they spread like a cancer, crowding out the native
species, reducing diversity, and producing a landscape that is not only un-
productive but also unattractive. With the progress of the restoration, the
prairie has assumed a fresh new face. Native prairies are rich in biodiversity,
and as the prairie has established itself and flourished, many native species
of birds, butterflies, bees and other insects, once absent, are returning, attracted to the opening of new niches and food sources. This morning the
prairie is alive with a symphony of birds. As I walk through quietly, they

1. Francis, *Christus vivit*, #174. Here he quotes from his *Address at the Prayer Vigil
of the XXVIIII World Youth Day in Rio de Janeiro*, July 27, 2013.

sing wholeheartedly, flitting from ground to branch, spikes of grass bowing under their weight, calling back and forth to one another, and occasionally crossing in front of me. Red-winged blackbirds, white-crowned sparrows, song sparrows, tree swallows, bluebirds . . . Even a pair of meadowlarks, a species in decline, has returned to the prairie, hopefully to nest. This morning, as if celebrating, they sing musically and break out into gliding flight. I feel honored to be a silent partner in this symphony.

The difference between this landscape and what it was before its restoration is palpable. The beauty and richness, the noise and activity that greet me this morning are a stark contrast to the sterility and homogeneity of the former pasture. This prairie restoration project has reintroduced species native to the area and brought new life to what was a declining ecosystem.

Pausing for a moment to reflect on the gift of this extravagant moment, I receive a sudden small insight, a glimpse into the analogical connectedness between the ecological landscape and the "cultural-religious landscape" in which we are now living. As America's ecological landscapes are changing, so is its religious landscape. As ecosystems are losing species and experiencing ecological extinctions, so the Church is also suffering a loss, especially among her younger members. The statistics bear it out: According to the PEW 2014 Religious Landscape Study, "the Christian share of the U.S. population is declining, while the number of U.S. adults who do not identify with any organized religion is growing."[2] In just seven years from 2007 to 2014, the percentage of Christians in the U.S. declined almost 8 percent, from 78.4 to 70.6 percent. This decline includes a 4.8 percent decline in Protestant Christians and a 3.1 percent decline in Catholics (from 23.9 to 20.8 percent). At the same time, the percentage of Americans who identify as "religiously unaffiliated"—popularly called the "nones"—jumped 6.7 percent from 16.1 to 22.8 percent.[3] By 2016, it had risen to 25%, according a Public Religion Research Institute (PRRI) study.[4] It is a sobering statistic that 25% of Americans, or 80 million people, now identify themselves as "nones," more in absolute numbers than either Catholics or mainline Protestants.[5] The percentage is even higher for those age thirty years old and under: A shocking forty percent of that group currently do not subscribe to any religion.[6]

2. *PEW Research Center*, "America's Changing Religious Landscape," 3.

3. *PEW Research Center*, "America's Changing Religious Landscape," 3.

4. Jones et al., "Exodus," 2.

5. Jones et al., "Exodus," 2. See also *PEW Research Center*, "America's Changing Religious Landscape," 10.

6. Jones et al., "Exodus," 3.

The bottom line is that the sector of the religiously unaffiliated is on the rise, especially among the millennials and younger generations. Why is this? What factors in the cultural landscape are driving young people to disaffiliate from the Church? And what restoration techniques or programs of evangelization are needed to bring them back, to restore the "ecology of the Catholic landscape," if you will?

In this chapter, I address these questions from my perspective as a religious woman and a scientist, drawing upon the Final Document of the 2018 Synod on Young People[7] and *Christus Vivit*, Pope Francis' post-synodal apostolic exhortation to youth. Through the Synodal process, the Bishops sought to avoid "the tendency to provide prepackaged answers and ready-made solutions;" rather, they committed to listening attentively to young people in order to allow "their real questions to emerge" and to honestly face as a Church the challenges their questions pose.[8] In *Christus Vivit*, Pope Francis responded to the findings of the Synod, expressing concern that "we can, in fact, spend our youth being distracted, skimming the surface of life, half-asleep, incapable of cultivating meaningful relationships or experiencing the deeper things in life."[9] Further, he says plainly: "Dear young people . . . [d]on't observe life from a balcony. Don't confuse happiness with an armchair, or live your life behind a screen . . . Don't go through life anaesthetized or approach the world like tourists . . . Cast out the fears that paralyze you, so that you don't become young mummies."[10] Instead, he exhorted youth to return to Christ and to "start over," to converse with the Lord about the realities of their lives, assuring them that "Christ is alive and he wants you to be alive!"[11] Later in the document, he reiterated: "Dear young people, please, do not be bystanders in life. Get involved! Jesus was not a bystander. He got involved. Don't stand aloof, but immerse yourselves in the reality of life, as Jesus did."[12]

In response to the Holy Father's exhortation, this chapter explores the lack of engagement of youth, not only with the Church, but underlying this, with the very incarnational realities of life.[13] The chapter begins by highlighting three cultural challenges that have been significant in precipitating this

7. 2018 Synod of Bishops, *Final Document.*

8. Francis, *Christus vivit*, #65.

9. Francis, *Christus vivit*, #19.

10. Francis, *Christus vivit*, #143.

11. Francis, *Christus vivit*, #1–2, 124, 129.

12. Pope Francis, *Christus vivit*, 174. Here he quotes from his *Address at the Prayer Vigil of the XXVIIII World Youth Day in Rio de Janeiro*, July 27, 2013,

13. Throughout *Christus vivit*, Pope Francis exhorts youth to engage with the reality of their lives. See, for example, #1–2, 19, 71, 75, 88, 110, 129.

cultural disengagement and that represent distinct threats to contemporary evangelizing efforts. In response, two strategies for evangelization specifically geared to reconnecting youth with reality are proposed. First, land-based experiences are explored as a means for bringing youth into deeper relationship with the realities of life. Secondly, the chapter proposes that dialogue with science could be an effective strategy for reconnecting youth with concrete realities, one that might be particularly attractive in today's science-dominated culture. Without predetermining or limiting the outcomes of these strategies, they could accomplish several auspicious goals: namely, to show young people that the Church takes reality seriously; to attract young people to concrete realities; and finally, *through* that attraction, to guide them on the path to deeper relationship with the realities of life and ultimately with transcendent realities. As the Catholic Church is a fundamentally incarnational church, it would seem that an essential element for restoring the ecology of the Catholic landscape is to re-prioritize incarnational realities and experiences, especially if cultural analysis indicates that they are being "crowded out" by other invasive influences. Viewed through this lens, land-based experiences and dialogue with science could be two significant strategies for enriching and diversifying Catholic evangelizing efforts and for restoring a vital culture of formation in the Church.

Cultural Challenges

What are the primary cultural challenges that pose a threat to deeper engagement of youth with reality and with their faith? Based upon *Christus Vivit* and the 2018 Synod, and as relevant for this proposal, they coalesce around three main invasive influences: (1) the digitalized culture; (2) a culture of the ephemeral; and (3) a science-dominated culture. In recent decades, these cultural influences have become increasingly aggressive and have had a domineering, homogenizing effect on the Catholic landscape, analogically similar to the effects of invasive species on ecological landscapes.

The digital environment was one of three primary areas of concern that emerged out of the synodal process.[14] As reported in the *Final Document* and echoed by the Holy Father in *Christus Vivit*, "[i]t is no longer merely about 'using' instruments of communication, but living in a highly digitalized culture that has had a profound impact on ideas of time and space, on self-understanding, on understanding of others and of the world, on how to communicate, to learn, to inform oneself, to enter into relationship with

14. See 2018 Synod of Bishops, *Final Document*, #21–24, 145–46; *Christus vivit*, #86–90; Synod of Bishops, *Instrumentum Laboris*, #34–35, 54–58, 134, 154, 160–61.

others."[15] This prevailing digital environment, says Pope Francis, while it has had positive effects in creating "new ways to communicate and bond," also has "its share of limitations and deficiencies," including "exposing people to the risk of addiction, isolation, and gradual loss of contact with concrete reality," . . . "favoring encounter between persons who think alike, shielding them from debate," . . . and creating "a delusional parallel reality that ignores human dignity."[16] This results, he continues, in a kind of "digital migration" that leaves youth "feeling rootless while remaining physically in one place."[17] It is a culture of "zapping," in which youth can interact simultaneously with multiple screens but are not discerning in terms of critical thinking.[18] Later in the document, the Pope refers to the "anesthetizing" influences of such a culture, when life is lived from behind a screen, susceptible to the distractions and banality of every passing trend.[19] He also laments the "homogenizing" influence of the digitalized culture,[20] which threatens youth with becoming "photocopies,"[21] "blurring what is distinctive about their origins and back-grounds, and turning them into a new line of malleable goods." This, he says, "produces a cultural devastation that is just as serious as the disappearance of species of animals and plants."[22]

Secular researchers have also elaborated on the effects of the digital culture on our youth. Luciani Floridi, Professor of Philosophy and Ethics of Information at the University of Oxford, coined the term, "onlife," to refer to the fact that so many of today's daily activities—shopping, work, study, health, entertainment, even conversations—are on-line.[23] In addition, the personas people adopt on social media are increasingly coloring their lives, so the distinction between "online" and "offline" is disintegrating. They are in effect living "onlife." Floridi and others have compiled the "On-Life Manifesto," which aims to launch public debate about the radical effects technology is having on the human condition.[24] He argues we are entering into a fourth revolution similar in scale to the Copernican and Darwinian evolutions.

---

15. 2018 Synod of Bishops, *Final Document*, #21. Also quoted by the Holy Father in *Christus vivit*, #86.

16. Francis, *Christus civit*, #87–90.

17. Francis, *Christus vivit*, #87–90.

18. Francis, *Christus vivit*, #86, 279.

19. Francis, *Christus vivit*, #75, 143, 233.

20. Francis, *Christus vivit*, #186.

21. Francis, *Christus vivit*, #106, 107, 162.

22. Francis, *Christus vivit*, #186.

23. Floridi, *The Fourth Revolution*.

24. Floridi, ed., *The Onlife Manifesto*.

Jean Twenge, Professor of Psychology at San Diego State University, has done research on generational differences and the effects of technology on youth. Her latest book focuses on iGen-ers—those "born in 1995 and later, who grew up with cell phones, had an Instagram page before they started high school, and do not remember a time before the Internet."[25] She makes the case that smartphones and other screens promote antisocial behavior, prolong childhood, and increase loneliness, depression and political disengagement. The results of these and other research studies increasingly indicate that although youth are hyper-connected, they are feeling more disconnected than ever before.

Another outgrowth of the digital culture is that extensive use of technology is profoundly distorting our perception of reality, blurring the distinction between the real and the virtual, and between human, non-human creation, and machine, and even causing people to disengage from reality itself. In the third chapter of his encyclical *Laudato Si'*, Pope Francis proposes that under the influence of the technocratic paradigm, we tend to "ignore or forget the reality in front of us," while falling prey to the notion that "reality, goodness and truth automatically flow from technological and economic power as such."[26] As a result, Pope Francis laments in *Christus Vivit*, "[t]oday, a culture of the ephemeral dominates, but it is an illusion."[27] The isolation that comes with digital preoccupation, he says, can cause young people to lose their sense of reality and succumb to shallow self-absorption and concupiscence.[28] Driven by the immediacy and dominance of technology, the impulse to enjoy the moment, and the mistaken notion that "nothing can be definitive," youth can thus readily become transfixed by a flattened, ephemeral culture.[29]

Such a culture, for its part, manifests itself in a number of ways. For one, it easily develops into a throwaway culture which discards human beings as readily as things, since nothing has value beyond itself in the moment. Even the human body loses its meaning.[30]

An ephemeral culture also easily succumbs to the temptation of relativism. Relativism catches people in distorted notions of the truth, or even in the conviction that there is no such thing as truth. In his book *Navigating*

---

25. Twenge, *iGen*, 2.

26. Francis, *Laudato Si*, #105–6.

27. Francis, *Christus vivit*, #264.

28. Francis, *Christus vivit*, #110.

29. Francis, *Christus vivit*, #264.

30. See, for example, 2018 Synod of Bishops, *Final Document*, #37–39 and *Christus vivit*, #81, 90.

the New Evangelization, Father Cantalamessa, the preacher for the Papal Household, identifies three forms of relativism, each of which reinforces a culture of the ephemeral: scientism, rationalism, and secularism.[31] His concerns and those of Pope Francis are related because each of these "isms" represents a deformation of its real counterpart: scientism a distortion of science; rationalism a distortion of reason; and secularism a distortion of secularization. Scientism is the philosophical notion that science is the only valid way of knowing reality and that there is no need for the "hypothesis of God." Similarly, rationalism is a kind of absolutism which sees reason as the primary source and arbiter of knowledge. Says Father Cantalamessa, rationalism is "an attitude of isolationism, of enclosure within reason itself. . . [I]t consists in refusing to acknowledge that there can be any truth outside of what passes through human reason."[32] While secularism and secularization are both derived from the word "saeculum," meaning the "present time," secularism distorts the true meaning of secularization by reducing reality to the here and now; it effectively excludes the possibility of eternity.[33] In another of his writings, Father Cantalamessa says that "the word that ought to be shouted today to wake up those of her children who have fallen asleep . . . is 'Eternity!' . . . "[W]e need to set about shouting 'Eternity, eternity!' to the people of today."[34] These three branches of relativism engender a severely constricted, ephemeral view of reality, one that puts outside of its brackets everything but the here and now or that which can be seen and touched.

A third cultural challenge is a strange twist: The culture of the ephemeral, while denying or minimizing the reality of perduring truth, also seems to seek it intently. And to what truth has the culture entrusted itself? The truth of science. In August 2019, *Science News* reported the results of a PEW Research Center Study about public trust in different professionals in the U.S. The result: "When it comes to overall confidence that professionals act in the public good, scientists scored the highest among respondents, followed closely by the military. Trust in the motivations of journalists and politicians trailed, by comparison," as did trust in religious leaders.[35]

One outgrowth of the growing cultural faith in scientists over religious leaders is a perceived cultural war between science and religion. It seems that in the minds of many, science has replaced religion as the arbiter of

---

31. Cantalamessa, *Navigating the New Evangelization.*

32. Cantalamessa, *Navigating the New Evangelization,* 69.

33. Cantalamessa, *Navigating the New Evangelization,* 84–85.

34. Cantalamessa, *Jesus Christ, The Holy One of God,* quoted in May 2020 *Magnificat,* 364.

35. Daigle, "Public Trust," 5.

all truth. Recent research undertaken by CARA, the Center for Applied Research in the Apostolate, found that the most common answer given by respondents to the question of why they are no longer Catholic was that they no longer believe in God or religion. The reason? In their own words:

> "Catholic beliefs aren't based on fact. Everything is hearsay from back before anything could be documented, so nothing can be disproved, but it certainly shouldn't be taken seriously."
> "It no longer fits into what I understand of the universe."
> "I realized that religion is in complete contradiction with the rational and scientific world, and to continue to subscribe to a religion would be hypocritical."[36]

When asked what they would need to come back to the Church in the future, the respondents indicated that they would need evidence, "replicable, peer-reviewed, conclusive proof" of God and of the afterlife.[37] For those with this perception, the decision for or against the Church is an "either-or"– either faith or science, but not both. The scientific paradigm is so inflated in their minds that it has crowded out faith, leaving no room for God.

These three cultural challenges pose significant threats to evangelization efforts and present to us a culture fundamentally disengaged from the realities of life. The following section considers two strategies for reengaging youth with the Church by reengaging them with concrete realities. This task is not foreign to the mission for the Church, for the Church has always sought to engage with reality, to listen to it and discern its truth.[38] This does not mean that the Church adopts every passing trend, but rather that "[w]hat calls [the Church] to action are realities illumined by reason."[39]

Two Strategies for Evangelizing in the Spirit of *Christus Vivit*

Pope Francis has on many occasions throughout his pontificate spoken about the importance of engaging with concrete realities and situations in living and teaching about the faith.[40] Perhaps he models himself on his

---

36. Gray, "Young people are leaving the faith."

37. Gray, "Young people are leaving the faith."

38. 2018 Synod of Bishops, *Instrumentum Laboris*, #4, 57, 88, 118.

39. Francis, *Evangelium Gaudium*, #231–33.

40. See, for example: Francis, *Lumen Fidei* #12, 22, 46, 47, 51, 54, 55; *Misericoriae Vultus*; *Evangelium Gaudium* #95, 115, 181, 182, 193, 283; *Laudato Si* #15, 110, 112, 140, 172; *Amoris Laetitia* #31, 36, 90, 121, 162, 203, 204, 218, 223, 229, 300, 303, 304, 311, 315, 321; Brockhaus, "Pope Francis on sharing the Christian message in reality;" Ivereigh, "The Papal obsession."

namesake, St. Francis of Assisi, whose spirituality was manifestly concrete and embodied. Think of St. Francis first being impelled to rebuild the Church through physically rebuilding churches around Assisi, his embrace of the leper and consequent commitment that the friars should care for lepers, his inspiration to create the first living crèche at Greccio, or his final marking with the Stigmata. One of the key distinguishing features of Francis' life and spirituality is its incarnational stamp.

There is also of course a scriptural basis to this incarnational approach. In his first letter to the Corinthians, St. Paul states plainly: "It is not the spiritual which is first but the physical, and then the spiritual."[41] Commenting on this passage in a series of homilies on creation then-Cardinal Joseph Ratzinger emphasized: "I believe that we must develop a Christian pedagogy that accepts creation . . . We must never try to take the second step before the first: *first the physical, then the spiritual.*"[42] This fundamental stance is also shared by John Paul II in his theology of the body.

Indeed, the importance of incarnational realities has been the refrain of the Church since its foundation. To be clear, material realities are important in themselves in the Catholic understanding, but not in isolation. Together, physical and spiritual realities make up the totality of reality which was brought into being and is continually sustained by God the Creator. Moreover, physical realities can serve as an entrance point to deeper spiritual realities. One of the most beautiful articulations of this is from the Church father St. Irenaeus: "He [God] kept calling them to what was primary by means of what was secondary, that is, through the foreshadowings to the reality, through things of time to things of eternity, through things of the flesh to things of the Spirit, through earthly things to the heavenly things."[43]

Applying this to the concrete situations of contemporary culture suggests that one avenue of evangelization is to bring people back to God and to the Church—to what is primary—through what is secondary—that is, through experiences of physical reality. This is how God has always guided his people. It is in this spirit, so dear to the heart of the Church, that I propose the following two strategies.

---

41. 1 Cor 15:46 (RSV).

42. Cardinal Joseph Ratzinger, "*In the Beginning. . .*," 94. Italics mine.

43. St. Irenaeus, *Against Heresies.*

Evangelizing through Elemental Land Experiences

Throughout his pontificate, Pope Francis has emphasized the importance of caring for creation.[44] In this mission, there is a need to develop programs for youth which build on their natural attraction to nature. As Pope Francis writes in *Christus Vivit*: "Nature holds a special attraction for many adolescents and young people who recognize our need to care for the environment. Such is the case with the scouting movement and other groups that encourage closeness to nature, camping trips, hiking, expeditions and campaigns to improve the environment."[45] Consequently, in *Christus Vivit*, the Holy Father proposes that one area of youth ministry that needs to be developed is experiences with nature.[46] How can this benefit youth? As Pope Francis says in *Laudato Si'*: "Nobody is suggesting a return to the Stone Age, but we do need to slow down and look at reality in a different way."[47] Experiences in the natural world can assist youth in reconnecting with concrete realities. Moreover, "in the spirit of Saint Francis of Assisi, these experiences can be a real initiation into the school of universal fraternity and contemplative prayer."[48]

One of the first goals and primary benefits of engaging youth with nature, then, is providing them with opportunities for contemplation. Such opportunities are rare in in an ephemeral, digitalized culture that perpetuates itself by trapping persons into shallow, quick exchanges. Yet the simple experience of beauty is a catechetical tool. Bringing youth into concrete experiences of the natural world using all of their senses can help reorient their understanding of reality and of their place in the world. When youth encounter the beauty and complexity of nature, that encounter can scratch the tightly stretched surface of their lives and stimulate questions as to why there is so much beauty and how this beauty came to be. One hopes that the attractions to nature that young people feel can be the foundation for deeper movement into an aesthetic of care. Further, since the beauty and complexity of nature evinces a design far more complex and beautiful than any human designs, experiencing nature can also engender in young people a sense of awe—a powerful antidote to the spirit of indifferentism

---

44. The most obvious example of this is his encyclical *Laudato Si'*, the first in the history of the Church to focus on environmental issues and creation care. He also joined other Christian denominations in becoming part of the ecumenical "Season of Creation" (seasonofcreation.org) and has made numerous statements throughout his pontificate on the centrality of caring for creation as Catholics.

45. Francis, *Christus vivit*, #228.

46. Francis, *Christus vivit*, #228.

47. Francis, *Laudato Si'*, #114.

48. Francis, *Christus vivit*, #228.

and disengagement currently dominating the culture. The experience of the awesomeness of the beauty of nature can revive in youth what Guardini calls a "youthful and still untested yearning for the infinite."[49] Once the desire for the transcendent is enkindled, young people may progress interiorly to the fire of longing for the Creator God, the one who created such beauty.

As the Holy Father indicates, Franciscan spirituality is a key door into this "school" of contemplation through nature.[50] As Chesterton said so eloquently: "The whole philosophy of St. Francis revolved around the idea of a new supernatural light on natural things, which meant the ultimate recovery, not the ultimate refusal, of natural things."[51] For St. Francis, creation is "stamped," if you will, with the Creator's signature; in other words, when we look at creation we see the footprints of God. St. Bonaventure, the great Franciscan theologian who put into words what St. Francis lived, explained creation as a "book" in which the Creator can be "read" through the "words" of the created world.[52] Through the diversity and beauty of their many created forms, created realities constantly "shout out" praises of their Creator.[53] In Franciscan spirituality, creation itself is fundamentally expressive, mirroring the expressiveness of the Father, Son, and Holy Spirit.[54] Bringing youth into contemplative experiences of nature could thus be a tool for helping them learn how to perceive and read the expressive language of creation and thereby be led back to the author of this book, who is the Trinitarian God.

A second, and often over-looked, goal and benefit of engaging youth in land-based experiences is the opportunity to provide them with hands-on work. In *Christus Vivit*, the Pope includes a section on work in which he emphasizes the importance of honest work in the evangelization of youth.[55] Work is important, he says, for forming youth into their own self-identity and providing meaning and fulfillment in their lives.[56] It is "the place where friendships and other relationships develop because generally it is not done alone."[57] Learning how to work "in a truly personal and life-giving way"

49. Cf. *Christus vivit*, #290. Quoting from Guardini, *Die Lebensalter*, 20.

50. *Christus vivit*, #228, 269.

51. Chesterton, *St. Thomas Aquinas and St. Francis of Assisi*, 232.

52. Savino and Hittinger, "Loss of Creation and its Recovery," 11.

53. Savino and Hittinger, "Loss of Creation and its Recovery," 11.

54. LaNave, "God, Creation and Philosophical Wisdom: Bonaventure and Aquinas," 828–30.

55. Francis, *Christus vivit*, #268–73.

56. Francis, *Christus vivit*, #268–69.

57. Francis, *Christus vivit*, #268.

helps youth to see a vision for their lives and to discern God's call.[58] It should be noted that this, too, is Franciscan at heart because from the beginning of his order, St. Francis emphasized the priority of manual labor over begging as a means of support and spiritual centering.[59]

Evangelizing through work is a particular focus of my religious community, the Franciscan Sisters of the Eucharist.[60] Through the Franciscan Land Program as well as regular work periods on the lands of the sisters, the Franciscan Sisters of the Eucharist (FSE) provide elemental land experiences which guide young people into relationship with nature and with others. The goal of the experiences is to counter the current cultural tendency "to use virtual reality as a substitute for real, personal relationships, by promoting persons-centered community experiences with soil, plants, animals, food, tools, and media."[61] Such elemental experiences as planting, weeding, and harvesting, growing food and flowers, picking fruit, making jam, caring for animals, baking bread, and building simple structures help youth disconnect from their technology and reconnect with each other and with the natural world. Through these projects, youth are encouraged to replace shallow, consumeristic activities with relational, hands-on ones.

Mother Shaun Vergauwen, F.S.E., co-foundress of the Franciscan Sisters of the Eucharist, relates that the land programs began out of a need when the Franciscan Sisters of the Eucharist were first founded in 1973 and the community acquired lands on which to live and support themselves.[62] The Sisters, many of whom came from farming backgrounds in the Midwestern United States, were familiar with caring for land and had a pressing need for assistance with concrete work projects. In response, lay persons volunteered to help. The starting point was that there was an honest need for work, and this is important for evangelizing youth because they desire authenticity.[63] Although it began with the work, it soon became something more as the sisters realized that they were teaching those who came, *through* the work experiences.[64] Not only were they teaching them concrete skills in relation to caring for lands and buildings, but they were also teaching them about themselves and their relationships. The land experiences and

58. Francis, *Christus vivit*, #268. See also #170, 174, 253–58.

59. Thompson, OP, *Francis of Assisi*, 37–38.

60. "Franciscan Sisters of the Eucharist: Our Charism is . . . "; www.fsecommunity.org.

61. "Franciscan Sisters of the Eucharist: Joy in Mission;" www.fsecommunity.org/joy-in-mission.

62. Mother Shaun Vergauwen, FSE, Co-Foundress of Franciscan Sisters of the Eucharist, personal communication, March 31, 2020.

63. *Instrumentum Laboris*, #21, 66–67, 142.

64. Mother Shaun Vergauwen, F.S.E., personal communication.

relationships that developed through them were helping to form the young people as whole persons and teaching them the value of community. They learned teamwork and how to channel their energy, and even how to work through the disappointments and sufferings of life through their physical work. Hands-on work experiences can also lead persons organically to a healthier understanding of who they are as human beings and what their role is in nature—that is, they could discover themselves in the role, not of dominators, but more as gardeners working by the sweat of their brow to bring forth the fertility of creation.

The skills and discipline involved in working the land assist youth in developing new habits and discovering their individual gifts. Even discovering where their particular responses lie is important for youth, who have become "anaesthetized" by the digitalized, ephemeral culture. The physical work is, if you will, a "wake-up call," in the spirit of Pope Francis' exhortation to youth to wake up from their "lethargy" and become fully alive.[65] By working side-by-side on the land with young people, the sisters assist youth in this process of re-awakening and self-discovery. For example, some youth might have a native response to flowers, or to the vegetable garden, or to carpentry, or to a particular animal like the chickens or the goats. Others may discover a special giftedness with a particular tool, such as loppers or the chain saw. Engaging in this process of self-discovery through work on the land in a community setting is an important antidote to the homogenizing effects of consumeristic culture in which, as the Holy Father laments, youth are tempted to become "photocopies," "running after whatever the powerful set before them with the mechanisms of consumerism and distraction."[66] Instead, through concrete work experiences on the sisters' land, youth are encouraged to develop their unique God-given gifts and talents and use them for the good of others.

Engaging in these pursuits with others and under the guidance of the sisters exposes youth to natural rhythms and organic cycles in the earth, providing a "grounding" for them that has been lost in the ephemeral, digitalized culture in which they are growing up. This grounding also has a scientific base since it requires understanding and working with the laws in nature, and so it helps counter the prevailing cultural mindset that science and religion are at war with one another. Further, many of the land-based experiences undertaken by the sisters are pre-sacramental and can be a way of making Scripture and the sacraments more alive, real and relevant for today's young people.

65. *Instrumentum Laboris*, #1, 49, 130.
66. Francis, *Christus vivit*, #106.

Two particular aspects of the land-based approach of the Franciscan Sisters of the Eucharist deserve special mention. The first is the value of introducing youth to elemental technique—that is, the use of basic elemental tools in working the land as opposed to more advanced technologies. This is not because those technologies are bad in themselves, but rather because the advanced technologies have physically separated persons from natural realities, and returning to elemental methods can help persons physically reconnect with those realities. It can also aid persons in understanding better the basic principles of how to work fruitfully with those particular realities or elements of creation. For example, turning the soil with a hoe or small hand-operated rototiller, rather than a plow, brings persons closer to the soil rather than separating them from it and helps them to realize more immediately the role of soil in receiving the seed, as well as the need to preserve that soil's structure and fertility. In addition, according to Mother Shaun, understanding the elemental piece helps persons be creative. "Young people can do things, but do they understand the principle of what is happening? . . . "You can't make things happen without really understanding the elemental principles."[67]

A second distinguishing aspect of the FSE land programs is the practice of making spiritual analogies related to the particular work project. For example, if I am weeding, I might reflect with the group or sister with whom I am working about what the weeds are in my life and what needs to be weeded out at this time. Or if I am on the orchard pruning team, we might reflect on what in our lives could be pruned back; if I am clearing a new trail, what paths are emerging in my life in terms of vocation? Mother Shaun comments that one of the basic analogies that flows out of the land is "the honesty of sexuality in nature."[68] There is masculine and feminine everywhere: the pistil and stamen in the flower; the fertilized egg in the chicken coop; the flower and fruit in the garden or orchard; the seed in the soil. Sexuality is part of the pattern inscribed by God in nature. This is an important natural, embodied truth which one cannot escape when working closely with creation.

It should be noted that this approach to evangelizing through elemental land experiences need not be confined to rural areas. One compelling example is that of Father Raymond Ellis at St. Cecilia's parish, an impoverished African-American parish in downtown Detroit. In the late 1960s and early 1970s, Father Ellis worked with the youth of his parish to clean up the garbage on the parish grounds and used that concrete experience as a teaching

67. Francis, *Christus vivit*, #106.
68. Francis, *Christus vivit*, #106.

tool. Through the body experience of the unpleasant, smelly work in the intense summer heat of urban Detroit, Father Ellis shared with the youth a profound spiritual reflection on "the theology of garbage." In his own words:

> Garbage is a most graphic sign of death. And death is total self-gift . . . So too, garbage is a sign of love poured out . . . Egg shells are nothing other than eggs which have given their all on behalf of man . . . Coffee grinds, bones, empty bottles and cans, orange peelings, apple cores, watermelon rinds and all the other assorted things that make up the contents of the average garbage can, they all tell the same story: Death, self-gift, emptying oneself on behalf of others. A religious person will never be far from Christ or the meaning of His life and death even when he is busy with garbage.[69]

Land-based experiences such as those recounted here are tangible examples of evangelizing by reconnecting youth with concrete realities and opening them up to the spiritual realities, *through* the physical reality, in the spirit of St. Irenaeus. The next section explores the opportunity the Church has to do this by embracing science.

Evangelizing through Dialogue with Science

How could dialogue with science be an effective strategy for evangelization, since science is one of the cultural challenges causing the exodus of young people from the Church? To begin with, it is important that the Church view the scientific culture, not only as a challenge "but also, and even more, as a significant *opportunity*."[70] Since young people today have grown up with a scientific frame of mind, it is important for the Church to speak their language in order to reach them. This is the starting point for meaningful dialogue. This means that Catholic schools, colleges and seminaries should educate widely in the sciences; priests should present homilies addressing questions of science and technology; parishes should offer study groups and talks by scientists as part of their catechetical programs. In short, the Catholic Church needs to intensify its efforts to foster a science-educated Catholic populace.

This education should be founded on the conviction that science itself is not the problem. The problem is the ideology of scientism—or, as Father Cantalamessa articulated, the triple ideologies of scientism, rationalism,

---

69. Fr. Ellis, "The Theology of Garbage," 4.

70. Tanzella-Nitti, "Some Reflections on Scientific Thought in the New Evangelization," 235.

and secularism. These ideologies have compromised the contemporary understanding of science and reason and do not represent the fullness of what the Catholic intellectual tradition has to offer.

There are multiple ways that authentic science can be a tool for evangelization, but I propose three here: (1) science as opening to Pope Emeritus Benedict XVI's vision of "expanded reason;" (2) science as "sign," pointing beyond itself; and (3) science as "witness" of the faith.

Throughout his pontificate, Pope Benedict XVI advocated for an "expanded reason."[71] This understanding of reason is fundamentally different from rationalism. Expanded reason is not closed in on itself. Rather, science as an expression of expanded reason explicates "the rational structures on which creation is founded."[72] The Church has always supported this conception of science and of a Creating Reason at the heart of the world. Indeed, one of the great historical contributions of the Catholic Church is its demystifying of creation, demonstrating that creation is not the product of mythical forces and beings, but of a loving, creating, reasonable God. Building upon Greek philosophy, the Church has also carefully and consistently articulated the distinction between primary and secondary causes—an especially significant distinction for contemporary culture since it clears a space for the scientific enterprise. In essence, science is the study of secondary causes in the created world.

For Pope Emeritus Benedict, expanded reason is open to beauty. In a 2008 address to Italian priests he said: "We are fighting to expand reason, and hence for a reason which is also open to the beautiful . . . I think these two things go hand in hand: reason . . . and beauty. Reason that intended to strip itself of beauty would be halved; it would be a blinded reason."[73] Beauty is indeed not far from science: Think of the beauty of the constellations, the DNA helix, the spiral structures of the Fibonacci sequence, the systems of the human body, and so on.

Science as an expression of expanded reason is also connected to the truth. Science pursues the truth hidden in the structures and forms of created world. In a disengaged, relativistic culture of the ephemeral, the bond between science and truth is very important. Even acknowledging that there is such a thing as truth can be a monumental step in evangelization. We could use science to help present the reality of truth to our young people— to lead them, in the spirit of St. Irenaeus, to what is primary through what is secondary. For example, the particularity of science is a gentle corrective

71. Benedict XVI, *A Reason Open to God*, 17–18.
72. 2012 Synod of Catholic Bishops, *Message*, 10.
73. Pope Benedict XVI, *2008 Meeting with Clergy of Bolzano-Bressanone.*

to the prevailing homogenizing influences of the digital culture, for the laws of nature, from the macro to the micro level, demonstrate that each species in unique and occupies a unique niche. Exploring the connection of science with the truth, through the lens of expanded reason, could also be a powerful antidote to scientism and rationalism, demonstrating the harmony of faith and reason in a culture that pits them against one other.

This leads to the second aspect of science as "sign." As Max Planck, founder of quantum mechanics, rightly said: "And so we arrive at a point where science acknowledges the boundary beyond which it may not pass, while it points to those farther regions which lie outside the sphere of its activities."[74] In short, science points beyond itself. Most, though admittedly not all, scientists would agree that science will never be able to understand everything; there is always something larger or smaller beyond its grasp. Articulating the "sign value" of creation to our young people could help them recapture a sense of awe and mystery at the created world and might open them to the possibility of transcendent realities—again, leading to the primary through the secondary. In fact, the notion of science as sign suggests an intriguing catechetical strategy. Could we teach about the attributes of God through His signs in the created world? Can science assist us in "reading reality" and leading young people into a deeper experience of that reality?

For example, consider the human experience of awe and wonder at the extravagance of nature. Think of the number of leaves that fall from just one tree, the number of seeds produced by one plant, the tremendous energy in the clouds, the millions of collisions of charged particles that produce the Northern lights. As Annie Dillard puts it in *Pilgrim at Tinker Creek*: "This is a spendthrift economy. Though nothing is lost, all is spent."[75] Does this not point us analogically to the infinite greatness and extravagance of the Trinitarian God, who gave all, spent all, for our salvation?

Another example is the analogy of the "cruciform creation" proposed by philosopher and Templeton Prize winner Holmes Rolston.[76] Evolution, he says, is natural selection, but also something more: it can be viewed philosophically as one level of life laying down its life for another to survive. Can this reality be a vehicle for teaching young people about the sacrificial nature of Christ and awakening in them a desire to live a sacrificial life? Could this be a foundation for catechesis on the sacraments, especially the Eucharist?

---

74. Planck, *Where Is Science Going?*, 105–6.

75. Dillard, *Pilgrim at Tinker Creek*, 66.

76. Holmes Rolston, "Kenosis and Nature," 43–65. See also: "Does Nature Need to Be Redeemed?," 205–29; and "Perpetual Perishing, Perpetual Renewal," 113–15.

Finally, science can be an evangelizing force through its witness. This includes its witness of being at the service of the common good and of helping others. It also includes the witness of many faithful Catholic scientists and even Catholic scientist-saints. And there are more in the historical record than people realize.[77] Here one contemporary example could be highlighted—that of the brilliant scientist and geneticist Jerome Lejeune.[78] He discovered the cause of Down's syndrome and was also a devout Catholic who became dismayed that his genetic discoveries were being used to electively abort children with disabilities. Through his science he understood that life begins at conception and was a fearless advocate of that position, even when it meant being ostracized by his peers. Through his faith he upheld the inherent dignity of all human persons, including those with Down's syndrome and other disabilities. Although rejected by many of his peers, Jerome Lejeune was embraced by the Church. His cause for canonization is underway and he is now a Servant of God.[79] Teaching our young people about the courageous witness of Catholic scientists and scientist-saints such as Jerome Lejeune could be another way of countering the disengagement of the digitalized culture with a real and personal witness of conviction and sacrificial love.

Conclusion: Rebuilding the Future of the Catholic Landscape

Restoring the ecology of the Catholic landscape, like restoring ecological landscapes, is a complex task that will demand from the Church long-term commitment and vigilance as well as an infusion of grace. Yet, as I walk through the prairie, the book of nature speaks a number of gentle but clear messages about what sets a landscape on a trajectory toward restoration. First, the press in nature is toward diversity, not homogeneity. In nature, no creature is a photocopy of any other, and each creature has its own place and role in the ecosystem. When an ecosystem moves toward homogeneity, as by the invasive influences of particular introduced species (which if unchecked can even cause the extinction of native species), the ecological health of the whole system suffers as a result. This should put us on guard against the invasive influences of the digitalized culture and enliven efforts to support personalized approaches and communication with youth. Science or land-based programs that build community, provide youth with the skills to develop their God-given gifts, and encourage them to embrace the

77. Baglow, *Faith, Science, and Reason*, 108–14.

78. Google, "Professor Jerome LeJeune."

79. Google, "Association Les Amis du Professeur Jerome LeJeune."

reality of their particular calling in the Church can help counter the invasive, homogenizing influences of the contemporary culture.

Secondly, nature is extravagant in its diversity and fruitfulness. Nature does not hold back or stand aloof. It pours itself out totally and excessively, in ways that are often quite beautiful and awe-inspiring. What a corrective this image could provide if flashed across the gray screen of an indifferent, anaesthetized culture! The fruitfulness of nature flows out of enduring cycles which, although repetitive, allow for unique expressions. In its resilience and adaptability, the natural "programming" in nature is fundamentally different from the programming of digital content. Creation is naturally creative, the words "creation" and "creative" deriving from the same Latin root *creare*, meaning to "bring into being or to bring forth something new."[80] What a contrast to the ephemeral satisfaction of self-focused transitory pleasures that make a temporary "splash" but do not bring forth anything really new or lasting!

Finally, creation is translucent: it allows the light of the Creator to shine through it. It reveals its material truth to those who seek to understand it through their science, while at the same time pointing beyond itself to the extravagant Creator who originally brought it into being. Creation speaks both languages, if you will—the language of concrete matter and the language of the eternal. It is pre-sacramental, pointing to the mystery of the incarnation and the sacramental realities that are so much at the heart of the Catholic faith.

In conclusion, in the spirit of St. Irenaeus—that God leads us from the foreshadowings to the reality, from the secondary to the primary—land-based experiences and dialogue with science are two "restoration" strategies with real potential for rejuvenating the Catholic landscape. In fact, the Church needs more rather than less science—but science as expanded reason, as sign, and as witness. Further, authentic science, alongside or grounded in land-based experiential catechetical programs, could bring young people back to the Church. Together these two could be effective catechetical strategies for the New Evangelization.

---

80. Google, "Online etymology dictionary: Create."

Listen to Me

The Soteriology of Johann Baptist Metz and Its Effect on
Ministry with Adolescents[1]

DONALD WALLENFANG, OCDS _____

Abstract

ONE OF THE MOST vital ministries within the Church is its ministry to adolescents. As an unquestionably turbulent time of life, adolescence consists of a host of issues which must be navigated with great pastoral care on the part of elder members of the faith community. Taking as its starting point the particularities of an affluent parochial context in the Midwestern United States, this essay submits a prescription for transformative healing in response to the rampant self-injurious practices of young people today. The work of Johann Baptist Metz is called upon to deliver the necessary framework for facing the overwhelming suffering of young people head on. Metz's emphasis on narrative memory, solidarity and hope provides a compelling Christian formula to counteract self-destructive habits and tendencies toward isolation, especially within the post-pandemic milieu of the present. By attuning ministry with adolescents to the power of storytelling and empathy, this essay offers further insights about how to adapt the culture effectively to the Gospel through contemporary pastoral strategies.

---

1. At the time of this essay's original composition (2009), Donald Wallenfang was serving as full-time Director of Youth Ministry at Holy Spirit Catholic Community in Naperville, Illinois, U.S.A.

Introduction

In the parochial context of Holy Spirit Catholic Community located in Naperville, Illinois, teenagers hurt themselves. Self-injury, a rapidly growing phenomenon among teens in the United States, takes many forms: cutting, burning, drug and alcohol use, sexual experimentation, excessive body piercing and tattooing, embedding objects under one's skin, anorexia, bulimia, and attempting suicide. Such phenomena are often rendered taboo— things that are not to be talked about in public—by the general population, especially by adults. People who engage in such unorthodox and uncanny practices become strangers to the façade of the community at large and to themselves; they become stigmatized as weird, shameful and entirely other. Yet the behaviors of these young people express a cry for empathy and help: listen to me and love me! Given such a cry, Christian youth ministry must find ways to offer the listening ears and hearts for which young people are literally starving and dying.

The mystical-prophetic theology of Johann Baptist Metz offers key forms for realizing the saving power of the Christian proclamation: narrative, memory and solidarity. In providing a secure and non-judgmental space for young people to share the historical, metaphorical and symbolic narratives of their personal lives through an active and conscious communal memory, a community of faith is able to empathetically co-journey with one another as Christ journeyed alongside Cleopas and the unnamed disciple on their walk toward Emmaus. Through a committed empathetic solidarity, a space for authentic disclosure is opened—one in which human narratives intermingle with the dramatic cosmic narrative of the Word made flesh, who for us and for our salvation came down from heaven. Through empathy and solidarity, an opening is made for the mystical-prophetic spirit of the Gospel to offer healing and empowerment for the desperate, anguished lives of so many young people.

Demographics and Hope

Naperville, Illinois, is one of the most affluent communities in the United States of America. With a population of roughly 147,500 residents, a median household income of over $126,000, and a median real estate price tag of >$400,000, Naperville was ranked third among the 2008 best places to live in the United States by *Money Magazine*.[2] Home to six large Catholic churches and a myriad of non-Catholic Christian churches, Naperville is

2. CNNMoney.com, "Best Places to Live."

a place where the Gospel of Jesus Christ is freely proclaimed. The teenage population of Naperville is characterized as highly educated and replete with opportunities for personal advancement and community involvement. Neuqua Valley High School, which the majority of teenagers from Holy Spirit Catholic Community attend, boasts a state-of-the-art $65 million facility and a 97 percent graduation rate.[3] Yet despite its excessive material affluence and abundant vocational resources for young people, not a few teens find themselves living as invisible nomads, lost identities in a land of excess, dissipation, and waning temporality, whereby they go as unknown and unnoticed among family and their 100-plus so-called followers on Facebook and other social media platforms—going unknown even to themselves. Furthermore, beneath the veneer of self-sufficiency, success and the elusive arrival of "The American Dream" lies trouble in the "bubble": the scourges of gossip-violence, bullying, irredeemable self-image, pressure and insurmountable stress to achieve still higher, sexual abuse, parental neglect, and the real and lasting effects of addictive behaviors among family members and friends (for example, addiction to alcohol, drugs and pornography). All conditions taken together, Naperville presents itself as an ambivalent setting for a young person to grow and develop within.

Ensconced in such opulent and saturating circumstances of material prosperity, teens are crying out to be noticed, to be listened to, and perhaps even to be loved. Yet their cries often take on an inverted form in which anguish and internal suffering fail to meet an empathetic other and so metamorphose into a pattern of self-loathing and a groping for validated existence. Teens claim as their own the lyrics of the song *Iris* by the pop rock-and-roll band, *Goo Goo Dolls*:

> And you can't fight the tears that ain't coming,
> Or the moments of truth in your lies
> When everything feels like the movies
> Yeah, you bleed just to know you're alive.
>
> And I don't want the world to see me,
> Cause I don't think that they'd understand
> When everything's made to be broken,
> I just want you to know who I am.[4]

Tragically, teens are in fact "bleeding just to know they're alive." It is a similar phenomenon to that of pinching oneself to verify the reality versus the

---

3. Schools-Data, "Neuqua Valley High School, Naperville, IL"; Oprah.com, "Failing Grade."

4. Rzeznik, "Iris."

illusion of an experience, yet in the case of self-injurious practices among teens, the self-inflicted injury is exacted in proportion to the internal pain they feel—sometimes to the degree of death as in the case of suicide.

While the intent of this essay is not to identify adequately the psychological genesis of self-injurious behaviors among teens, an additional point of clarification must be stated: teens hurt themselves as a mode of communication.[5] The logic at work is a transfer from internal invisibility to external visibility; if one's internal pain is not recognized or validated, perhaps an external display of hurting may merit attention. In working as the Director of Youth Ministry at Holy Spirit Catholic Community in Naperville, I have recognized such an etiology on numerous occasions. For instance, once before a youth meeting at the parish, a teenage girl approached me and asked for a Band-Aid. I asked why she needed a Band-Aid and she replied that she had just been cutting herself. Surely, she did not need to ask me, an adult youth minister, for a Band-Aid, but I believe she asked me because she wanted me to know that she was hurting herself and she wanted me to respond. She was crying out for intervention, and this is how she communicated her cry for help. When their words fail to find an empathetic other who takes the time to listen and respond in a compassionate way, teens convert their expressions of pain and loneliness to a form of body language that speaks the urgent color red.

Given such a sobering vocation simply to listen and to love, how can a real empathetic receptivity emerge to affirm, accept and encourage a young person in his or her personal goodness and unrepeatable uniqueness? Two conditions must be met in order for this redemptive and transformative process to occur. First, a young person must be given the dialogical and trustworthy space to share his or her personal story—to share his or her personal journey of joy, pain, sorrow, fear and hope. Without such a secure space for disclosing one's personal and intimate story, genuine empathy cannot occur because without this essential space, there is nothing to be heard. Second, a spirit of judgment must be banished in order to make room for a spirit of acceptance and validation to preside within the space of dialogical disclosure. As Paul writes in his first epistle to the church in Corinth:

> But with me it is a very small thing that I should be judged by you or by any human court. I do not even judge myself. I am not aware of anything against myself, but I am not thereby acquitted. It is the Lord who judges me. Therefore do not pronounce judgment before the time, before the Lord comes, who

5. See Nock, "Why Do People Hurt Themselves? New Insights into the Nature and Functions of Self-Injury."

will bring to light the things now hidden in darkness and will disclose the purposes of the heart. Then every man will receive his commendation from God.[6]

Paul insists on assigning the task of personal judgment to God alone rather than to any human tribunal or even to a probing self-appraisal. It stands to reason and experience that a person is not able to share his or her personal story openly and without hindrance unless a spirit of love, acceptance and compassion prevails throughout the course of self-revelation. A self-affirming and non-judgmental space is a necessary condition of possibility for vulnerable self-disclosure.

A third vital component is required to actualize peace, healing and empowerment in the wounded lives of young people: the Spirit of the living God as revealed in and through Jesus of Nazareth. For this Spirit, in Christ, has assumed a history—a life-narrative that is not confined to a dead letter but lives in the active and intentional memory of a people united in a common bond of faith. In Jesus of Nazareth, the eternal God has become irreversibly enmeshed and embodied in creative history—a history commenced in the *ex nihilo* creative act of God (*creatio originalis*), continued in evolutionary patterns of living existence (*creatio continua*), and destined for an eternal rendezvous of re-creation (*creatio nova*). Precisely in this indissoluble movement of redemption does God open the possibility of historical metamorphosis: history can be rewritten and redeemed. The contours of the life-narrative of Jesus of Nazareth—contours marked by descent followed by ascent—bear the very potency of vital transformation. When the form of the narrative of Jesus coincides with the personal narrative of a hurting young person, an enigmatic commingling occurs whereby a little leaven raises the whole batch of dough.[7] Just as water and wine are together mingled at the heart of eucharistic liturgy to signify the redeeming logic of the paschal mystery, whereby divinity descends to become human in order for humanity to ascend to become divine, so too are the life-narratives of Christ and the Church interwoven.[8] Through a commingling of narratives, the life-giving

6. 1 Cor 4:3–5 (RSV).

7. See Matt 13:33: "(Jesus) told them another parable. 'The kingdom of heaven is like leaven which a woman took and hid in three measures of meal, till it was all leavened'" (RSV).

8. See Irenaeus of Lyons, *Adversus haereses*, Book V (Preface): "*Factus est quod sumus nos, uti nos perficeret quod et ipse*" ("He was made what we are, in order to perfect us into what he himself is" [translation my own]); Athanasius of Alexandria, *De incarnatione Verbi*, 54, 3: "He became man so that we might be made God; and He manifested Himself in the flesh, so that we might grasp the idea of the unseen Father; and He endured the insolence of men, so that we might receive the inheritance of immortality" [translation taken from Jurgens, *Faith of the Early Fathers*, 322]).

seeds of resurrection are planted within the vulnerability and brokenness of the human heart, acquiescing to the warm movement of God's eternal Spirit who comes to cultivate the fallowness of cynicism and indignation, calling forth the germination of mortal kernels into immortal resurrection bloom.[9] This logic of commingling narratives is most poignantly portrayed in the writing of Johann Baptist Metz. The application of Metzian mystical-prophetic theology in the field of pastoral ministry bears great potential for developing more holistic practices for ministering to people who are found in the valley of the shadow of death.[10]

The Soteriological Form of Johann Baptist Metz

Methodology: *Geschichte* and Incarnation

The question of relevance is essential for the theological method of Johann Baptist Metz. For Metz, soteriology must not be regarded as concerning another world or a merely coterminous process vis-à-vis actual human history, but rather as an evolving process occurring in and through human history. Any soteriological presentation which claims to hold demands upon the human conscience but remains detached from real, concrete, historical life is to be regarded as irrelevant and superfluous.[11] For Metz, the question of salvation must be fundamentally anthropocentric, falling under "the primacy of the subject, of praxis, and of alterity."[12] Metz is clear that his theological method has been branded by the horrors of World War II, signaled by the name Auschwitz: "To be true to the situation, *after Auschwitz* means nothing other than this: finally to accept the fact that concrete history, and the theological experience of nonidentity connected with it, have broken into theology's logos."[13] Metz's hermeneutic process is thus enmeshed within the bloody tapestry of human history—a history that is comprised of sorrow, joy and acute human experiences, especially that of suffering. With his piqued awareness of the question of the meaning of common (and even horrific) human experiences, Metz cautions against "falling under a soteriological

---

9. See John 12:24: "Truly, truly, I say to you, unless a grain of wheat falls into the earth and dies, it remains alone; but if it dies, it bears much fruit" (RSV).

10. See Ps 23.

11. In agreement with Metz, see Rahner, *Foundations of Christian Faith*, 230: "But a question which by its very nature challenges and confronts the whole of human existence cannot be posed to begin with as a question for which particular elements of the concrete existence of the subject doing the asking can be put in parentheses."

12. Metz, *Passion for God*, 24.

13. Metz, *Passion for God*, 25.

spell" whereby theology dispenses with the theodicy question in favor of a hypersensitive hamartiology.[14] An overemphasis on hamartiology avoids what is, for Metz, the foundational task of constructing an adequate, credible and relevant soteriology: relating the cross of Christ to the sum total of the unspeakable sufferings of humanity. The cross serves as the semiotic interpretive key to understanding history, "the sign of the constant protest within the world against God," and "the constant existential of the Christian economy of history."[15] Within this existential framework of ambivalence, Metz posits a human history which is engaged in suffering, sin and protest against God while at the same time experiences the redemptive process of handing sin over to God. Through its constant state of ambivalent tension, history is able to have both salvation and damnation open to it.[16]

According to Metz, it is precisely in and through its ambivalent historical state that God accepts the world: "in his son, Jesus Christ, God accepted the world with eschatological definitiveness."[17] God's unconditional acceptance of the world is essentially the "how" of Metz's soteriology. Following the traditional notion of incarnational theology articulated in the ancient baptismal creeds of the Church, Metz views the incarnation of Jesus as the axiomatic event of salvation history (*Geschichte*):

> Thus the Incarnation is not a "principle" that is *applied* subsequently *within* history (to particular phenomena), but the inner principle of history itself: its coordinating point (Col 1:17), its final ground (Rev 3:14), the dynamic reason for everything, its "Alpha and Omega" (Rev 1:8), its "fulfillment" (Gal 4:4; Mk 1:15), its absolute concretion, in which alone what is earlier and what is later in time become genuine history. Only if the

14. Schuster and Boschert-Kimmig, eds., *Hope Against Hope*, 49–50. Cf. Metz, *A Passion for God*, 4, 14, 23. Here Metz critiques theologies that are "idealistically closed-off systems" by proposing a postidealist and political theology that seeks to be informed by and draw in the non-Western world through irruptions which challenge typical Western bourgeois theologizing. The term "hamartiology" signifies a soteriology transfixed on forgiveness of sins in a metaphysical and abstract sense alone, rather than a concern for a kind of liberation theology in the *hic et nunc*.

15. Metz, *Theology of the World*, 17. Cf. John 15:18: "'If the world hates you, know that it has hated me before it hated you'" (RSV).

16. Metz, *Theology of the World*, 18. Cf. Metz, *Faith in History and Society*, 211: "The question of how history and salvation can be related without each being diminished may be regarded as of central importance in contemporary theology. History is the experience of reality in conflict and contradiction, whereas salvation is, theologically speaking, their reconciliation by the act of God in Jesus Christ."

17. Metz, *Theology of the World*, 19. See footnote 8 here for Metz's meaning of God's acceptance of the world. Cf. Rom 5:8: "But God shows his love for us in that while we were yet sinners Christ died for us" (RSV).

constant ground of history is itself conceived historically does the nature of history fully appear.[18]

It is evident that, for Metz, the incarnation of the divine Logos introduces the fullness of meaningfulness and coherency into history itself. If the meaning-making principle of history were to remain outside of history, the tapestry of human history would remain unintelligible. History demands that its ground and source become manifest and proclaimed precisely in history to make its raison d'être known. By the event of divine incarnation, God's coming "is indelibly inscribed in man's conscience as part of man's future," "God Himself has stepped into the historical process of human existence," and God becomes "Emmanuel, God with us. . .becomes visible in our horizon. . .forms part of our future. . .is ever coming down to us and weaving Himself into our historical pageant."[19] Through God's assumption of human nature God reveals the glory of the Most Holy Trinity and at the same time redeems humanity as that which is radically other than divinity.[20] According to Metz, the process of human redemption does not consist of apotheosis or divinization—in the sense of humanity becoming something ontologically new and identical to the divine nature—but is rather constituted by God's graceful affirmation and acceptance of humanity as humanity created in the *imago Dei*.[21] The grace of God's will is operative and efficacious in and through Jesus Christ, for God accepts the whole of humanity in the incarnate Christ. It is Christ who is the archetype of perfected humanity—a humanity perfected through obedience to God and voluntary involuntary suffering.[22] Metz, in effect, paints a picture of Christ which is vulnerability, helplessness,

18. Metz, *Theology of the World*, 23.

19. Metz, *Advent of God*, 4–8.

20. Metz, *Theology of the World*, 26: "God's divinity consists in the fact that he does not remove the difference between himself and what is other, but rather accepts the other *precisely as different from himself.*"

21. Metz, *Theology of the World*, 29: "God did not let the infralapsarian (fallen) order of nature be totally alienated from him because the sin which disturbed this order still remains held by his continuing saving will in Jesus Christ, so that the whole infralapsarian state of nature and of creation appears finally theologically as the expression of the grace of God's will in salvation history."

22. Metz, *Theology of the World*, 30: "Christ entered into the flesh of sin, he became open to suffering; his 'integrity' (as the power to give the *whole* of his being to the obedient love of God) is simultaneously his openness to suffering: his exposure to the fate which came upon him from outside, which is not simply summoned 'from within'; a death to which he is not reconciled from the beginning as his own, but is the chalice that he asks to pass from him; temptation that must be answered by obedience, that is, by accepting the contradictory."

and yet a mysterious and paradoxical power working through weakness.[23] Christ is observed as standing in solidarity with people who are oppressed, marginalized and powerless in the face of persecution—with people who suffer absurdly, obscenely and traumatically. "Thus in his humanity (Christ) accepts the world in that 'infralapsarian' distance from God" in and through human suffering and radical ambiguity.[24] Paul says as much in his epistle to the church of Rome: "While we were yet helpless, at the right time Christ died for the ungodly. . .But God shows his love for us in that while we were yet sinners Christ died for us."[25] God accepts the world in the dregs of its waywardness—a world utterly helpless to save itself. God's yes to the world in spite of the world's no to God opens a future leavened with the promise of redemption. God's affirmation of the world's inherent goodness subverts the unwarranted suspicion of the world's no in favor of the affirmation of eternal Goodness. It is this affirmative response to goodness which is enunciated in the historical life of Christ. The life-narrative of Jesus of Nazareth is that testimony to the goodness of existence which is resolute to its tragic end—a resoluteness of such conviction that it speaks beyond the grave. Yet before this "beyond" appears the present experience of suffering here below.

Locus of Suffering

Metz derives the relevance of his soteriology from the theodicy question. He situates the relationship between God and humanity in the context of senseless and absurd suffering—a "form of presence to God (taking) the form of protest, of insistent questioning: How long, oh Lord?"[26] Metz considers any soteriology which does not honestly grapple with this question to be irrelevant. "This insistent turning of one's question toward God finally contextualizes suffering as a *suffering unto God (Leiden an Gott)*."[27] Suffering unto God "defines for (Metz) the primordial, authentic way of being human in a world and church that lives inescapably after Auschwitz."[28] The mystery of human suffering is indispensable. Upon reflecting on life and its

23. See 2 Cor 12:8–10: "Three times I begged the Lord about this, that it should leave me: but he said to me, 'My grace is sufficient for you, for my power is made perfect in weakness.' I will all the more gladly boast of my weaknesses, that the power of Christ may rest upon me. For the sake of Christ, then, I am content with weaknesses, insults, hardships, persecutions, and calamities; for when I am weak, then I am strong" (RSV).

24. Metz, *Theology of the World*, 30.

25. Rom 5:6, 8 (RSV).

26. Metz, *A Passion for God*, 14.

27. Metz, *A Passion for God*, 14.

28. Metz, *A Passion for God*, 14–15.

entire array of experiences and the meaning of those experiences, one must halt before those miserable experiences of pain, suffering and death—especially highly traumatic suffering involving intense levels of pain, shock and horror. Such traumatic experiences constitute that part of life which all would rather avoid but nonetheless must inescapably undergo.[29] It is these experiences that cause one to face the rawness and harshness of reality while moving from insobriety to stupor. Pain, suffering and death cause one to question the reality of God and the meaning of life. These experiences, in the depths of their depravity, derangement and obscenity, drain the human spirit of all that is good, leaving it languishing and desperate for any scent of hope. It is at this threshold between despair and hope where Metz looks to the Christian kerygma to speak a good word to a wounded and numb humanity.[30] For teetering on this threshold between despair and hope, humanity is on the brink of viewing itself as inhuman, and life as without sense. It is here at this point of tension and desperation where Metz cries out: let there be a theology that is relevant for suffering humanity! It is here that Metz is able to appeal to a humanizing suffering unto God in solidarity with a suffering Savior. Whereas Karl Rahner writes, "the death of Jesus is such that by its very nature it is subsumed into the resurrection," Metz suggests a significant, lengthy and reverent pause on the death of Jesus before speaking of a subsummation.[31]

Not only does Metz suggest a pause on the death of Jesus but also on the suffering and death of all humanity of all times: Metz looks to the "concrete and all-encompassing history of suffering" to adequately treat the

29. Crucial to Metz's soteriological method is the decision not to evade the natural experiences of pain, suffering and death. See Metz and Moltmann, *Meditations on the Passion*, 29–30: "For us to take one step following the suffering Son of Man, we must first break free from the silent decree of our 'progressive' societies which forbid us to suffer, and we must do this, not by some abstract counter-cult of suffering, but so as to make ourselves capable, through our own ability to suffer, of suffering for the sorrows of others and in this way drawing close to the mystery of the suffering of the Man of Sorrows. We can achieve advances in technology, in civilization without this ability to suffer; but when we are concerned with truth and with freedom, without it we cannot progress, nor shall we come a single pace closer to the Son of Man."

30. See Metz and Moltmann, *Meditations on the Passion*, 31–32: "If we assent too long to the senselessness of death and of the dead, we shall in the end have nothing to offer the living but used-up secrets. It is not only the growth of our economic potentiality which is limited, as people today insist to us; the potentiality of our thinking seems also to be limited, and it is as if our reserves were dwindling, as if there were the danger that the big words with which we made our history—'freedom', 'emancipation', 'justice', 'happiness'—in the end will have no sense which has not been exhausted and dispersed."

31. Rahner, *Foundations of Christian Faith*, 266.

question of the meaning and redemptive value of suffering.[32] Metz acknowledges the entire history (past, present and future) of human suffering and the complex relationships among its various dimensions.[33] Suffering is redemptive inasmuch as it gives rise to the most profound occasion to exercise filial trust in the God of deliverance.[34] Suffering can be endured because the one who suffers unwaveringly trusts that this suffering will soon be alleviated and healed. While Metz links together the human existentials of sin, guilt and suffering in their coexistence as ontological counterparts, he does not reduce the experience of suffering to merely an effect of sin.[35] Though he admits that without sin there would be no guilt or suffering, he does not naïvely interpret suffering as a meaningless byproduct of humanity's destitution.[36] From a Christian perspective, for suffering to fulfill its redemptive character, it is necessary to place the many crosses of humanity beside the one cross of Christ: "the nameless history of the world's sufferings: of the many crosses beside the one Cross, of the countless, nameless perishings, of the speechless, stifled sufferings, of the massacred children from Herod's days to Auschwitz and Vietnam."[37] An adequate appropriation of human suffering must include a thorough and constant remembering of the concrete, historical sufferings of humanity. Without such tragic remembering, the power of salvation in Christ remains fallow.

Memory and Solidarity

While future sufferings of humanity have not yet been actualized, past sufferings have. Metz finds it essential to remember actively and remain in solidarity with the past sufferings of humanity. Anamnestic dialogue—dialogue which refuses to forget—becomes critical to Metz's soteriological project:

32. Metz, *Faith in History and Society*, 128.

33. Metz, *Faith in History and Society*, 123–24: "These histories of suffering are here understood as embracing all the actually experienced histories of suffering. . .a history of suffering as a history of guilt and as the fated destiny of finitude and of death."

34. Metz, *Faith in History and Society*, 124: "Redemption becomes an assured deliverance from the suffering of guilt and from the sinful self-degeneration of man, aspects elaborated in the so-called staurological (satisfactory) soteriology and as an assured deliverance from the suffering of finitude, of mortality, of that inner corroding nihilism of created being, as these are emphasized in the so-called incarnational soteriologies."

35. See Metz, *Poverty of Spirit*, 17–18: "By sinning we make a secret compromise with the offspring of sin—the forces of suffering and death; we join forces with them before they can assault us and make us truly poor."

36. See Rom 6:23: "For the wages of sin is death, but the gift of God is eternal life in Christ Jesus our Lord" (NAB).

37. Metz and Moltmann, *Meditations on the Passion*, 37.

the sufferings undergone by humanity cannot be forgotten lest we forget what it is to be truly human. Anamnestic dialogue requires a bounded, temporal and historical sense of time that is evident throughout the whole of the Hebrew and Christian Scriptures—a sense of time in and through which salvation history is actualized.[38] For Metz time is not as soft clay that can be reshaped and remolded anew with each successive generation, but rather as clay that is shaped, formed and then fired in the kiln of suffering, affliction and adversity, followed by cracking, scuffing and shattering: life-pottery that is both beautiful and marred and must be remembered in its actualized and definitive finality.[39] Metz refers to this act of active remembering of the past sufferings of humanity as *memoria passionis*. "Remembrance, which is always on the trail of the forgotten, (is). . .the organ of theology which, as theodicy, tries to confront our most progressive consciousness with what has been forgotten in it: the grievances and complaints of the past," and thus "*memoria passionis*, a profoundly biblical category, turns out to be a universal category, a category of salvation."[40] *Memoria passionis* saves humanity from its own hubris and self-sufficiency, preventing us from pursuing the realization of the *Übermensch* and becoming "like gods who know what is good and what is bad."[41] For Metz, striving toward the attainment of the arrogant and forgetful *Übermensch* is the antithesis of true humanity:

38. Metz offers a critique of various theological applications of non-temporal understandings of time in Metz, *A Passion for God*, 87: "Theology frequently lives off foreign, borrowed understandings of time, making it questionable how the God of biblical tradition can possibly be thought of in connection with them. This is true of cyclical time, as well as of time sheltered within a cosmos of preestablished harmony, of linear-teleological time. It is true of any progressive continuum, whether it be one that extends into infinitude, evolutionistically empty, or one that is dialectically slowed and interrupted; it is true also of biographically individualized time that is decoupled from nature's and the world's time. And I think it is true of the completely mythical representations of time, which seem to be coming to the fore again."

39. See 1 Cor 3:12–13: "Now if any one builds on the foundation with gold, silver, precious stones, wood, hay, straw—each man's work will become manifest; for the Day will disclose it, because it will be revealed with fire, and the fire will test what sort of work each one has done" (RSV).

40. Metz, *A Passion for God*, 65 and 41, respectively. Cf. ibid., 26: "A theology after Auschwitz wants to draw our attention to a principle that, because of the way Christianity became theological, fell more and more into oblivion: namely, that even the logos of Christian theology is formed not simply by subjectless and historyless ideas, but rather at its very roots by remembrancing (*Eingedenken*)." Also cf. Schuster and Boschert-Kimmig, *Hope Against Hope*, 24: "I know of really only one absolutely universal category: it is the *memoria passionis*. And I know of only one authority which cannot be revoked by any Enlightenment or emancipation: the authority of those who suffer."

41. Gen 3:5 (NAB); cf. Metz, *A Passion for God*, 41.

It is deeply inhuman to forget or suppress this question of the life of the dead, because it implies a forgetfulness and a suppression of past suffering and an acceptance of the meaninglessness of that suffering. Finally, the happiness of the descendants cannot compensate for the suffering of the ancestors and social progress cannot make up for the injustice done to the dead. If we accept for too long that death is meaningless and are indifferent towards the dead, we shall in the end only be able to offer trivial promises to the living.[42]

In other words, it is irresponsible to forget the suffering of past generations, even in the name of happiness and progress. A genuine humanity is built on the conscious memory of the hope-laden suffering of ancestors. Without such an active *memoria passionis*, present generations are unable to understand the redemptive meaning of suffering as well as endure their given lot of suffering. Just as the "non-identity of human suffering cannot be cancelled out" to maintain an authentically human anthropology, the "non-identity of the human history of suffering is, in the light of the *kenosis* of God in the cross of Jesus, taken up into the Trinitarian history of God," and thereby constitutes the way in which remembrancing (*Eingedenken*) united to the cross of Jesus is salvific.[43] The history of human suffering is thereby incarnated within the life of the Trinity insofar as "the Father's power 'raised up' Christ his Son and by doing so perfectly introduced his Son's humanity, including his body, into the Trinity."[44] A great subversion transpires in which the world's no to God is converted into a yes through a resolute suffering unto God.[45] Thus Jesus lives in solidarity with suffering sinners through his experience of maltreatment, humiliation, torture, crucifixion and death, promising to all sufferers that their suffering has meaning and will be vindicated.

"In every thing there is always a loud, or at times a silent, cry."[46] There is even "a nameless suffering which cannot be identified as Christian; (a)

42. Metz, *Faith in History and Society*, 75.

43. Metz, *Faith in History and Society*, 132. Cf. Metz and Moltmann, *Meditations on the Passion*, 39: "Only when we Christians give ear to the dark prophecy of the nameless, unrecognized, misunderstood and misprized Passion do we hear aright the message of his suffering."

44. *Catechism of the Catholic Church*, 648.

45. Metz, *A Passion for God*, 42: "This theology conceives of the Yes to God in history as a suffering unto God that ultimately approaches even the suffering of abandonment by God that has become unforgettable to us in Jesus' cry from the cross."

46. Ibid., 5. Cf. Rom 8:22: "We know that the whole creation has been groaning with labor pains together until now; and not only the creation, but we ourselves, who have the first fruits of the Spirit, groan inwardly as we wait for adoption as sons, the redemption of our bodies" (RSV).

universality of suffering."[47] If all human beings—past, present and future—experience suffering, and if suffering has salvific meaning and bears within it a promise of vindication, then it is possible for us to have compassion for one another and live in solidarity with one another in and through each other's personal suffering.[48] The past sufferings of humanity bespeak a message of horror and hope to the sufferings of those now present.[49] "The dead, after all, also belong equally to the universal community of all men in solidarity with each other," and "solidarity here should be understood in a strictly universal sense as a solidarity that has to justify itself not only with regard to the living and future generations, but also with regard to the dead."[50] This liberating hope of justification applies to, and unites, past, present and future generations:

> There is in the light of this history of redemption not only a "forward solidarity" with the coming generations but also a "backward solidarity" with the silent and forgotten dead. The latter is a practical solidarity of memory which looks from the standpoint of the conquered and the victims sacrificed in the world theatre of history. It does not only expose the non-sense of history against the probing optimism of the victor. . .It narrates the counter-meaning of redemption.[51]

In narrating the counter-meaning of redemption and the antithesis of true humanity, the tale of salvation history is simultaneously told and authentic humanity is brought to light. Human memory serves to illuminate the true human self, created *in imago Dei*.[52] Human memory serves to recall the true

47. Metz and Moltmann, *Meditations on the Passion*, 38.

48. See Rahner, *Foundations of Christian Faith*, 251: ". . .this situation of salvation is always of very short duration for the individual person, who can never lose himself in the crowd of all mankind." This is to say, vis-à-vis Metz's soteriological vision, that the suffering of each individual person in history should never go unnoticed or regarded as insignificant and meaningless. The suffering of each individual person has a *sui generis* character and a personal and incommunicable bearing on the whole of humanity in its potent particularity.

49. See Metz, *Faith in History and Society*, 76: "In this hope, then, the Christian does not primarily hope for himself—he also has to hope for others and, in this hope, for himself. The hope of Christians in a God of the living and the dead is a hope in a revolution for all men, including those who suffer and have suffered unjustly, those who have long been forgotten and even the dead."

50. Metz, *Faith in History and Society*, 75–76.

51. Metz, *Faith in History and Society*, 129–30.

52. Cf. Gen 1:27; 5:1; 9:6. For an example of liberating memory, see Deut 5:15: "For remember that you too were once slaves in Egypt, and the LORD, your God, brought you from there with his strong hand and outstretched arm" (NAB).

origin of life and divine nomological precepts.[53] This recollection is itself salvific in providing godly direction for human ethics that leads to eternal life. However, Metz identifies this memory as dangerous: "Where salvation approaches, there danger grows as well."[54] Persecution threatens the authentic follower of Christ just as it threatened him and, in the end, tried to stamp out his life. For the Christian narrative, the Christian kerygma—the proclamation of the cross—is "the power of God and the wisdom of God," and is for this reason threatening for the *Übermenschen* and dangerous for its adherents who are in constant spiritual warfare with the "principalities, with the powers, with the world rulers of this present darkness, with the evil spirits in the heavens."[55] The Christian message bears within itself the transformative power of redemption.

Narrative and Eschatology

According to Metz, *memoria passionis*, activated and expressed in and through narrative, substantiates the power to liberate and to redeem. For Metz humanity is a soteriological condition of possibility: "you shall lovingly accept the humanity entrusted to you!"[56] The anthropological categorical imperative is to accept the "chalice of existence":

> Man's self-acceptance is the basis of the Christian creed. Assent to God starts in man's sincere assent to himself, just as sinful flight from God starts in man's flight from himself. In accepting the chalice of his existence, man shows his obedience to the will of his Father in heaven (cf. Mt 26:39,42); in rejecting it, he rejects God. . .Man must learn to accept the painful experiment of his living.[57]

53. See Ps 119:93: "I will never forget your precepts; through them you give me life" (NAB).

54. Metz, *A Passion for God*, 49.

55. 1 Cor 1:24; Eph 6:12. Cf. Moltmann, *Crucified God*, 326: "The memory of the passion and resurrection of Christ is at the same time both dangerous and liberating. It endangers a church which is adapted to the religious politics of its time and brings it into fellowship with the sufferers of its time."

56. Metz, *Poverty of Spirit*, 7. Cf. Metz, *Advent of God*, 25. Here Metz identifies humanity as "a locale for God's advent"; cf. Metz, *Advent of God*, 31: "In the last analysis, we need only say yes to what we are: beings who can never completely reject or deny their true nature"; and cf. Metz, *Advent of God*, 33: "When we become the hope-filled poor of which the Gospel speaks, when we dare to embark upon the great adventure of God's coming, then we shall begin to taste some of the happiness that comes with advent existence."

57. Metz, *Poverty of Spirit*, 7–8.

Metz sums up this anthropological existential receptivity to the gift of God in the phrase "poverty of spirit": "poverty of spirit is the meeting point of heaven and earth, the mysterious place where God and man encounter each other, the point where infinite mystery meets concrete existence."[58] To live in poverty of spirit requires a decisive act of the will: "(man) makes (the unlimited potentialities of the future his own) by his historically unique and irrevocable personal decision, through which he finds a foothold in the thrust of his existence."[59] Through voluntary self-emptying, becoming spiritually impoverished and humiliated, one submits oneself to the potency of the Christian narrative. The story of salvation history is none other than a dialogical unfolding of alterity:

> Only when man commits himself without reservation to the recognition of this "Thou" does he hear himself endlessly called to the full taking possession of that priceless, irreplaceable "I" whom he is meant to be. In the great hours of a man's life this "I" announces itself, not as achieved reality, but as the possibility man is endlessly called to realize. It is when man, in the poverty of his worshipping spirit, treads before the face of God's freedom, into the mystery of that impenetrable "Thou"—it is then that he finds access to the depths of his own Being and worth. Then he really becomes a man.[60]

Metz attests to the pathway which leads to an authenticated humanity— a redeemed humanity that lives in hope toward the infinite horizon of its possibilities. "It is precisely because Christians believe in an eschatological meaning for history that they can risk historical consciousness: looking into the abyss. . .even Christian hope remains accountable to an apocalyptic conscience."[61] In other words, if vindication and revelation of the meaning of immense human suffering is but a bereft dream, why should we remember our voluminous sufferings? Would it not be better to forget them and move on with the only hope being to avoid future suffering? On the contrary, Christian faith extends the hopeful promise that our sufferings are not in vain or meaningless but rather "fill up what is lacking in the afflictions of Christ on behalf of his body, which is the church."[62] The Gospel of Christ is based on the future hope of resurrection: "in a word from the future-proof of Christianity is the hope of Christians forming an alliance with the fate of

58. Metz, *Poverty of Spirit*, 26.

59. Metz, *Poverty of Spirit*, 44.

60. Metz, *Poverty of Spirit*, 52.

61. Metz, *A Passion for God*, 40, 71.

62. Col 1:24.

humanity."[63] A Christian teleology of hope is tethered to an eschatological rendezvous of vindication. Senseless suffering and despair do not have the final say. Rather, the entire cosmos awaits the final pronouncement of eternity which will bring all history—with all its ambiguity and obscurity—into the light of truth.

Poverty of spirit entails living in solidarity with fellow sufferers and not forgetting the collective sufferings of life's pilgrims of the past. Christian faith offers a model and brother in the struggle of existence entailing suffering: Jesus Christ. "Messianic history is no history of success leading on to success, but a history of suffering, of rejection and of decline; there can be no talk of salvation and of life except by and through that history."[64] Through Jesus's poverty of spirit, "our human brother now becomes a 'sacrament' of God's hidden presence among us, a mediator between God and man," whereby the world accepts God and God accepts the world through Christ.[65] However, "Christianity in its message of redemption, does not offer definitive meaning for the unexpiated sufferings of the past. It narrates rather a distinct history of freedom: freedom on the basis of a redeeming liberation through God in the cross of Jesus."[66] Yet through the Christian narrative believers are inspired to live in solidarity with one other through their sufferings because God, in and through Jesus, lives in solidarity with humanity in their sufferings. For "Christian community is one gathered around the Eucharist, memory and communal narrative in undivided imitation of Jesus."[67] The Christian narrative serves as the bridge between orthodoxy and orthopraxy:

> Christianity as a community of those who believe in Jesus Christ
> has, from the very beginning, not been primarily a community
> interpreting and arguing, but a community remembering and
> narrating with a practical intention—a narrative and evocative
> memory of the passion, death and resurrection of Jesus. The lo-
> gos of the cross and resurrection has a narrative structure. Faith
> in the redemption of history and in the new man can, because
> of the history of human suffering, be translated into dangerously

63. Metz and Kaufmann, *Zukunftsfähigkeit*, 124: "*Im Wort von der Zukunftsfähigkeit des Christentums ist die Hoffnung der Christen mit dem Geschick der Menschheit verbunden*" (translation my own).

64. Metz and Moltmann, *Meditations on the Passion*, 27.

65. Metz and Moltmann, *Meditations on the Passion*, 35.

66. Metz, *Faith in History and Society*, 129.

67. Metz and Kaufmann, *Zukunftsfähigkeit*, 155: "*Christliche Gemeinde ist eine um die Eucharistie versammelte Erinnerungs- und Erzählgemeinschaft in der ungeteilten Nachfolge Jesu*" (translation my own).

liberating stories, the hearer who is affected by them becoming not simply a hearer, but a doer of the word.[68]

Christian kerygma, especially in its narrative form, operates as a performative discourse. It embodies the earthy history of its protagonists—especially that of Jesus of Nazareth—and further is sown as a living seed within its listeners. Those who affirmatively respond to the summons of the Gospel of Christ are converted radically and configured dramatically to the pattern of kenotic and self-abandoning love. The Gospel is ever dangerous due to the world's innate hostility to it, though it ironically remains addressed to the world it intends to liberate.

Liberation and Praxis

Metz's vision of salvation is concretized in the rawness of human history and in the pragmatic effect of the Gospel on every-day life. Authentic followers of Christ engage in an ongoing *mimesis*, or imitation, of the life of Christ. Metz defines the Christian faith in the following way:

> The faith of Christians is a praxis in history and society that is to be understood as hope in solidarity in the God of Jesus as a God of the living and the dead who calls all men to be subjects in his presence. Christians justify themselves in this essentially apocalyptical praxis (of imitation) in their historical struggle for their fellow men. They stand up for all men in their attempt to become subjects in solidarity with each other.[69]

For Metz, each person is indeed one's brother's and sister's keeper.[70] It is in and through the bond of mystical fraternal union among the diverse members of the Body of Christ that salvation is here and now enacted, as well as promised for the future.[71] Living solidarity with one another is an image of *agape* love through which all the divine precepts are lived. *Agape* love seeks not only its own interests and good, but the common good—the true good of one another. *Agape* love embraces the vocation to poverty of spirit that resists hubris and does not forget one's siblings in Christ who are afflicted, marginalized and oppressed. This kind of love speaks out on behalf

68. Metz and Kaufmann, *Zukunftsfähigkeit*, 212.

69. Metz, *Faith in History and Society*, 73.

70. See Gen 4:9.

71. See 1 Cor 12; Luke 19:9: "And Jesus said to him, 'Today salvation has come to this house because this man too is a descendant of Abraham. For the Son of Man came to seek and to save what was lost'" (NAB).

of those who are not able to advocate for themselves and is never personally content due to the awareness that one's fellows in Christ are not at peace. Metz insists that "if it is not to remain at the level of a pure assertion that is suspected of ideology, theology must be able to define and call upon a praxis in which Christians can break through the complex social, historical and psychological conditions governing history and society."[72] In order for Christian theology to be relevant it must be transformed from impersonal paper to embodied praxis—a praxis informed by its cognitive correlates of memory and narrative.[73] The power of praxis is generated from faith in the resurrected Christ accomplished in and through human subjectivity and daily phenomena: "this faith into which Jesus is risen is not really and directly faith in this resurrection, but is that faith which knows itself to be a divinely effected liberation from all the powers of finiteness, of guilt and of death, and knows itself to be empowered for this by the fact that this liberation has taken place in Jesus himself and has become manifest for us."[74] Faith in the resurrection of the body is the anchor of a hope which does not disappoint because it is a hope rooted in the fidelity and constancy of divine goodness, uncreated love, and boundless mercy.[75]

It is precisely in the disclosure of the dangerously liberating stories of young people that their histories are not forgotten nor rendered irrelevant but imbued with the transformative power of resurrection when told vis-à-vis the dangerously liberating story of Jesus. For Metz insists that "the category of narrative memory both prevents salvation and redemption from becoming paradoxically unhistorical and subordinates them to the logical identity of dialectical mediation."[76] Narrative memory is the sine qua non of conversion and salvation. The dialectic between salvation (at once

72. Metz, *Faith in History and Society*, 76–77.

73. See Metz, *Faith in History and Society*, 120–23.

74. Rahner, *Foundations of Christian Faith*, 268.

75. See Rom 5:1–5: "Therefore, since we have been justified by faith, we have peace with God through our Lord Jesus Christ, through whom we have gained access [by faith] to this grace in which we stand, and we boast in hope of the glory of God. Not only that, but we even boast of our afflictions, knowing that affliction produces endurance, and endurance, proven character, and proven character, hope, and hope does not disappoint, because the love of God has been poured out into our hearts through the holy Spirit that has been given to us" (NAB).

76. Metz and Jossua, eds., *Crisis of Religious Language*, 92; cf. 95: "In this perception, history, as a remembered history of suffering, acquires for reason the form of a 'dangerous tradition,' which is passed on not in a purely argumentative manner, but as narrative, that is, in 'dangerous stories'. . .These dangerous stories. . .show that man's consciousness which is 'entwined in stories,' which always has to rely on narrative identification and which, when the relative importance of the magisterium of history has been recognized, cannot entirely do without the magisterium of stories."

eschatological and proleptic) and suffering engenders the fruit of hope, yet only through the empathetic solidarity of a community of faith. It is only through the telling and re-telling of both particular personal narratives and Jesus's universal narrative (which is at once our narrative) that faith comes alive, validating its history and raison d'être. The process of storytelling, and ensuing compassionate empathy, thus serves as a pivotal breakthrough in validating the precious personal and communal identities of young people, allowing them to own their unique personal histories and to embrace Jesus's cosmic history and the salvific history of the Church as their own. In this way the community of faith grows in its love for one another, actively and intentionally listening to and empathizing with its younger members: "for the kingdom of God belongs to such as these."[77]

77. Mk 10:14 (NAB).

Bibliography

Abrahams, Roger D. *Everyday Life: A Poetics of Vernacular Practices*. Philadelphia: University of Pennsylvania Press, 2005.

Ammerman, Nancy Tatom. "Religious Identity and Religious Institutions." In *Handbook of the Sociology of Religion*, edited by Michele Dillon, 207–24. Cambridge: Cambridge University Press, 2003.

———. *Sacred Stories, Spiritual Tribes: Finding Religion in Everyday Life*. Oxford: Oxford University Press, 2013.

Anderson, Benedict. *Imagined Communities: Reflections on the Origin and Spread of Nationalism*. Revised edition. New York: Verso, 2016.

Antonovsky, Aaron. *Unraveling the Mystery of Health: How People Manage Stress and Stay Well*. San Francisco: Jossey-Bass, 1987.

Asad, Talal. "Thinking about Religion, Belief, and Politics." In *Cambridge Companion to Religious Studies*, edited by Robert A. Orsi, 36–57. Cambridge Companions to Religion. New York: Cambridge University Press, 2012.

Association Les Amis du Professeur Jerome LeJeune. "The Cause." http://amislejeune. org/index.php/en/the-cause-of-beatification/the-cause/90-le-proces-de-beati fication/le-proces/ou-en-est-on

Augustine. *City of God*. Translated Marcus Dods. 1950. Reprint. New York: Random House, 2000. Originally published in 1950.

———. *Essential Sermons*. Translated by Edmund Hill. The Works of Saint Augustine: A Translation for the 21st century. Hyde Park, NY: New City, 2007.

Baglow, Christopher T. *Faith, Science, and Reason: Theology on the Cutting Edge*. 2nd ed. Downers Grove, IL: Midwest Theological Forum, 2019.

Bartkus, Justin, & Christian Smith. *A Report on American Catholic Religious Parenting*. University of Notre Dame (2017). https://churchlife-info.nd.edu/a-report-on-american-catholic-religious-parenting

Bartlett, Robert. *The Making of Europe: Conquest, Colonization, and Cultural Change, 950–1350*, Princeton, NJ: Princeton University Press, 1993.

Bauman, Zygmunt. *Liquid Modernity*. Cambridge: Polity, 2000.

Bellah, Robert N., et al. *The Good Society*. NY: Vintage, 1992.

Benardete, Seth. *The Tragedy and Comedy of Life: Plato's Philebus*. University of Chicago Press, 2009.

Benedict XVI, Pope. *Deus caritas est Encyclical Letter*. Washington, DC: United States Conference of Catholic Bishops, 2005.

―――. *Meeting of the Holy Father Benedict XVI with the Clergy of Diocese of Bolzano-Bressanone*. August 6, 2008. http://www.vatican.va/content/benedict-xvi/en/speeches/2008/august/documents/hf_ben-xvi_spe_20080806_clero-bressanone.html

―――. "Faith, Reason and the University―Memories and Reflections," 2004.

―――. *A Reason Open to God: On Universities, Education, and Culture*. Edited by J. Stephen Brown. Washington, D.C.: The Catholic University of America Press, 2013.

―――. "The University: The House where One Seeks the Truth Proper to the Human Person," from "Address to Young University Professors, Apostolic Journey to Madrid on the Occasion of the 26th World Youth Day, August 19, 2011."

Bengtson, Vern L., et al. *Families and Faith: How Religion is Passed Down across Generations*. Oxford: Oxford University Press, 2014.

Berger, Peter L. *The Sacred Canopy: Elements of a Sociological Theory of Religion*. Reprint edition. New York, New York: Anchor, 1990.

―――. *The Heretical Imperative: Contemporary Possibilities of Religious Affirmation*. Garden City, NY: Anchor, 1979.

Bilgrami, Akeel. "What Is Enchantment?" In *Varieties of Secularism in a Secular Age*, 145–65. Cambridge, MA: Harvard University Press, 2010.

Bourdieu, Pierre. "The Forms of Capital." In *Handbook of the Theory and Research for the Sociology of Education*, edited by J.G. Richardson, 241–158. New York: Greenwood, 1986.

Boyd, Dana. *It's Complicated: The Social Lives of Networked Teens*. New Haven, CT: Yale University Press, 2014.

Brague, Rémi. *Eccentric Culture: A Theory of Western Civilization*. Translated by Samuel Lester. South Bend, IN: St. Augustine's, 2009.

Brassai, László, et al. "Meaning in Life: Is It a Protective Factor for Adolescents' Psychological Health?" *International Journal of Behavioral Medicine* 18.1 (2011) 44–51.

"A Brief Biological Sketch of G. Stanley Hall." American Psychological Association. http://teachpsych.org/page-1562855.

Briel, Don. "The University and the Church." *Logos: A Journal of Catholic Thought and Culture* 18.4 (2015) 15–31.

Brockhaus, Hanna. "Pope Francis on sharing the Christian message in 'reality.'" *Catholic News Agency*, December 6, 2019. https://www.catholicnewsagency.com/news/pope-francis-on-sharing-the-christian-message-in-reality-52683.

Bronk, Kendall Cotton, et al. "An Introduction to Exemplar Research: A Definition, Rationale, and Conceptual Issues." *New directions for child and adolescent development* 142 (2013) 1–12.

Bronk, Kendall Cotton, et al. "Purpose, Hope, and Life Satisfaction in Three Age Groups." *The Journal of Positive Psychology* 4.6 (2009) 500–510.

Brown, Peter. *The Cult of the Saints: Its Rise and Function in Latin Christianity*. Chicago: University of Chicago Press, 1981.

Brown, Wendy. *Undoing the Demos: Neoliberalism's Stealth Revolution*. New York: Zone, 2015.

Brumfield, Joshua. *The Benedict Proposal: Church as Creative Minority in the Thought of Pope Benedict XVI*. Eugene, OR: Pickwick, 2020.

Bryce, Mary Charles. *Pride of Place: The Role of the Bishops in the Development of Catechesis in the United States*. Washington DC: The Catholic University of America Press, 1984.

Canales, Arthur David. "The Ten-Year Anniversary of Renewing the Vision: Reflection on Its Impact for Catholic Youth Ministry." *New Theology Review* 20 (2007) 58–69.

Cantalamessa, Raniero. *Navigating the New Evangelization*. Boston: Pauline Books & Media, 2014.

Casanova, José. *Public Religions in the Modern World*. Chicago: University of Chicago Press, 1994.

Casarella, Peter. "The Expression and Form of the Word: Trinitarian Hermeneutics and the Sacramentality of Language in Hans Urs von Balthasar's Theology." *Renascence* 48.2 (1996) 111–135.

Catechism of the Catholic Church: Vatican City: Libreria Editrice Vaticana

Cavanaugh, William T. *Being Consumed: Economics and Christian Desire*. Grand Rapids, MI: Eerdmans, 2008.

Certeau, Michel de. *The Certeau Reader*. Edited by Graham Ward. Malden, MA: Blackwell, 2000.

Chaput, Charles J. *Strangers in a Strange Land: Living the Catholic Faith in a Post-Christian World*. New York: Henry Holt and Co., 2017.

"Charter for the Protection of Children and Young People." United States Conference of Catholic Bishops. http://www.usccb.org/issues-and-action/child-and-youth-protection/upload/Charter-for-the-Protection-of-Children-and-Young-People-revised-2011.pdf

Cherry, Stephen M., & Tricia C. Bruce. "Asian and Pacific Islander American Catholic young adults: Perspectives and challenges." In *Young adult American Catholics: explaining vocation in their own words*, edited by Maureen K. Day, ##–##. New York: Paulist, 2018.

Chesterton, G.K. *St. Thomas Aquinas and St. Francis of Assisi*. San Franciscan, CA: Ignatius, 2002.

———. *Tremendous Trifles*. Unknown City: Cavalier Classics, 2015.

CNNMoney.com. "Best Places to Live." http://money.cnn.com/magazines/moneymag/bplive/2008/snapshots/PL1751622.html.

Colby, Anne, and William Damon. *Some Do Care: Contemporary Lives of Moral Commitment*. New York: Free, 1992.

Connerton, Paul. *How Societies Remember*. Cambridge: Cambridge University Press, 1989.

Constable, Giles. *The Abbey of Cluny: A Collection of Essays to Mark the Eleven-Hundredth Anniversary of Its Founding*. Vita Regularis 43. Berlin: Lit, 2010.

Cowdrey, H.E.J. *The Cluniacs and the Gregorian Reform*. Oxford: Clarendon, 1970.

———. "The Peace and the Truce of God in the Eleventh Century." *Past and Present* 46 (1970) 42–67.

D'Antonio, William V., et al. *American Catholics in transition*. Lanham, MD: Rowman & Littlefield, 2013.

Daigle, Katy. "Public trust that scientists work for the good of society is growing." *Science News* 196.4 (2019) 5. https://www.sciencenews.org/article/public-trust-scientists-work-good-society-growing.

Damon, William. *The Path to Purpose: Helping Our Children Find Their Calling in Life*. New York: Simon and Schuster, 2008.

Damon, William, and Anne Colby. *The Power of Ideals: The Real Story of Moral Choice.* Oxford: Oxford University Press, 2015.

"Data and Information." *National Catholic Education Association.* http://www.ncea.org/data-information/catholic-school-data

Day, Dorothy. *The Reckless Way of Love: Notes on Following Jesus.* Edited by Carolyn Kurtz. Walden, NY: Plough, 2017.

Day, Maureen K. "Going, going, and some are gone: Marginal and former young adult Catholics." In *Young adult American Catholics: Explaining vocation in their own words,* edited by Maureen K. Day, ##–##. New York: Paulist, 2018.

Dawkins, Richard. *The God Delusion.* New York: Houghton Mifflin Harcourt, 2006.

Dawson, Christopher. *The Historic Reality of Christian Culture.* New York: Harper, 1960.

Delio, David. *An Aristocracy of Exalted Spirits: The Idea of the Church in Newman's Tamworth Reading Room.* London: Gracewing, 2016.

Department of Education, United States Catholic Conference. *A Vision of Youth Ministry, Bilingual Edition.* Washington, D.C.: United States Catholic Conference, 1986.

Dillard, Annie. *Holy the Firm.* New York: Harper and Row, 1977.

———. *Pilgrim at Tinker Creek.* New York: Harper Collins, 2007.

———. *Three by Annie Dillard: The Writing Life, An American Childhood, Pilgrim at Tinker Creek.* New York: Harper Perennial, 1990.

Dodd, C. H. *Parables of the Kingdom.* Rev. ed. New York: Charles Scribner's Sons, 1961.

Dollahite, David C., and Loren D. Marks. "Positive Youth Religious and Spiritual Development: What We Have Learned from Religious Families." *Religions,* 10.10 (2019) 548.

Drake, Tim. *Young and Catholic: The Face of Tomorrow's Church.* Manchester, NH: Sophia Institute, 2004.

Dreher, Rod. *The Benedict Option: A Strategy for Christians in a Post-Christian Nation.* New York: Sentinel, 2017.

Dupre, Louis. *Passage to Modernity: An Essay in the Hermeneutics of Nature and Culture.* New Haven, CT: Yale University Press, 1993.

Durkheim, Emile. *The Division of Labor in Society.* New York: Free, 1997.

East, Thomas, ed. *Leadership for Catholic Youth Ministry: Second Edition.* New London, CT: Twenty-Third, 2013.

Eco, Umberto. *Art and Beauty in the Middle Ages.* Translated by Hugh Bredin. New Haven, CT: Yale University Press, 1986.

Eisenstadt, S. N. "Multiple Modernities." *Daedalus* 129.1 (2000) 1–29.

Elias, Norbert. *The Civilizing Process: Sociogenetic and Psychogenetic Investigations.* Rev. ed. Malden, MA: Blackwell, 2000.

Ellis, Raymond. "The Theology of Garbage." *The Beacon. The Weekly Newspaper of St. Cecilia Parish, Detroit,* July 19, 1970.

Erikson, E. H. *Identity: Youth and crisis* (No. 7). WW Norton & Company, 1968.

Esolen, Anthony. *Out of the Ashes: Rebuilding American Culture.* Washington, DC: Regnery, 2017.

"Fact Sheet: Hispanics in the U.S." *Center for Applied Research in the Apostolate.* http://cara.georgetown.edu/staff/webpages/Hispanic percent20Catholic percent20Fact percent20Sheet.pdf

Fee, Joan L., et al. *Young Catholics in the United States and Canada*. William H. Sadlier, Inc., 1981.

Fitzgerald, F. Scott. *The Great Gatsby*, New York: Scribner, 1999.

Floridi, Luciani. *The Fourth Revolution: How the Infosphere is Reshaping Human Reality*. Oxford: Oxford University Press, 2014.

Francis, Pope. *Address at the Prayer Vigil of the XXVIIII World Youth Day in Rio de Janeiro*. July 27, 2013. http://www.vatican.va/content/francesco/en/speeches/2013/july/documents/papa-francesco_20130727_gmg-veglia-giovani.html.

———. "Address at the Meeting with Students and Representatives of the Academic World in Piazza San Domenico, Bologna" *AAS* 109 (2017) 1115.

———. *Amoris Laetitia*. Vatican City: Liberia Editrice Vaticana, 2016.

———. *Christus Vivit*. Vatican City: Liberia Editrice Vaticana, 2019.

———. *Evangelii Gaudium*. Vatican City: Liberia Editrice Vaticana, 2013.

———. *Gaudete et Exsultate*. Vatican City: Liberia Editrice Vaticana, 2018.

———. *Laudato Si*. Vatican City: Liberia Editrice Vaticana, 2015. http://www.vatican.va/content/francesco/en/encyclicals/documents/papa-francesco_20150524_enciclica-laudato-si.html.

———. *Letter of His Holiness Pope Francis on the Occasion of the Presentation of the Preparatory Document of the 15th Ordinary General Assembly of the Synod of Bishops*. January 13, 2017. http://www.vatican.va/content/francesco/en/letters/2017/documents/papa-francesco_20170113_lettera-giovani-doc-sinodo.html.

———. *Lumen Fidei*. Vatican City: Liberia Editrice Vaticana, 2013. http://www.vatican.va/content/francesco/en/encyclicals/documents/papa-francesco_20130629_enciclica-lumen-fidei.html

———. "Meeting with the Participants in the 5th Convention of the Italian Church," November 10, 2015. http://w2.vatican.va/content/francesco/en/speeches/2015/november/documents/papa-francesco_20151110_firenze-convegno-chiesa-italiana.html.

———. *Misericordiae Vultus*. Vatican City: Liberia Editrice Vaticana, 2015.

"Franciscan Sisters of the Eucharist: Our Charism is . . . "; www.fsecommunity.org.

"Franciscan Sisters of the Eucharist: Joy in Mission;" www.fsecommunity.org/joy-in-mission.

Frankl, Viktor E. *Man's Search for Meaning*. 1st ed. Boston: Beacon, 2006.

Frimer, Jeremy A., and Lawrence J. Walker, "Reconciling the self and morality: An empirical model of moral centrality development." *Developmental Psychology* 45.6 (2009) 1669–81.

Frimer, Jeremy A., et al. "Hierarchical integration of agency and communion: A study of influential moral figures." *Journal of Personality* 80.4 (2012) 1117–45.

Gable, Shelly, and Jonathan Haidt. "What (and Why) Is Positive Psychology." *Review of General Psychology* 9.2 (2005) 103–110.

Garfinkel, Harold. *Studies in Ethnomethodology*. Englewood Cliffs, NJ: Prentice-Hall, Inc., 1967.

Gerard Manley Hopkins: The Major Works. Edited by Catherine Phillips. New York: Oxford University Press, 2009.

Gibson, David. "Duluth Catholic diocese latest to file for bankruptcy over sex abuse payouts." *Religion News Service*. http://www.religionnews.com/2015/12/07/duluth-catholic-diocese-latest-file-bankruptcy-sex-abuse-payouts

Gray, Mark M. "Young people are leaving the faith. Here's why." *Our Sunday Visitor,* August 27, 2016. https://osvnews.com/2016/08/27/young-people-are-leaving-the-faith-heres-why/.

Gray, Mark M., and Hannah Hagan. "Catholicism: The next generation?" June 2, 2017 *Nineteen Sixty-four.* http://nineteensixty-four.blogspot.com/2017/06/catholicism-next-generation.html

Greeley, Andrew M. *The young Catholic family: Religious images and marriage fulfillment.* Chicago: Thomas More, 1980.

Guardini, Romano. *The End of The Modern World.* Rev. ed. Wilmington, DE: Intercollegiate Studies Institute, 2001.

———. *Die Lebensalter. Ihre ethische und pädagogische Bedeutung.* 3rd ed. Würzburg: Werkbund Verlag, 1955.

Habermas, Jürgen. *The Structural Transformation of the Public Sphere: An Inquiry into a Category of Bourgeois Society.* Sixth Printing edition. Cambridge, MA: The MIT Press, 1991.

Haile, Beth. "Catholic Moral Theology." *Reflections on a Terminal Diagnosis* (2018). https://catholicmoraltheology.com/reflections-on-a-terminal-diagnosis/.

Hall, G. Stanley. *Adolescence: Its Psychology and Its Relations to Physiology, Anthropology, Sociology, Sex, Crime, and Religion.* New York: Read, 1931.

Han, Byung-Chul. *The Burnout Society.* Translated by Erik Butler. Stanford: Stanford University Press, 2015.

Hardy, Sam A., and Pamela Ebstyne King. "Processes of Religious and Spiritual Influence in Adolescence: Introduction to a Special Section." *Journal of Research on Adolescence* 29.2 (2019) 244–53.

Hervieu-Leger, Daniele. *Religion as a Chain of Memory.* Translated by Simon Lee. New Brunswick, NJ: Rutgers University Press, 2000.

Hill, Patrick L., et al. "Purpose in Life in Emerging Adulthood: Development and Validation of a New Brief Measure." *The Journal of Positive Psychology* 11.3 (2016) 237–45. https://doi.org/10.1080/17439760.2015.1048817.

Hine, Thomas. *The Rise and Fall of the American Teenager.* New York: Perennial, 1999.

Hoge, D.R., et al. *Young Adult Catholics: Religion in the culture of choice.* Notre Dame, IN: University of Notre Dame Press, 2001.

Hourlier, Jacques. *Saint Odilon, abbé de Cluny.* Louvain: Publications universitaires de Louvain, 1964.

Howe, John. "The Nobility's Reform of the Medieval Church." *American Historical Review* 93.2 (1988) 317–339.

Hütter, Reinhard. "Polytechnic Utiliversity," *First Things* (2013) 47–52.

———. "University Education, Unity of Knowledge, and Theology." *Nova et Vetera* 11.4 (2013) 1017–56.

Irenaeus. *Against Heresies.*

Ivereigh, Austin. "'The Papal obsession with getting close and concrete." *Crux,* January 24, 2017. https://cruxnow.com/analysis/2017/01/papal-obsession-getting-close-concrete/.

Jerome LeJeune Foundation. "Professor Jerome LeJeune." https://lejeunefoundation.org/jerome-lejeune/.

John Dewey Project. *A brief overview of progressive education.* http://www.uvm.edu/~dewey/articles/proged.html

John Jay College of Criminal Justice. "The Nature and Scope of Sexual Abuse of Minors by Catholic Priests and Deacons 1950–2002." United States Conference of Catholic Bishops.   http://www.usccb.org/issues-and-action/child-and-youth-protection/ upload/The-Nature-and-Scope-of-Sexual-Abuse-of-Minors-by-Catholic-Priests-and-Deacons-in-the-United-States-1950–2002.pdf

John Paul II, Pope. *Iuvenum Patris*. Vatican City: Liberia Editrice Vaticana, 1988.

———. *Pastores Dabo Vobis*. Vatican City: Liberia Editrice Vaticana, 1992.

Johnson-Mondragón, Ken. "Hispanic Youth and Young Adult Ministry: Recent Findings." Instituto Fe y Vida. http://www.feyvida.org/documents/Perspectives6. pdf

Jones, Robert P., et al. "Exodus. Why Americans are Leaving Religion—And Why They're Unlikely to Come Back." Washington, DC: Public Religion Research Institute (PRRI), 2016. https://www.prri.org/wp-content/uploads/2016/09/PRRI-RNS-Unaffiliated-Report.pdf

Jurgens, William A. *The Faith of the Early Fathers, Vol. 1*. Collegeville, MN: The Liturgical Press, 1970.

Kant, Immanuel. *Critique of the Power of Judgment*. Translated by Paul Guyer and Eric Matthews. Cambridge: Cambridge University Press, 2000.

Kaplan, Grant. "What has Ethics to Do with Rhetoric?: Prolegomena to any Future Just War Theory." *Political Theology* 6:1 (2005) 31–49.

Kegan, Robert. *The Evolving Self: Problem and Process in Human Development*. Cambridge, MA: Harvard University Press, 1982.

Keles, Betul, et al. "A Systematic Review: The Influence of Social Media on Depression, Anxiety and Psychological Distress in Adolescents." *International Journal of Adolescence and Youth* 25.1 (2020) 79–93.

Kett, Joseph F. *Rites of Passage: 1790 to the Present*. New York: Basic, 1977.

Kettlekamp, Theresa M. "Ten Points to Create Safe Environment for Children." *United States Conference of Catholic Bishops*. http://www.usccb.org/issues-and-action/ child-and-youth-protection/child-abuse-prevention/ten-points-to-create-safe-environments-for-children.cfm

Kilbane, Clare. *The 4Cs: Critical Thinking*. Arlington, VA: National Catholic Education Association, 2017.

King, P. E., et al. "Adolescent spiritual exemplars: Exploring spirituality in the lives of diverse youth." *Journal of Adolescent Research* 29.2 (2014) 186–212.

King, Pamela Ebstyne, and Frederic Defoy. "Joy as a virtue: The means and ends of joy." *Journal of psychology and theology* 48.4 (2020) 308–31.

Krogstad, Jens Manuel and Mark Hugo Lopez. "Hispanic population reaches 55 million, but growth has cooled." *Pew Research Center*. http://www.pewresearch. org/fact-tank/2015/06/25/u-s-hispanic-population-growth-surge-cools/

LaNave, Gregory F. "God, Creation, and the Possibility of Philosophical Wisdom: The Perspectives of Bonaventure and Aquinas." *Theological Studies* 69 (2008) 828–30.

Land, Kenneth C. "Child and Youth Well-Being Index." Duke University. http://www. soc.duke.edu/~cwi/

Le Goff, Jacques. *The Birth of Europe*. Translated by Janet Lloyd. Oxford: Blackwell, 2005.

———. *The Birth of Purgatory*. Translated by Arthur Goldhammer. Chicago: University of Chicago Press, 1984.

Lear, Jonathan. *Radical Hope: Ethics in the Face of Cultural Devastation*. Cambridge, MA: Harvard University Press, 2006.

Lipka, Michael. "Millennials Increasingly are Driving the Growth of 'Nones.'" *Pew Research Center*. http://www.pewresearch.org/fact-tank/2015/05/12/millennials-increasingly-are-driving-growth-of-nones

Locke, Ben. "Center for Collegiate Mental Health Annual Report 2014." *Publication No. STA 15–30* (2015) 44.

Lonergan, Bernard. *Method in Theology*. Toronto: University of Toronto Press, 1990.

Lopez, Kathryn Jean. "Coherency in Higher Education & the Integrated Life of Faith." The Corner (blog). *National Review* (2014). https://www.nationalreview.com/blog/corner /coherency-higher-education-integrated-life-faith-kathryn-jean-lopez/.

Lugo, Luis. "Becoming Latino: the Transformation of U.S. Catholicism." *Fordham Center on Religion and Culture*. http://digital.library.fordham.edu/cdm/ref/collection/rc/id/28

Mabbe, E., et al. "Day-to-day variation in autonomy-supportive and psychologically controlling parenting: The role of parents' daily experiences of need satisfaction and need frustration." *Parenting* 18.2 (2018) 86–109.

MacIntyre, Alasdair. *After Virtue: A Study in Moral Theory*. Notre Dame, IN: University of Notre Dame Press, 1981.

———. *Dependent Rational Animals: Why Human Beings Need the Virtues*. Chicago: Open Court, 2001.

Madan, Anjana, et al. "The Effects of Media Violence on Anxiety in Late Adolescence." *Journal of Youth and Adolescence* 43.1 (2014) 116–26.

Mahan, Brian J., et al. *Awakening Youth Discipleship: Christian Resistance in a Consumer Culture*. Eugene: OR: Cascade, 2008.

Mahmood, Saba. *Politics of Piety: The Islamic Revival and the Feminist Subject*. Rev. ed. Princeton, N.J: Princeton University Press, 2011.

Manglos-Weber, Nicolette and Christian Smith. *Understanding former young Catholics: Findings from a national study of American emerging adults*. University of Notre Dame, 2015. https://mcgrath.nd.edu/assets/170517/icl_former_catholics_final_web.pdf

Manning, Patrick R. *Converting the Imagination: Teaching to Recover Jesus' Vision for Fullness of Life*. Eugene, OR: Pickwick, 2020.

Marcia, J. E. "Development and validation of ego-identity status." *Journal of personality and social psychology* 3.5 (1966) 551.

McCarraher, Eugene. *The Enchantments of Mammon: How Capitalism Became the Religion of Modernity*. Cambridge, MA: Belknap, 2019.

Meeus, Wim H. J., et al. "On the progression and stability of adolescent identity formation: A five-wave longitudinal study in early-to-middle and middle-to-late adolescence." *Child development* 81.5 (2010) 1565–1581.

Mercandante, Frank. *Engaging a New Generation: A Vision for Reaching Catholic Teens*. Huntington, IN: Our Sunday Visitor, 2012.

Metz, Johann Baptist. *The Advent of God*. New York: Newman, 1970.

———, ed. "Christianity and the Bourgeoisie" in *Concilium: Religion in the Seventies, Vol. 125*. New York: Seabury, 1979.

———. *The Emergent Church: The Future of Christianity in a Postbourgeois World*. New York: Crossroad, 1981.

————. *Faith in History and Society: Toward a Practical Fundamental Theology*. New York: Seabury, 1980.

————, ed. "Fundamental Theology: The Church and the World" in *Concilium: Theology in the Age of Renewal, Vol. 6*. New York: Paulist, 1965.

————, ed. "New Questions on God" in *Concilium: Religion in the Seventies, Vol. 76*. New York: Herder & Herder, 1972.

————. *A Passion for God: The Mystical-Political Dimension of Christianity*. New York: Paulist, 1998.

————. *Poverty of Spirit*. New York: Newman, 1968.

————. *Theology of the World*. New York: Herder and Herder, 1969.

———— and Jean-Pierre Jossua, eds. "The Crisis of Religious Language" in *Concilium: Religion in the Seventies, Vol. 85*. New York: Herder & Herder, 1973.

———— and Franz-Xaver Kaufmann. *Zukunftsfähigkeit*. Freiburg: Herder, 1987.

———— and Jürgen Moltmann. *Faith and the Future: Essays on Theology, Solidarity, and Modernity*. New York: Orbis, 1995.

———— and Jürgen Moltmann. *Meditations on the Passion*. New York: Paulist, 1979.

———— and Karl Rahner. *The Courage to Pray*. New York: Crossroad, 1981.

Milbank, John. *Theology and Social Theory: Beyond Secular Reason*. 2nd ed. Malden, MA: Wiley-Blackwell, 2006.

Mirowski, Philip. *Never Let a Serious Crisis Go to Waste: How Neoliberalism Survived the Financial Meltdown*. 1st ed. London; New York: Verso, 2013.

Mojtabai, R., et al. "National Trends in the Prevalence and Treatment of Depression in Adolescents and Young Adults." *PEDIATRICS* 138.6 (2016) e20161878–e20161878.

Moltmann, Jürgen. *The Crucified God*. Minneapolis: Fortress, 1993.

————. *Theology of Hope: On the Ground and Implications of a Christian Eschatology*. New York: Harper & Row, 1967.

Murphy, Ella, et al, eds. *Hope for the Decade: A Look at the Issues Facing Catholic Youth Ministry*. Washington DC: National Catholic Youth Organization Federation, 1980.

National Association for the Education of Young Children (2008). *Overview of the NAEYC Early Childhood Program Standards*. https://www.naeyc.org/files/academy/file/OverviewStandards.pdf

National Catholic Network de Pastoral Juvenil Hispana. *Conclusions: First National Encounter for Hispanic Youth and Young Adult Ministry*. Washington DC: USCCB, 2008.

National Conference of Catholic Bishops. *To Teach as Jesus Did*. Washington DC: United States Catholic Conference, 1972.

National Council for the Social Studies. "The College, Career, and Civic Life (C3) Framework for Social Studies State Standards: Guidance for Enhancing the Rigor of K-12 Civics, Economics, Geography, and History." Silver Springs, MD: NCSS, 2013.

National Governors Association Center for Best Practices & Council of Chief State School Officers. *Common Core State Standards*. Washington, DC: Authors, 2004. http://www.corestandards.org/standards-in-your-state/

National Governors Association Center for Best Practices & Council of Chief State School Officers. *Common Core State Standards for Mathematics*. Washington, DC: Authors, 2010.

Newman, St. John Henry. *The Idea of a University*. New York: Longmans, Green, and Co., 1907.

Nock, Matthew K. "Why Do People Hurt Themselves? New Insights in to the Nature and Functions of Self-Injury." *Current Directions in Psychological Science* (April 2009). http://www.psychologicalscience.org/journals/cd/18_2_inpress/Nock.pdf.

Nolan, Hugh J., ed. *Pastoral Letters of the United States Catholic Bishops, vol. 1*. Washington DC: National Conference of Catholic Bishops, 1984.

———. *Pastoral Letters of the United States Catholic Bishops, vol. 2*. Washington DC: United States Catholic Conference, 1984.

Ong, Walter J. *Orality and Literacy*. 30th anniversary ed. New York: Routledge, 2012.

On-line Etymology Dictionary. https://www.etymonline.com.

Oprah.com. "Failing Grade." http://www.oprah.com/slideshow/oprahshow/oprahshow1_ss_20060411/3.

Floridi, Luciani, ed. *The Onlife Manifesto: Being Human in a Hyperconnected Era*. London: SpringerOpen, 2015.

Origen of Alexandria, *Contra Celsum*. Translated by Henry Chadwick. 1953. Reprint. Cambridge: Cambridge University Press, 1980.

Ospino, H. "Hispanic young Catholics." In *Young adult Catholics: Explaining vocation in their own words*, edited by Maureen K. Day, ##–##. New York: Paulist, 2018.

Palladino, Grace. *Teenagers: An American History*. New York: Basic, 1996.

Paradis, Wilfred H. and Andrew D. Thompson. *Where Are the 6.6 Million? A Statistical Survey of Catholic Elementary and Secondary Formal Religious Education 1965–1974*. Washington DC: United States Catholic Conference, 1975.

"Partnership for 21st Century Skills," *Framework for 21st Century Learning*. (2004). http:// www.21stcenturyskills.org/

Pascione, Mark. "25th Anniversary Review, 1992–1997." *National Federation of Catholic Youth Ministry*. http://nfcym.org/about/history.htm

Paul VI, Pope. *Apostolicam Actuositam*. Vatican City: Liberia Editrice Vaticana, 1965.

Paxton, Frederick S., and Isabelle Cochelin, *The Death Ritual at Cluny in the Central Middle Ages*. Disciplina Monastica 9. Fontes 2. Turnhout: Brepols, 2013.

Pew Research Center. "America's Changing Religious Landscape" (2015). https://www.pewforum.org/2015/05/12/americas-changing-religious-landscape/

———. "Columbine Shooting Biggest News Draw of 1999." http://www.people-press.org/1999/12/28/columbine-shooting-biggest-news-draw-of-1999

———. "Most U.S. Teens See Anxiety and Depression as a Major Problem Among Their Peers" (2019).

———. "The Shifting Religious Identity of Latinos in the United States." http://www.pewforum.org/files/2014/05/Latinos-Religion-07-22-full-report.pdf

———. *U.S. Catholics open to non-traditional families* (2015). https://www.pewforum.org/wp-content/uploads/sites/7/2015/09/Catholics-and-Family-Life-09-01-2015.pdf

Pinker, Steven. *The Better Angels of Our Nature: Why Violence Has Declined*. New York: Penguin, 2011.

Pius X, Pope. *Acerbo Nimis*. Vatican City: Liberia Editrice Vaticana, 1905.

Pius XI, Pope. *Caritate Christi Compulsi*. Vatican City: Liberia Editrice Vaticana, 1932.

Planck, Max. *Where Is Science Going?* Oxford: Oxbow, 1981.

Plante, Thomas G. and Kathleen L. McChesney, eds. *Sexual Abuse in the Catholic Church: A Decade of Crisis, 2002–2012*. Santa Barbara: Praeger, 2012.

Podles, Leon J. *Sacrilege: Sexual Abuse in the Catholic Church.* Baltimore: Crossland, 2008.

Pohier, Jacques and Dietmar Mieth, eds. "Suicide and the Right to Die" in *Concilium: Religion in the Eighties, Vol. 179.* Edinburgh: T. & T. Clark, 1985.

Polanyi, Karl. *The Great Transformation: The Political and Economic Origins of Our Time.* 2nd ed. Boston, MA: Beacon, 2001.

Pontifical Council for the Promotion of the New Evangelization. *Directory for Catechesis.* Washington DC: United States Conference of Catholic Bishops, 2020.

Pratt, T.N. "Black Catholic young adult Catholics: A broader context." In *Young adult American Catholics: explaining vocation in their own words,* edited by Maureen K. Day, ##-##. New York: Paulist, 2018.

Rahner, Karl. *Foundations of Christian Faith: An Introduction to the Idea of Christianity.* New York: Crossroad, 2005.

Ratzinger, Joseph. *Das neue Volk Gottes: Entwurfe zur ekklesiologie.* Dusseldorf: Patmos, 1977.

———. *'In the Beginning . . . ': A Catholic Understanding of the Story of Creation and the Fall.* Translated by Boniface Ramsey, O.P. Grand Rapids, MI: Eerdmans, 1995.

———. *Introduction to Christianity.* San Francisco: Ignatius, 2004.

———. *Principles of Catholic Theology: Building Stones for a Fundamental Theology.* Translated by Mary Frances McCarthy. San Francisco: Ignatius, 1987.

———. *Pilgrim Fellowship of Faith: The Church as Communion.* Translated by Henry Taylor. San Francisco: Ignatius, 2005.

Ratzinger, Joseph, and Marcello Pera. *Without Roots: The West, Relativism, Christianity, Islam.* Translated by Michael Moore. New York: Basic, 2006.

Ricoeur, Paul. *Time and Narrative, Volume 1.* Translated by Kathleen McLaughlin and David Pellauer. Chicago: University of Chicago Press, 1990.

Rolston, Holmes, III. "Does Nature Need to Be Redeemed?" *Zygon* 29.2 (1994) 205-229.

———. "Kenosis and Nature." In *The Work of Love: Creation as Kenosis,* edited by John Polkinghorne, 43-65. Grand Rapids, MI: Eerdmans, 2001.

———. "Perpetual Perishing, Perpetual Renewal." *The Northern Review* 28 (2008) 111-23.

Root, Andrew. *Revisiting Relational Youth Ministry: From a Strategy of Influence to a Theology of Incarnation.* Downers Grove, IL: IVP, 2007.

Root, Andrew and Kendra Creasy Dean. *The Theological Turn in Youth Ministry.* Downers Grove, IL: InterVarsity, 2011.

Rosenwein, Barbara H. "Feudal War and Monastic Peace: Cluniac Liturgy as Ritual Aggression." *Viator* 2 (1972) 129-157.

Rzeznik, Johnny. "Iris" from *Dizzy Up the Girl.* Warner Bros. Records, 1998.

Sackur, Ernst. *Die Cluniacenser in ihrer kirchlichen und allgemeingeschichtlichen Wirksamkeit bis zur mitte des elften Jahrhunderts,* 2 vols. Halle: M. Niemeyer, 1892.

Santrock, John W. *Adolescence: Fifteenth Edition.* New York: McGraw Hill, 2014.

Satlow, Michael L. "Tradition: The Power of Constraint." In *The Cambridge Companion to Religious Studies,* edited by Robert A. Orsi, 130-150. Cambridge Companions to Religion. New York: Cambridge University Press, 2012.

Savage, Jon. *Teenage: The Creation of Youth Culture: 1875-1945.* New York: Penguin, 2007.

Savino F.S.E., Sr. Damien Marie, and John Hittinger. "Loss of Creation and its Recovery Through Aquinas and Bonaventure." *New Blackfriars* 19.1067 (2016) 5–21.

Schmemann, Serge. "Hapsburg Grandeur is Dusted Off for Burial of "Our Sister the Empress Zita," in *The New York Times* (1989) 3. https://www.nytimes.com/1989/04/02/world/hapsburg-grandeur-is-dusted-off-for-burial-of-our-sister-the-empress-zita.html#:~:text=The%20Empress%20Zita%2C%20as%20she,she%20lived%20her%20last%20years.

Schmid, Karl and Joachim Wollasch, "Die Gemeinschaft der Lebenden und Verstorbenen in Zeugnissen des Mittelalters." *Frühmittelalterliche Studien* 1 (1967) 365–405.

Schools-Data.com. "Neuqua Valley High School, Naperville, IL." http://www.schools-data.com/schools/NEUQUA-VALLEY-HS-NAPERVILLE.html.

Schuster, Ekkehard and Reinhold Boschert-Kimmig, eds. *Hope Against Hope: Johann Baptist Metz and Elie Wiesel Speak Out on the Holocaust*. New York: Paulist Press, 1999.

Schwartz, Seth J., et al. "Identity and agency in emerging adulthood: Two developmental routes in the individualization process." *Youth & Society* 37.2 (2005) 201–229.

Second Vatican Council, *Message to Young Men and Women* #18.

Silver, Harold and Pamela Silver. *An Educational war on poverty: American and British policy-making 1960–1980*. Cambridge: Cambridge University Press, 1991.

Smith, Christian, and Melinda Lundquist Denton. *Soul Searching: The Religious and Spiritual Lives of American Teenagers*. New York: Oxford University Press, 2005.

Smith, Christian, et al. *Religious parenting: Transmitting Faith and Values in Contemporary America*. Princeton, NJ: Princeton University Press, 2020.

Smith, Christian, et al. *Young Catholic America: Emerging Adults In, Out of, and Gone from the Church*. Oxford: Oxford University Press, 2014

Smith, James K. A. *Desiring the Kingdom*. Grand Rapids, MI: Baker Academic, 2009.

Sobrino, Jon. *Christology at the Crossroads: A Latin American Approach*. New York: Orbis, 1982.

———. *Christ the Liberator: A View from the Victims*. New York: Orbis, 2001.

Somers, Margaret R. "The Narrative Constitution of Identity: A Relational and Network Approach." *Theory and Society* 23 (1994) 605–49.

Soni, Varun. "There's a Loneliness Crisis on College Campuses." *Los Angeles Times*. https://www.latimes.com/opinion/op-ed/la-oe-soni-campus-student-loneliness-20190714-story.html.

Synod of Bishops. (2017, January 13). Young people, the Faith, and vocational discernment. http://www.vatican.va/roman_curia/synod/documents/rc_synod_doc_20170113_documento-preparatorio-xv_en.html

Synod of Bishops, "Preparatory Document -Young People, the Faith and Vocational Discernment," # 4. http://www.vatican.va/roman_curia/synod/documents/rc_synod_doc_20170113_documento-preparatorio-xv_en.html.

Synod of Bishops: XII Ordinary General Assembly. *Message*. October 7–28, 2012. http://www.vatican.va/roman_curia/synod/documents/rc_synod_doc_20121026_message-synod_en.html

Synod of Bishops. XV Ordinary General Assembly. *Final Document: Young People, the Faith, and Vocational Discernment*. October 27, 2018. http://www.vatican.va/roman_curia/synod/documents/rc_synod_doc_20181027_doc-final-instrumentum-xvassemblea-giovani_en.html

Synod of Bishops: XV Ordinary General Assembly. *Instrumentum Laboris. Young People, the Faith, and Vocational Discernment.* 2018. http://www.vatican.va/roman_curia/synod/documents/rc_synod_doc_20180508_instrumentum-xvassemblea-giovani_en.html.

Swedberg, Richard. *Tocqueville's Political Economy.* Princeton, NJ: Princeton University Press, 2018.

Swidler, Ann. "Culture in Action: Symbols and Strategies." *American Sociological Review* 51.2 (1986) 273–86.

Taba, Hilda. *Curriculum Development. Theory and Practice.* New York: Harcourt, Brace & World, 1962.

Taylor, Charles. *A Secular Age.* 1st ed. Cambridge, MA: Belknap, 2007.

———. *Sources of the Self: The Making of the Modern Identity.* Cambridge, MA: Harvard University Press, 1992.

Thompson, Augustine, O.P. *Francis of Assisi: A New Biography.* Ithaca, NY: Cornell University Press, 2012.

Thompson, Janice Allison. "Making Room for the Other: Maternal Mourning and Eschatological Hope." *Modern Theology* 27:3 (July 2011) 395–413.

Tocqueville, Alexis de. *The Ancien Regime and the French Revolution.* Cambridge Texts in the History of Political Thought. New York: Cambridge University Press, 2011.

Twenge, Jean. "The Mental Health Crisis among America's Youth Is Real—and Staggering." *The Conversation.* http://theconversation.com/the-mental-health-crisis-among-americas-youth-is-real-and-staggering-113239.

Twenge, Jean M., et al. "Age, Period, and Cohort Trends in Mood Disorder Indicators and Suicide-Related Outcomes in a Nationally Representative Dataset, 2005–2017." *Journal of Abnormal Psychology* 128.3 (2019) 185–99.

Twinge, Jean. *iGen.* New York: Atria, 2017.

United States Conference of Catholic Bishops. *Synod of Bishops—1974.* Washington, D.C.: United States Conference of Catholic Bishops, 1975.

———. *Renewing the Vision: A Framework for Catholic Youth Ministry.* Washington DC: United States Conference of Catholic Bishops, 1997.

Vogt, Brandon. "New Stats on Why Young People Leave the Church." https://brandonvogt.com/new-stats-young-people-leave-church/.

Voragine, Jacobus de. *The Golden Legend.*

Von Balthasar, Hans Urs. *The Glory of the Lord, Vol. 1: Seeing the Form.* Translated by Erasmo Leiva-Merikakis, 2nd ed. New York: Ignatius, 2009.

Warren, Michael. *Youth Ministry: A Book of Readings.* New York: Paulist, 1975.

Watson, Justin. *The Martyrs of Columbine: Faith and the Politics of Tragedy.* New York: Palgrave MacMillian, 2002.

Weber, Max. "Politics as a Vocation." In *From Max Weber: Essays in Sociology,* edited by H.H. Gerth and C. Wright Mills, 77–128. New York: Oxford University Press, 1958.

———. *The Protestant Ethic and the Spirit of Capitalism.* BN Publishing, 2008.

———. "Science as a Vocation." In *From Max Weber: Essays in Sociology,* edited by H.H. Gerth and C. Wright Mills, 129–56. New York: Oxford University Press, 1958.

Weddell, Sherry A. *Forming Intentional Disciples: The Path to Knowing and Following Jesus.* Huntington, IN: Our Sunday Visitor, 2012.

Weigel, George. *Witness to Hope, the Biography of John Paul II.* New York: Cliff Street, 1999.

Weil, Simone. *Gravity and Grace*. 1st ed. London; New York: Routledge, 2002.

———. *Waiting for God*. Translated by Emma Craufurd and Kegan Paul. New York: Routledge, 210.

Wilson, Mark. "Measuring progressions: Assessment structures underlying a learning progression." *Journal of Research in Science Teaching* 46.6 (2009) 716–730.

Wittberg, Patricia. *Catholic Cultures: How Parishes can Respond to the Changing Face of Catholicism*. Collegeville, MN: Liturgical, 2016.

Wollasch, Joachim. "Monasticism: The First Wave of Reform," in *New Cambridge Medieval History*, vol. 3, edited by Timothy Reuter, 163–185. Cambridge: Cambridge University Press, 2008.

Wynn, Phillip. *Augustine on War and Military Service*. Minneapolis, MN: Fortress, 2013.

Index